Praise for *MY LONG TRIP HOME*:

"This is one of the most beautifully written and skillfully reported memoirs I have ever read. Searching to unlock the puzzle of his parents' lives, Whitaker writes with empathy and insight, shifting seamlessly between a child's recollection and an adult perspective. This story will capture your heart from start to finish."

—**Doris Kearns Goodwin, author of *Team of Rivals***

"A book filled with as much family tumult as Jeannette Walls described in *The Glass Castle* and a racial factor to boot. It's a story that registers not only for its shock value but also for the perspective and wisdom with which it can now be told. . . . Mr. Whitaker . . . is well justified in thinking that his family's unusual history warrants book-length treatment. *My Long Trip Home* is full of remarkable stories."

—*The New York Times*

"A thoughtful account of growing up bi-racial at a point in this country's history when racial identities are in flux and when people of mixed race are ever more common. . . . For the most part Whitaker's tone is objective, almost reportorial, which permits the reader to see his story clearly rather than through the mists of hyperventilated emotion. It's a good book."

—*The Washington Post*

"Though Whitaker may be familiar to many who followed his trajectories at *Newsweek* and CNN, this book is less about the journalist's storied career than his gut-wrenching saga of family and racial identity . . . . In reading *My Long Trip Home,* you can feel him smarting as he rips off one Band-Aid after another." (Grade: A-)

—*Entertainment Weekly*

"With the skill of a seasoned reporter, Whitaker delivers a heartfelt treatise on growing up in a biracial family, drawing on emotional and factual truths to examine how his dysfunctional childhood ultimately inspired his achievements."

—Daily Beast.com

"[A] poignant memoir . . . Whitaker is unsparing in his account of his father's sins and the scars they inflicted . . . but the author filters his profile through a rich reflection and understanding. Like Barack Obama's *Dreams from My Father,* Whitaker's memoir is in many ways an iconic story of the post—civil rights era, one in which transcending racial barriers liberates people to succeed—and fail—in their own peculiar ways."

—*Publishers Weekly* (starred review)

"A heavily detailed and highly readable account of the author's lineage . . . the writing comes across as honest and wholly engaging. A fascinating personal treatise on racial identity and complicated father-son dynamics."

—*Kirkus Reviews*

"A deeply moving history of family relations and racial identity."

—*Booklist* (starred review)

"Told straightforwardly, Whitaker's stories of life and work in proximity to power will appeal to government and media junkies. . . . The parallels to another high-achieving, mixed-race public figure are hard to ignore. Whitaker's retelling of his journalistic triumphs and missteps will remind readers that the face of America's elite is changing."

—*Library Journal*

"[Whitaker's] thoughtful writing is straightforward and easy to read. *My Long Trip Home* is a paean to one man's struggle to find his place in the world."

—*Charleston Post & Courier*

"Like Obama's, Whitaker's heritage is complicated and fascinating . . . Whitaker's ability to move forward shows that anger can be transformed into sheer determination and, ultimately, success and understanding."

—Barnes and Noble Review.com

"Reflecting both a reporter's painstaking attention to detail and a prodigal son's sincere search for closure and redemption, *My Long Trip Home* is a riveting, revealing, and heartbreaking memoir affirming the potential of even the messiest of lives to blossom belatedly into something satisfying and beautiful."

—*Baret News Service*

"[A] remarkable memoir. . . . Anyone who cares about the subjects of race, family and growing up multiracial in America should read this absorbing book. In his memoir, Whitaker reveals the whole story in an unflinching look at his life and that of his caucasian mother and African-American father. Whitaker's roots form the core of this fascinating memoir but this skillful storyteller uses it as a launching point to write, too, about life in America during the oft-chaotic '60s and '70s."

—Marketwatch.com

"In a poignant family memoir, veteran journalist Mark Whitaker describes his long road to truth and reconciliation with his parents, a biracial couple brought together by a shared faith and torn apart by their separate frailties. . . . Whitaker knows how to work a story. Although here he is investigating his own personal history, he approaches it in the same manner he would for any other journalistic assignment: carefully, candidly, and with reasoned prose."

—In The Fray.com

"A universal story about the relationship between a son and his parents. Whitaker is a great journalist, so the research is impeccable, and it's beautifully written. Really worth getting."

—Fareed Zakaria's GPS: Book of the Week

My Long

A Family

Trip Home

Memoir

MARK WHITAKER

Simon & Schuster Paperbacks

New York   London   Toronto   Sydney   New Delhi

Simon & Schuster Paperbacks
A Division of Simon & Schuster, Inc.
1230 Avenue of the Americas
New York, NY 10020

First Simon & Schuster trade paperback edition January 2013

SIMON & SCHUSTER PAPERBACKS and colophon are registered
trademarks of Simon & Schuster, Inc.

For information about special discounts for bulk purchases,
please contact Simon & Schuster Special Sales at
1-866-506-1949 or *business@simonandschuster.com*.

The Simon & Schuster Speakers Bureau can bring authors
to your live event. For more information or to book an event,
contact the Simon & Schuster Speakers Bureau at 1-866-248-3049
or visit our website at *www.simonspeakers.com*.

Designed by Ruth Lee-Mui

Manufactured in the United States of America

3   5   7   9   10   8   6   4   2

The Library of Congress has cataloged the hardcover edition as follows:

Whitaker, Mark.
My long trip home / by Mark Whitaker.—1st Simon & Schuster hardcover ed.
p. cm.
1. Whitaker, Mark. 2. Television journalists—United States—Biography.
3. African American journalists—United States—Biography.
4. Journalists—United States—Biography. I. Title.
PN4874.W475A3 2011
070.92—dc22
[B]
2011002645

ISBN 978-1-4516-2754-1
ISBN 978-1-4516-2755-8 (pbk)
ISBN 978-1-4516-2756-5 (ebook)

All photographs except the one on page 190 are from the author's collection.

For Alexis, Rachel, and Matthew

My Long Trip Home

1

Growing up, I always took it for granted that it was my mother who was first attracted to my father. After all, he was the exotic one, the gregarious one, the charm machine. She was the shy one, the one who stuttered so badly as a child that her parents sent her away to be treated by doctors in Paris and who still got self-conscious when she couldn't get her words out quickly. But when I went back and investigated, it turned out that it was the other way around: He became obsessed with her.

She had noticed him around campus, of course. As one of the few black students at Swarthmore College in the mid-1950s, he was hard to miss. She had heard him perform once or twice: He played the guitar and sang folk songs. For a while, he earned pocket money by recording radio commercials, and later she would hear one of his jingles playing on the air and feel a shiver of pride when the announcer said that if the young man with that voice ever turned professional he would give him a contract. But that was news to me too, since I have no memories of my father singing.

They met in his junior year, thanks to a play. Jeanne Theis was a French instructor in her fourth year of teaching at Swarthmore. She was also the faculty adviser for the French Club and she decided that it would be fun to help the students put on a production in the original. She chose a satirical one-act play by Jean Giraudoux called *Supplément au voyage de Cook* that recounts the fanciful story of Captain Cook's arrival in the tropics. To direct, she enlisted Michael DeLaszlo, a junior from England who had taken one of her classes as a freshman. They cast most of the parts but didn't have anyone to play Chief Outourou, the tribal leader who greets the explorers. DeLaszlo said he knew someone who had the perfect look for the part: his roommate, Syl Whitaker.

The only hitch was that he didn't speak French. When he agreed to take on the role, she had to coach him so he could learn his lines and speak with a convincing accent. They met before rehearsals and several times in her apartment, in a dorm called Roberts, where she oversaw "French Hall," a suite of rooms for students who wanted to speak the language and attend her weekly teas. She was impressed by how quickly he learned and by what a good mimic he was. They laughed at the part where the chief, to show hospitality, offers his daughters to the flustered, repressed Englishmen. She noticed how his cheeks dimpled when he smiled and how the worry lines in his forehead creased when he was making a serious point. In all, there was no mistaking how handsome he was, particularly when he put on his grass-skirt costume for rehearsals and bared his dark, muscular chest.

But she was startled the night of the wrap party, which she threw at Roberts, when they were talking in a corner of her crowded apartment and all of a sudden he kissed her.

She pulled back, looking confused.

"I thought you wanted me to do that," he said. "The other day, when you touched my arm, I thought it was a signal."

"I'm sorry," she said. "That's just something I have the habit of doing when I'm talking to people."

He must have seen her blushing, since her skin was fair and freckled and framed by black hair that she wore, Jean Seberg–style, in a short bob. But her diffidence didn't deter him. In fact, it may have been part of the allure when he had fantasized about wooing her, as he must have done, since in 1955 a black student would hardly have dared to kiss his white teacher on the lips simply on a spur-of-the-moment whim.

"Would you mind if I visited you here again?" he asked.

"I suppose that would be all right," she replied.

He started to come by Roberts every few days, for an hour or so at a time. They would listen to music, and he brought his favorite 45s and introduced her to black jazz singers like the infectious Nellie Lutcher and Eartha Kitt, with her seductive purr. Sometimes he would kiss her or hold her hand, and she would primly consent, but mostly they talked.

He told her about growing up in Pittsburgh, about his parents the morticians and what it was like to live above a funeral parlor. When his mother came to visit friends in Philadelphia, he arranged for them to meet. My mother was instantly impressed by Grandmother Edith's light-skinned beauty and her elegant manner and entertaining way of speaking. He rarely mentioned C.S., the man he was named for, except to say that they didn't get along and that his parents were divorced. He confessed that his father had beaten him as a child. Eventually they discovered what was for him a humiliating coincidence: My mother had gone to graduate school at Bryn Mawr with a girl who came from Harrisburg and whose family had employed Granddad as a butler after he lost his business.

She told him about her parents, about how they met as Protestant missionaries in Africa, where she was born and spent much of her childhood before they moved to France. She described how she came to America on a boat with five of her little sisters when she was fourteen and went to live with the family of Dr. Enders, the Swarthmore biology professor, which was how she came to attend college there and later return to join the French Department. And she explained the reason her parents had sent her away, the dangerous work that caused Pastor Theis to be watched and arrested by the Vichy police. She told him how much she loved and admired her father and how sad she thought it was that he disliked his own so much.

They reminisced about student work camps. After the war, she had returned to France for several summers to attend the work camps at the boarding school that her father had founded in the mountains of central France, joining young people who came from across the country and as far away as Britain and America to build classrooms and dorm barracks. In high school, he had started going to summer work camps run by the Quakers. His Bible school teacher at Bethany Baptist, his family's church in Pittsburgh, had first told him about a Friends camp in Ithaca when he was fifteen. He decided to go there after some local Quakers offered to pay his way, although for the life of him he couldn't understand why well-to-do white kids from places like New York and Boston and Chicago would spend good money to do manual labor in the hot summer sun.

When he arrived in upstate New York and was first introduced to Quaker ideas about nonviolence, "I told them that I had never heard anything more preposterous," he would later tell the author of a book about the Friends. But before long he found himself drawn to the faith's teachings about simplicity and pacifism and the subtle power of silent prayer, so different from the raucous call-and-response of the black church services he was used to. Around the campfire at night, the work campers sang folk and protest songs, and when he returned to Pittsburgh he told his mother that he intended to worship as a Quaker and to teach himself how to play the guitar.

He recounted the harrowing time he had at a work camp the next summer, in the backwoods of Harlan County, Kentucky. A Pittsburgh Quaker named Spahr Hull, who later became my godfather, told him that the Friends were looking for a black student to integrate Pine Mountain, their first camp in the Deep South. Locating a *Time* magazine article about "Bloody Harlan," my father learned that there had been a murder indictment in the county every month for 132 years.

Still, he agreed to go, confident that the force of his goodwill and winning personality would see him through.

On his second night there, a dozen hillbilly kids came to the camp for a square dance. Seeing one of the local white girls sitting alone on the other side of the camp's lodge, my father worked up the courage to ask her to do-si-do. She nodded and he took her hand, but she never looked him in the eye, and her damp fingers and the red tips of her ears betrayed how nervous she was. Afterward he discovered that the night watchman, who was called Old Martin, had complained to a nurse at the infirmary. "I can't stand to see a nigger touch a white woman like that!" the guard said. "They'll soon run that nigger out of here, and I won't do a thing to stop them!"

Before long, a group of hillbilly boys started lurking on the outskirts of Pine Mountain day and night, asking where my father slept and once hanging a white rope over a tree. "Hey, which of you gals wrang that nigger's neck until it got black?" they called out to a group of girls as they passed by with a female counselor.

One day the work campers went on an overnight trip and had to search for hours to find a spot that wasn't marked "White" and "Colored" to set up their tents. In the middle of the night, four cars pulled up with headlights flashing. A dozen drunken men got out, announcing that they had come to get "that nigger." The camp director, a local Kentucky minister named Sandy Sandborne, grabbed a flashlight and went out to the road to talk to them. He calmly insisted that the person they were looking for wasn't there, and eventually the drunks got back in the cars and left, giving the campers a terrible scare but also an object lesson, as my father described it to my mother, in the power of nonviolent resistance.

He told her about another terrifying incident that happened later that summer. Toward the end of the eight-week camp, the brother of the girl he had asked to square-dance came back to town and joined the loitering pack of local white boys. All of a sudden, they started to be suspiciously nice to my father. They shouted out to invite him to join them on a hike, then on a rifle-shoot. The other campers told him to ignore them, especially a white Jewish girl from New York with whom he had been taking long walks. What if they were trying to lure him into an "accident"? she warned. But he replied that the whole point of work camping was to teach people from different backgrounds to get to know and respect each other. If he didn't go, he would always wonder what was really in their hearts. So when the local boys arrived in a car to pick him up, he climbed into the backseat.

They drove to a clearing in the woods with a big tree stump at the end. Shotguns were handed out and everyone took turns firing at cans placed on top of the wooden nub. Once all the cans were knocked down, one boy at a time would walk across the clearing and set them up again. When it was my father's turn, he set off slowly toward the stump, his back to the other boys.

He said that he never experienced so powerfully the physical effects of fear. Every muscle in his body tightened up, and he felt like he was going to vomit. After setting up the cans, he turned around and faced what looked like a hillbilly firing squad: six local boys with long scraggly hair, dressed in tattered overalls, holding shotguns. His breathing stopped and he almost fainted as he walked back toward them. But no one fired, and from then on the white boys treated him like one of them, as though he had passed a tribal test of manhood. On the last week of camp, the family of the girl at the square dance invited all the work campers to a chicken dinner. After that, he told my mother, he felt he really understood what the Quaker belief in searching for the Light in every human being was all about.

As they talked, visit after visit, my mother found herself falling in love. It was partly a physical condition, with all the usual symptoms: She couldn't stop thinking about him when they were apart, and she longed for their next rendezvous. As she walked across campus, she found herself humming a Nellie Lutcher tune: *"He's got a fine brown frame, I wonder what could be his name. He looks good to me, and all I can see is his fine brown frame. . . ."*

But for her, it was an intellectual process as well. She fell in love with the idea of him. He was handsome in a way that particularly appealed to her, perhaps because she had spent her early childhood in Africa. She respected his bravery in coming to a virtually all-white school like Swarthmore and good-naturedly confronting the racism he had encountered in his life. And she was moved that he took his faith so seriously, that coming from such different backgrounds they shared the same commitment to battling the world's evils by turning the other cheek rather than demanding an eye for an eye.

She was taken with his charisma and the almost chemical effect he had on other people. From the time he arrived at Swarthmore, he had "displaced a lot of water," as one of his friends described it. He told her the story of how, as a freshman, he had gone into the little barbershop in town for a trim and the barber had refused to serve him. Word spread across campus and soon scores of students joined a boycott. One Greek-American student from Massachusetts named Michael Dukakis even began offering haircuts in his dorm room, a story that decades later the Dukakis campaign would tout in his presidential run.

She saw that Syl Whitaker knew how to enjoy himself, when he would arrive with stories of sneaking off with Michael DeLaszlo in his roommate's car to go to a jazz club in Philadelphia or to get their favorite hoagie sandwiches at a delicatessen called Stacky's in Chester. (She didn't hear the story of how his roommates had once been shooting the bull late at night and played a game of How Would You Like to Die? "In an airplane crash while making love!" my father proclaimed, impressing them all with his bravado and the implicit implication that he *had* made love before.)

But she also saw him as possessing a maturity and talent for leadership beyond his years. That impression only deepened when, in the months they were meeting secretly, he was selected to run the Swarthmore Folk Festival. The three-day event had started in the mid-1940s, when she was an undergraduate, and by the time she came back to teach in the early 1950s it was the biggest thing on campus. Singers like Pete Seeger and Woody Guthrie and Leadbelly had all come to perform, and each year hundreds of young people from up and down the East Coast descended on the college, filling the walkways with their cars and littering the dorm rooms with their sleeping bags. To headline the 1955 festival, my father booked Josh White, one of my mother's favorites, and the black protest singer got the crowd stomping and clapping and singing along to his renditions of "Lonesome Road" and "On Top of Old Smokey."

Yet as soon as it was over, Swarthmore's president, Courtney Smith, sent word through his deans that the festival had become too big and disruptive. My father was chosen to mediate and he spent days crafting a proposal for new rules that would have limited the number of outside visitors and required registration in advance. But Smith rejected the compromise and eventually canceled the 1956 concert. My father concluded that the WASP-ish president, who had once decreed to the student body that he would tolerate "no ostentatious displays of affection," was simply a prude. He didn't like the fact that students held hands during the festival and wore blue jeans. The jeans issue rankled my father so much that he decided to visit Smith in his office in Parish Hall to discuss the matter. He pointed out that as a financially strapped student on a full scholarship, he wore jeans to cut down on his cleaning bills, but Smith was unimpressed and curtly dismissed him after a short conversation.

By the end of the school year, my mother had decided that her feelings for my father were strong enough that she needed to confide in someone. She chose Hal March, an older colleague in the French Department who had become somewhat of a professional father figure. March wasn't shocked or scandalized, but he expressed concern about what the consequences would be for her reputation if she were seen to have been in a frivolous affair with a student, especially one who happened to be black. So he summoned my father to a meeting in his office.

"Do you intend to marry her?" he asked.

My parents had never discussed the idea, and at that point it may well have never occurred to my father. But from the white professor's stern tone, he must have grasped that he had started something that could only be made respectable in the eyes of the college and the broader society of mid-1950s America by giving it the sanctity of an engagement.

"Yes, I would like to marry her," he answered.

The next time my parents met, my father recounted the discussion with Professor March and reiterated his matrimonial intentions. He didn't exactly propose, and my mother didn't exactly accept. It was as though they were at a Quaker Meeting and had reached consensus that they would eventually get married.

"I guess I just assumed everything would work out," my mother told me as she looked back. She hardly thought of herself as a spinster, but she was already twenty-eight. Some of her younger sisters were already married, and she always assumed that one day she would be too. She was in love with my father, as she understood it. She never stopped to think what marrying a black man might mean for her career or for any children they might have. And at the time, she didn't see what was so wrong with a teacher being involved with a student—male professors did it all the time—particularly if they waited until after he graduated for the wedding.

She also confessed that the engagement relieved her of another anxiety: what to do about sex. For someone of her religious upbringing, it wasn't something you did with a mere boyfriend. But now it could happen, and by the end of the semester it did.

What was my father thinking when they decided to get married? "He probably saw it as a big adventure that would impress his Quaker friends," my mother said. But I'm sure that it was more complicated than that. He must have believed that he was in love too, but at age twenty what did that mean? After all their long talks, did he think that he had found a soul mate, or was he still in the grip of infatuation? Had his summer in Pine Mountain stirred not only an attraction to white women but an appetite for risk? How noteworthy was it that she was an older, professional woman, someone like his mother, although as different from Grandmother Edith as she could be in outward appearance and personality? And how driven was he by his ambition and competitive insecurities, by the prospect that she could help him with advice and inside information on where he stood in relation to all the brainy white students of Swarthmore?

When classes were over, he returned to Pittsburgh to earn a few weeks' pay working in the post office, while she stayed in Swarthmore to grade exams. One night his roommates invited her for a drink at Sam's bar, a place that students went to in the nearby village of Media, because Swarthmore was a dry town. After a glass of whiskey, she momentarily forgot that not all of them were in on the secret.

"So you're the one who is going to work in East Harlem this summer!" she said when she was introduced to Knowles Dougherty, an all-American type with a big grin.

"How did you know that?" he asked.

"Uh, Syl told me," she said, recognizing her gaffe but not wanting to tell a lie.

Later in the conversation she recommended that they all read *Anti-Semite and Jew*, by Jean-Paul Sartre.

"Yes, Syl is reading it," said Paul Berry, a senior who was one of two roommates, along with Michael DeLaszlo, who knew about the romance.

This time she knew enough not to comment on the connection.

My father and his group lived in a dorm called Mary Lyons, and my mother had arranged to take a faculty apartment there in the fall so they could be closer together. But when she told Bob Cross, another professor who resided in the dorm, he asked teasingly: "What kind of immoral behavior are you planning to indulge in down there?" She didn't think he knew, but the remark disturbed her and made her realize how careful they had to be.

Hoping it would please him, she wrote my father to tell him how the graduating seniors he knew had done in their final honors exams. But then she made the mistake of revealing details of a faculty meeting about the junior honors exams that he and members of his class had just taken. She told him that he had received an "adequate" on one test and that the chair of the History Department had joked that she was going to write him a letter urging him to drop the honors track in political science in favor of history.

That night, he called her from Pittsburgh in a huff. What did "adequate" mean? he asked indignantly. Nothing bad, she comforted him; it was the standard grade for all tests except those deemed worthy of highest honors. And was the history chair suggesting that he couldn't cut it in poli-sci? he wanted to know. No, she replied; it was meant as a compliment, that surely the History Department just wanted to claim him because he was bound to have such impressive final results.

The phone conversation must have rattled her, because the next day she put off grading her comp and diction papers and sat down to write a letter that went on four pages in her tiny, tightly packed handwriting and took her six hours to finish. "Darling, please don't feel deflated," she wrote, "or I shall never again report what the faculty says in its curious, superficially supercilious language. . . . Heck, you're in a very strong position, don't be ultra-sensitive. I don't worry about you for a minute, except because you are so sensitive."

Then she talked about hearing an Eartha Kitt song and thinking about him. "Syl, I miss you so much," she wrote. "I can waste so much time just wishing I were with you, dammit. I shouldn't feel this way because it'll be so long before we can be together much. If I can't be more sensible I'll begin thinking loving you is unrealistic and wrong."

But his defensiveness must have hit a nerve with her too, because halfway through the letter she started venting some of her own resentments. She complained about the "clever self-protectiveness" that was "rampant" among her colleagues on the Swarthmore faculty. "I do mind eventually this too-too faddish and witty atmosphere among the faculty here," she wrote. "It finally amounts to conformism of a would-be superior kind. . . . Dismissing every problem with a joke becomes tiresome. . . . I also greatly minded a few comments I heard last night about Christianity not having a place in the modern world."

Then she said some things that suggested that her own earnest beliefs had started to become a source of friction between the two of them. "I realize that the feeling that this is God's world is essential to me . . ." she wrote. "I've also been thinking quite a bit about what the implications would be for the way we love each other under God, so to speak. I don't mean to be theological, or use high-sounding language. But it is very important—please understand . . . Syl, honest, I love you very much—but I don't love you more than I love God. This sentence sounds almost indecent, I know—but you understand what I mean. You think your most fundamental beliefs are important too. As a matter of fact, I think our fundamental beliefs are the same. But we've got to learn to talk about them without getting irritated by each other's language."

The moment of touchiness appears to have passed, and several weeks later she joined him in Pittsburgh and they set out on a trip to Mexico City. He was headed for a Quaker work camp in El Salvador, and she had decided to accompany him part of the way. Because Michael DeLaszlo had a car, he offered to drive them along with another of their roommates, David Steinmuller. His vehicle was a 1947 Town and Country that Michael's wealthy father had purchased from a used car salesman in Detroit but had smashed up in a minor accident almost as soon as it was off the lot. In a rush to get to freshman week at Swarthmore, they had bought the first replacement parts they could find: a red hood and blue fenders. So it was a wagon of many colors that carried the interracial band toward the Texas border, on a route that stretched through the Jim Crow South.

Although my father had a driver's license, he didn't dare take the wheel for fear that the Dixie cops would pull him over. DeLaszlo and Steinmuller took turns driving, while my father and mother sat on the red-leather seats in the back. To avoid having to use separate "White" and "Colored" eating areas and bathrooms, they ordered takeout dishes from roadside restaurants and ate the food in the car. When my father needed to relieve himself, the station wagon pulled over to the side of the road.

Once they reached Mexico, my mother returned to Pittsburgh while he went on to a work camp near San Salvador. There, young Friends were called *"Amigos,"* and a year later, when one of his Swarthmore classmates visited the village where he stayed, the locals were still talking about how charming he had been. "There was a young man called Agripino Flores who is now teaching in the *escuela segundaria* in Xochimilco," she wrote him. "He too was with the *Amigos* last summer and remembers you. He said what a *buen amigo* you had been, and *muy* sociable and how well you got on with the children playing basketball."

My mother returned to Pittsburgh to wait until he returned, riding a Greyhound bus that was crowded with women reading *True Romance* and *Confidential* and talkative soldiers on leave. As the bus retraced their car route, she counted the segregated rest stops all the way to St. Louis. Once she reached the funeral home that his mother ran then, at 616 Belmont Street in Belzhoover, she passed the time sewing dresses on an old foot-pedal machine and enjoying the salty soul food served up by Grandmother Edith and her mother, whom everyone called Gram. The two of them and my father's sisters, Gertrude, Della, and Cleo, all treated her like family, but she was still sometimes overcome by shyness and realized how much she was coming to depend on him to help her engage with the world. "You leave a big hole, you know," she wrote him wistfully.

When they got back to the college in the fall, he persuaded her to buy a car, even though she didn't drive, so they could spend time together away from prying eyes on campus. She dipped into her meager savings to purchase a used blue Kaiser coupe from a freshman for $250. They took the car to movies in Philadelphia and made two more trips across the state to Pittsburgh. Occasionally she accompanied him to Bryn Mawr, her graduate school alma mater, where he cross-registered in an anthropology course so as to have another excuse to leave Swarthmore.

One day as they drove along the Main Line, a white policeman pulled them over and asked where they were going. My father politely answered his questions, and the cop allowed them to move on. But once they were moving again, he exploded with rage. He hadn't been speeding or violating any traffic regulations! The only reason the cop had stopped them was that he was a black man in a car with a white woman! But then he shook his head and said that a black man could never "get lippy" with a police officer, a warning that he would pass on to me decades later.

By now my mother was all too aware of my father's brooding about his academic standing, but she still admired how hard he worked in Swarthmore's honors program. Juniors and seniors who were admitted into this select group met in small seminars, often in the homes of their professors. Rather than passively receiving instruction, they learned from each other, spending hours debating papers that a couple of students in each class were assigned to spark discussion. Before graduating, they sat for written and oral exams by visiting professors. Come spring, my father impressed the outside examiners enough to be awarded high honors. Yet privately, he fumed that he hadn't attained highest honors like his friend Norman Rush, an older student from San Francisco who had done jail time as a conscientious objector and would later become a novelist.

Finally, on a sunny day in June, Syl Whitaker donned his black commencement gown and cap and became one of only a handful of black students ever to receive a Swarthmore diploma. In the 1956 *Halcyon,* the college yearbook, his dark visage stands out among pages of white faces. The accompanying paragraph captures the many sides of his personality: a nickname, "The Whit," conveying his joviality: his favorite expression, "Hmmm . . . ," suggesting his thoughtfulness; and a final note whose irony jolted me when I read it: ". . . always a breath of sobriety."

Two months later, on August 18, my parents married on a rainy day in Le Chambon-sur-Lignon, the little mountain village in France where my grandfather was the assistant pastor and ran his secondary school. All six of my mother's sisters who lived in France were there, along with Michael DeLaszlo and a college friend of my mother's named Cushing Dolbeare and her husband. My father wore a light gray tie and a dark suit over his slender frame, and my mother looked radiant in a stylish white wedding dress that she had sewn herself. According to French custom, they went first to the mayor's office to sign an official marriage certificate, then they made their way under an umbrella down the slippery cobblestone streets to the small Protestant temple at the bottom of the village. A friend of Pastor Theis presided over an austere religious ceremony, and as he paused for a moment of silent prayer, a thunderclap cracked the sky outside and shook the windows of the church.

For their honeymoon, they visited one of my mother's college friends, Janet Nyholm, who had married a Danish artist and moved to Denmark. They spent several days under cloudy skies in Copenhagen and saw a flea circus that they thought was particularly hilarious.

They had kept their year-and-a-half courtship so quiet that most faculty and students at Swarthmore were stunned when they heard the news. But it didn't come as a surprise to school president Courtney Smith. Earlier in the year, my father had gone to Parish Hall to inform him of their intentions. It wasn't just the skirmishes over the folk festival and the blue jeans that had made him wary of how Smith would respond. It was also how unsympathetic the stiff-necked president had been toward another interracial couple on campus. When a Jewish senior named Edgar Cahn and a black junior named Jean Camper had begun dating, they had received an anonymous death threat, and one day someone had burned a cross outside her dorm room. Cahn had appealed to Smith to do something about it, but the president had refused, sniffily implying that they had only themselves to blame. One of his deans had even started calling Cahn's parents whenever the two lovebirds were seen together, in a ham-handed attempt to break them up.

Sure enough, President Smith confirmed my father's worst suspicions. Although my mother was coming up for tenure and had her department's support, he waffled about her prospects. My father was irate, and so were the friends he confided in. "Of course, going to Courtney was a basic error," his former roommate Paul Berry wrote from graduate school in Stanford. Then he added sarcastically: "I hereby propose that he be awarded the title of Courtney Craig Smith, R.Q., for Reluctant Quaker, an even more dangerous form than the Confused Quaker."

When my parents returned from their honeymoon in late August, they heard that Smith was whispering word of his disapproval. A friend and classmate named Annie Guerin wrote my father urging him not to do anything rash. "Don't get too angry at President Smith," she advised, teasing him that she wanted to see "faculty reactions to your highly reprehensible marriage!"

But my father wasn't about to take the situation lying down. He complained angrily about my mother's predicament to civil rights leaders whom he had met through Quaker circles.

One day the phone rang at my parents' apartment and my father picked up the receiver.

"Hello?" he said.

"Syyylvester!" a loud voice boomed at the other end of the line. "Bayaaard Rustin here!"

It took a second for it to sink in that one of America's foremost civil rights leaders, Bayard Rustin, the man who would organize Martin Luther King Jr.'s march on Washington seven years later, was on the line.

"I hear you're having some trouble there in Swarthmore!" Rustin said in his stentorian baritone.

Rustin's advice was to go over Smith's head to Swarthmore's board of directors. He reached out to other civil rights leaders who wrote letters on my parents' behalf, reminding them of the college's long history of championing racial equality. My father's Quaker mentors sent testimonials to his religious faith and work camp experience. In the end, the board told Smith to back off, and my mother received tenure after all.

That fall, my parents moved into one of the faculty apartments at 317 North Chester Road, in one of the big Dutch colonial revival houses that had been built in Swarthmore's West Hills at the turn of the century. My father started commuting in the Kaiser coupe to Princeton, where he had been admitted as the first black doctoral student in the history of its prestigious Department of Politics. Living on my mother's meager salary of just over $3,000 a year, they were poor enough that they drove to working-class Chester to buy groceries, and my father kept going home at Christmas to work in the Pittsburgh post office. But now at least they could be public about their relationship, and they found that most of the Swarthmore community was supportive. My mother's faculty friends told her how much they liked Syl and how much they admired their courage.

But there was one exception. Bob Enders, the biology professor whose family had taken my mother in during the war, was suspicious of my father. He thought he was a perfectly bright student and had no feelings of racial animus toward him, but when my mother told him about their engagement, he disapproved. As someone who was used to writing recommendations for medical school and sizing up which students would make good doctors, he prided himself on his judgments about character, and he wasn't sure about Syl Whitaker. He believed that he took advantage of my mother, as he had in pressuring her to buy the big blue car for his use as much as theirs. And he thought my father had a chip on his shoulder. Once, when they were visiting the Enders house for tea, he complained about how hard his father, C.S., had pushed him as a child, and Dr. Enders was alarmed to see how enraged he became. Uncle Bob, as she called him, was too fond of my mother to try to warn her off the marriage, but he expressed his concerns to his wife, Abbie.

"Angry men don't make good husbands," he said.

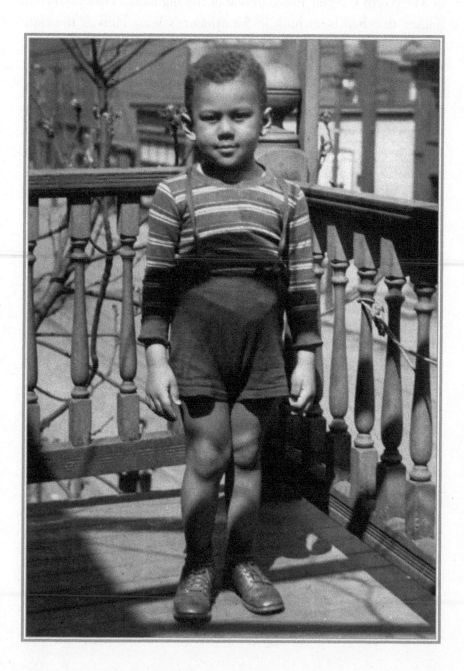

2

Another mistaken assumption: I always thought my father had inherited all of his magnetism from his mother. But that was before, a
year to the day after he died, on the Saturday after Thanksgiving, I
woke up in the middle of the night and decided that I wanted to tell
his story—a story that might remind others of a more famous biracial
child and his dreamt-of father, but that was so different, because I
had known mine for half a century, for better or, as was so often the
case, for worse. I got up in the darkness and groped for my laptop
to begin recording my memories. But my recollection only took me
so far, and there were too many blanks that had never been filled.
So I started to do what more than three decades as a journalist had
trained me to do: to interview, to collect letters and photographs, to
comb through historical records and newspapers clippings, in short,
to report. And as reporters invariably do, I discovered that the truth
was far more revealing than what I thought I knew and that the story
wasn't just about him, it was about all of us.

I had never considered the impact that my father's father had on his life. That's because when I was just a few years old, Granddad suffered a massive stroke that left him completely paralyzed on the left side of his body. From then on, his speech was labored and slurred, and his long, withered frame was confined to a wheelchair. If he was at home at Grandmother Edith's funeral home when we visited Pittsburgh for the holidays, he usually sat in the corner of the room, saying very little. Or he was staying at St. Barnabas, a depressing nursing home on the outskirts of the city, where Grandmother would take us to see him on visiting day.

It never would have occurred to me that on March 11, 1973, the day of his seventy-fifth birthday, he would have had the physical strength and mental capacity to compose an "autobiography." It was all of eleven pages long and neatly typed, so my guess is that he dictated it to a nurse at St. Barnabas. My uncle Gene searched through a desk drawer and produced it on the day I first went to interview him and my aunt Cleo for my research about my family, and for the first time I learned what a force of nature C.S. Whitaker Sr. was in his own right.

Granddad's testament begins as follows: "I hope that this autobiography will prove that I am still capable of doing something other than being here in this nursing home, at the age of 75, waiting for death."

He recorded that his father—my great-grandfather—was born a slave in the state of Texas in 1853. It wasn't until Frank Whitaker was twelve, when the Civil War ended, that he was set loose from the plantation. When he grew up he went to work on the John L. Thorn tenant farm, located in Leon County, about eight miles east of Jewett, a small town on the Great Northern Railroad line. Although he never attended school, he taught himself to write and became literate enough to submit articles to the *Jewett Messenger*, the local newspaper. "Anyone wanting to know anything about the history of Leon County would go to my father," Granddad wrote. Frank Whitaker married Della Sylman, who worked alongside him on the farm and earned extra money taking in laundry for white people in the area. In the spring of 1898, she gave birth to their eleventh and last child, Cleophaus Sylvester.

Granddad barely made it to his second birthday. "One of the earliest things I can remember," he wrote, "is being caught in a Texas hurricane and almost drowning. The rain was so intense one would strangle breathing. I am told that I almost died from malnutrition before I was two years old. My entire family, mother, father, and eleven children came down with typhoid fever at the same time but I survived the ordeal. There was only one death, my sister Julia, the oldest girl."

He began his education in a one-room schoolhouse built out of logs about five miles from the farm, where he learned the alphabet and mastered the first, second, and third "readers." A white teacher took a liking to him and sometimes invited him to spend weekends with her family. On the sly, he and his brothers and sisters made friends with some of the white children on the farm. "Although we were forbidden by our respective parents to play together, we would steal off and play together anyway," he recalled.

When young Cleophaus was thirteen years old, Frank Whitaker sent him to stay with his father-in-law in Oswego, Kansas, so that he could get a better education. At first the school there placed him in the third grade with younger and much smaller eight- and nine-year-olds. Ashamed, he asked to be promoted to the sixth grade with students closer to his own age and size. He could do most of the work at that level but struggled with mathematical fractions. Although my grandfather's grandfather was illiterate, he knew how to compute interest on money and he helped Granddad solve the problems. The next day Granddad wrote the solutions on the blackboard in class. "Then I was in trouble," he wrote, "for I could not explain how I got the answer!"

Homesick, he returned to the family farm and completed the seventh, eighth, and ninth grades in a school run by Wiley University, a black college in Marshall, Texas. But as he grew older, he realized how much his year in Oswego had opened his eyes to the backward conditions for black people in his home state. "Being able to compare the difference in civil rights in Kansas and Texas," he wrote, "I decided the South was not for me."

One of his older brothers had hopped the Great Northern line to Pittsburgh, like millions of Negroes who left the South looking for industrial jobs up the Mississippi and Ohio Rivers in the "great black migration." When Granddad arrived there in October 1916, at the age of eighteen, his brother offered him one week of free room and board but told him that he would have to pay his own way from that point on. He took a job on a construction crew for thirty cents an hour and then went to work for a floating labor gang that loaded and unloaded freight cars at the Westinghouse plant in East Pittsburgh.

Hearing that jobs inside the plant paid better and came with a free meal every day, he applied for a job in the storeroom. As he roamed around the plant on his lunch hour, he came upon a company magazine that advertised a training program open to "all employees." He went to the Education Department and said he wanted to learn how to become a machinist. But the director, a man named C.S. Coler, informed him that he was mistaken: The program was not available to black workers. "This upset me very much," Granddad recalled. "I showed him the magazine and insisted, which resulted in a controversial confrontation. We interrupted his entire office staff and I was ordered from his office."

After stewing for several days, he took a step that showed early signs of his self-confidence and prickly pride: He wrote a letter to the vice president of Westinghouse Electric, a Mr. H.P. Davis. Another black man in the storeroom had worked for Davis and assured Granddad that he was a reasonable man. The next day, he was startled to be summoned to the vice president's office at two o'clock in the afternoon.

"From this letter you seem to be dissatisfied," said Davis, a tall, wiry man with thinning white hair who struck Granddad as "the perfect executive type."

He replied that he was indeed restless and wished to get training to improve his situation.

A smile crossed Davis's face. Nothing wrong with that, he said. He gave his blessing to the machinist training but expressed wonder that a black man would be so forward. "He told me that my case was most unusual, that he never knew that any black people were dissatisfied or were not contented with their conditions," Granddad wrote. "I told him I only wished that he better understood the racial problem in America, especially the economic problem. He said that I must have some white blood and this was causing me some frustration."

Grateful for the opportunity, he enrolled in the class and was soon tracing blueprints, the first step toward becoming a machinist. Eventually he became skilled enough to work in the small industry motor division, where he was assigned to milling motor shafts slated for the navy. His foreman warned him that the material was very expensive and advised him to get regular inspection checks to avoid waste. One day, he asked the inspector to look over his first finished piece, but the man took forever examining it, turning it over and over in his hands. Since Granddad was paid on a piecework basis and the wait was costing him money, he grew impatient and kept milling shafts. When the job was done, the inspector placed the entire morning's work on his bench and marked it "ALL SCRAP."

Granddad expected to be fired on the spot. But then the general foreman of the plant appeared on the shop floor and took the inspector away to the superintendent's office. After waiting half an hour, Granddad found the suspense too much to bear and went to see what was happening.

The general foreman burst out of the superintendent's office holding a blueprint in his hand.

"Whitaker!" he shouted. "How did you make this costly mistake?"

"Why should I explain, as I am going to be fired anyway?" Granddad replied defiantly.

"Not until I hear your side of the story!" the foreman said.

Granddad asked to see the drawing and pointed out a red circle on it. "This is the item on which I was told to work," he said.

The general foreman grinned. "You're not fired," he said. "You are right. Go back to your department and go to work."

Granddad summed up the moral of the story: "I tell this incident to say that no matter how much racism we have, we still have some fair-minded white people. I never knew but have always believed that this incident was a trap, set up for me by the inspector, encouraged by my fellow workers, for within a few days the superintendent, Mr. Sharring, sent for me and said that the man on the machine next to me was spreading the rumor that I had said I could not be fired because I was his pet. I assured him that I had said nothing of the kind. He assured me he did not believe it and thought I was too smart to say anything like that."

When Granddad left Westinghouse a year later, he went to Mr. Sharring's office to thank him for his fairness. His next job was operating a crane in the foundry department of the Edgar Thomas United States Steel Works in Braddock, Pennsylvania. There too, he recalled, "I also had some difficult experiences, which makes me conclude that when and wherever a Negro has anything above a laborer's job, he will always be subject to harassment."

Granddad's "autobiography" spends nine pages recounting these early adventures and the light he believed they shed on racial attitudes. It devotes only one page to the rest of his career. He wrote that he apprenticed as an undertaker and opened two funeral homes before ill health forced him to sell the second one and that he eventually supported himself as a milk salesman. "Menzie Dairy gave me no problem," he said. "While on this job I suffered a severe stroke. . . ." It was as if that stroke had erased most of his memory of everything that happened in the half-century between the Westinghouse plant and Menzie Dairy, the years when he became wealthy and powerful and before his appetites caused it all to fall apart.

As for his personal life, he wrote that in September 1920 he had married a "wonderful" girl from Wilkinsburg named Anna Barnes. She gave birth to three "lovely daughters"—Gertrude, Della, and Cleo—before dying in 1932. Two and a half years later, he married his second wife, Edith. "She is at present in very bad health, suffering from arthritis," he wrote. "We have one son, who is teaching at the Woodrow Wilson School of Political Science at Princeton University in New Jersey." He never mentioned my father by name, and my brother Paul and I are the only ones among his nine grandchildren who were left out his last testament.

What that document doesn't record is how, after leaving the Braddock steel mill, Granddad discovered his life's calling. He had married Anna Barnes and moved to her hometown of Wilkinsburg, where he worked at the Walmer Hardware Store. To earn extra money for his young family, he took a part-time job as a chauffeur for a funeral home. It wasn't just any funeral home but Freyvogel's, the fanciest in Pittsburgh. The wealthy founder, John A. Freyvogel, had a thriving business but a looming problem: As more blacks moved into the area, prosperous colored families were coming to him to bury their loved ones. He had taken in two or three deceased Negroes, keeping the caskets empty and closed and stashing the bodies in the back of the home, but he worried that it would be bad for business if his white clients found out. What the city needed, he decided, were black funeral directors who could bury their own kind.

"Have you ever considered becoming an undertaker?" Freyvogel asked Granddad one day. They had chatted while driving around town and Freyvogel had concluded that the young black chauffeur was intelligent enough to master the art of embalming and to earn a funeral director's license. When his employer offered to arrange for an apprenticeship and to pay for his exam, Granddad seized the opportunity. He trained with Jenny Wood, one of Pittsburgh's first female undertakers, who taught him all aspects of the business, from interviewing the bereaved to staging the viewings to orchestrating the burials. Her embalmer, a Mr. Wareham, wasn't happy about having to tutor a black man but grudgingly taught him everything he needed to know about preparing the corpses: how to clean and arrange the table and the instruments, how to wash and disinfect the remains with formaldehyde, how to dispose of the human waste, and how to dress and tastefully set the facial features of the diseased. After Granddad had apprenticed for the requisite period and assisted in embalming a mandatory number of bodies, he was finally approved to take the mortician's exam and received his certificate.

Once he was licensed, he opened a funeral home in a frame house in Rankin, a small borough on the Monongahela River south of Pittsburgh. It was a mill town, with more Poles and Czechs than black folk, and he had no illusions that any of his white neighbors would give him business, but he calculated that his establishment would have more cachet with well-to-do blacks if it were located in a mixed neighborhood. Before long, other black funeral homes would open across Pittsburgh—McTurner's and West's and Gaines—but Whitaker's was one of the first.

Before he moved to Rankin, Anna Barnes had died of tuberculosis, six months after giving birth to their third child. When Granddad learned he had another daughter, he worried that he might never have a son and decided to give her the female version of his name, Cleo. Then not long after his first wife passed, he met a beautiful, fair-skinned young lady in her early twenties named Edith McColes. She was an accomplished pianist, gifted enough to earn money giving classical recitals. She grew up in the Hill District, the neighborhood in downtown Pittsburgh on the north side of the river that had become the hub of black life in the city. Her father came from Virginia and was light enough to pass as a white man at his job at the railroad company. Her mother, whose roots were on the eastern shore of Maryland, wasn't much darker, but just enough that she never dared visit her husband at his place of work. They both spoiled Edith, who was their only child.

For someone of Cleophaus Whitaker's background, it was a clear case of courting up. Edith McColes came from the black elite that had migrated to Pittsburgh before World War I, and her parents mixed with the well-to-do crowd of colored professionals on the Hill that belonged to restrictive clubs like the Loendi and the Frogs and the Greek letter societies. Although she never went to college, she was a graduate of Schenley High School, one of the city's finest, with its imposing limestone edifice on the edge of the Hill District in Oakland. When Granddad had arrived in Pittsburgh fifteen years earlier as just another southern migrant, he could never have aspired to woo a young woman of such refinement. But unlike so many of the young black men he had worked with then, he hadn't remained in the steel mills. He was now a successful businessman who called himself "C.S." like the white supervisor in the Westinghouse plant. He had learned to act and dress the part, and his intelligence and ardor and good looks won her over.

C.S. Whitaker and Edith McColes were wed in 1934, and less than a year later, on February 21, 1935, she gave birth to a son. Granddad was overjoyed to finally have a male heir and insisted on naming my father Cleophaus Sylvester Whitaker Jr.

Nicknamed "Junior," he immediately exhibited a sweet, engaging temperament. He was the baby of the family and his sister Cleo was only three years older, so the two became inseparable. In many of the family photographs from the Rankin days, they are posed together. In one picture taken as they set out for church on Easter Sunday, Cleo, already tall for her age, wears a long white dress and my father stands beside her in a white jacket and matching shorts. In another photo snapped on the front porch of their home, he sits atop a tricycle, dressed in a pair of short overalls, a striped shirt, and tiny patent leather shoes. His round face is framed by large, protruding ears, his distinctive worry lines already visible on his forehead, and he gazes at the camera with a precociously mature look.

In the 1930s, the spread of influenza and TB created a thriving trade for the Whitaker Funeral Home in Rankin. When FDR took America into World War II after Pearl Harbor, business boomed. Every week, it seemed, another family of a black serviceman killed in battle was calling to make arrangements. With a successful business and a growing nest egg to protect, Granddad began to worry about what would happen to his young family if he were no longer around. So he suggested to Grandmother that she earn an undertaker's degree as well. At first she demurred—it was hardly a refined pianist's dream—but he was so persistent that eventually she consented. Like him, she mastered every aspect of the profession, from the parlor to the grave, although she never had his stomach for embalming. She learned just enough about the procedure to pass the exam but afterward always insisted on hiring someone else to deal with the corpses.

By 1942, the Whitakers were flush with cash and decided that it was time to leave Rankin and move to a more prosperous area. They set their sights on a neighborhood in Pittsburgh called Homewood Brushton. Although the local population was still predominantly Italian, with a smattering of Irish and Jews, Homewood had a small, prosperous black community. Grandmother had heard that a local music teacher named Mary Cardwell Dawson was opening the National Negro Opera House on Apple Street. She thought the local high school, Westinghouse, would be a fine place to educate her children, with its long tradition of graduating talented Negro musicians like the jazz pianist Erroll Garner and Duke Ellington's collaborator Billy Strayhorn.

Granddad had long envied a property in Homewood, the Leslie Funeral Home on Bennett Street. It was a big, square, brown-brick house with three floors and a wide stone stairway leading down to the street. The first floor had a large viewing parlor, a business office, and an embalming room in the back, and the two upstairs floors would be more than ample for a family of six. There was only one catch: Bennett Street was an all-white block. Leslie would surely never sell his property to a Negro! But Granddad had an idea: He knew a white businessman who could buy the house as his proxy and then turn over the deed. His friend agreed to the scheme, and before anyone knew what was happening, the Whitakers had moved in as the first black family on the street.

At first the neighbors were furious. A group of men from the block tracked down Leslie, the former owner, and gave him a beating.

"For Sale" signs went up in front of some of the homes. But then the white families noticed how the Whitakers were fixing up their place. They painted the shutters on the windows white, planted flowers out front, and constructed an imposing green awning over the front steps with "Whitaker Funeral Home" emblazoned in bold script. Not to be outdone, other families on the street began making improvements to their houses, and with time they came to accept and even become friends with the black undertaker and his elegant wife and their well-behaved children. "The Whitakers are different from other Negroes," they told each other.

For Gertrude, Della, Cleo, and Junior, Bennett Street was a dream come true. They went to integrated local schools with clean hallways and up-to-date sports facilities: Homewood Elementary through sixth grade, then Westinghouse High. The teachers at both schools treated them with respect and expected them to do just as well as the white students. On Sundays, the family attended Bethany Baptist Church, where all the young Whitakers were baptized. While my grandparents worked the church pews upstairs, the children joined their black friends downstairs in Sunday school.

From the time the younger children could walk, Grandmother had taken them to classical music concerts; now, in Homewood, they were able to indulge their taste for popular culture. At the end of Bennett Street was not just one but two movie theaters: the Belmar, with its wide seats and a plush red carpet; and the Highland, just down the street, which was not as grand but charged five cents less per ticket. On Saturdays and Sundays after church, they and their friends had only to go down the block to see the latest movies starring Jimmy Cagney and Fred Astaire and Ginger Rogers.

At home, there was enough money to hire maids to clean the house and do the laundry, but Grandmother still insisted that the girls help in the kitchen and that Junior take out the garbage. "You may have enough money not to do chores," she told them, "but you should still get in the habit in case some day you don't!"

As partners in business, my grandparents made quite a team. To begin with, they were an exceptionally handsome couple. Granddad was over six feet tall, with a broad forehead and strong, square jaw. He wore a neat brush mustache and wire-rimmed glasses that added to his air of distinction. Grandmother had a beautiful round face and showed off her delicate, mocha-colored skin by plucking her eyebrows pencil thin and straightening her hair in a fashionable wave. Between them, they could handle any business or social occasion. C.S. was the master salesman and negotiator. He bargained hard with the car dealer who rented out hearses for burials and took other men out for drinks at the local pool hall. He cut a distinguished figure at the gravesites of dead soldiers, as he did in a picture that can still be found in the archives of Teenie Harris, the veteran black photographer for the *Pittsburgh Courier*.

With anyone who didn't appreciate her husband's brusqueness, Edith would take the lead. Everyone loved "Edie." She held hands and comforted the bereaved just as easily as she gossiped and told stories over games of bridge. Whether people liked doing business with the Whitakers because of C.S. or because of Edith, it was all the same to them. The money all went to the same place: the family bank account.

They were particularly skilled at cultivating one major source of business. Under the table, Granddad handed out generous referral fees to black clergymen for recommending his services. They went out of their way to entertain the good reverends, whether from Bethany or any Baptist or Methodist church with blacks in the congregation. Their home was always open, and so was their liquor cabinet. Black ministers never drank in front of their own parishioners and risked losing their jobs if word got out that they indulged in spirits. But late at night, when young Cleo and Junior crept down the stairway from their bedrooms in the attic, they often saw men they recognized from the pulpit sitting in the living room with their parents. The pastors held the fancy family crystal in their hands, and they nodded readily as Grandmother offered to refill the glasses.

"You are not to breathe a word of what you saw!" she would tell them if she caught them spying. If her guests ever noticed, she would assure them that they had nothing to worry about: Her children could keep a secret.

Grandmother herself had something to stay mum about: the women who were forever calling the house, asking for "Undertaker Whitaker" and pretending that it was about business. Still, she knew better. Her girlfriends in the neighborhood kept her up to date. Sometimes the ladies even informed on each other, out of jealousy or sheer maliciousness. But she kept playing bridge with all of them, as though nothing were amiss. Her husband's philandering gave her permission to engage in her own flirtations, she told herself, and if his way with women helped bring in customers, then so much the better for the family too.

By the late 1940s, the business on Bennett Street was doing so well that Granddad started talking about opening another funeral home. He suggested that Grandmother run it, since she had her own license. They decided to start the way they had in Rankin: with a small establishment outside of Pittsburgh, where there was less competition and real estate was cheaper. Since they catered to well-to-do blacks in Homewood, they set their sights on another market: the rapidly expanding postwar population of working-class Negroes. After some scouting, they settled on a town called Monessen, about twenty miles south of Pittsburgh, that was the headquarters of Pittsburgh Steel, the largest foundry in the area and employer to a growing black work force.

The Edith M. Whitaker Funeral Home in Monessen turned out to be good for the family's finances but not for the Whitaker marriage. The long commute kept Grandmother away from Bennett Street for long stretches of time. Granddad had more freedom to cat around and he grew more indiscreet. When she returned to Homewood, she had to suffer the indignity of hearing about his public goings-on from her friends and neighbors.

She confronted him, and they quarreled bitterly.

"Maybe I'll leave you!" she told him in the middle of an argument one night.

"You never would leave me!" he responded dismissively. "You couldn't make it on your own!"

"I wouldn't be so sure!" she said.

When they finally divorced, some of her girlfriends told each other that it all traced back to that dare. It wasn't just the infidelity that Edie couldn't forgive; it was the condescension.

Grandmother moved the children to a smaller house in Homewood so they could continue to go to Westinghouse High. Without the household help she was used to, she decided that maintaining a business miles away from Pittsburgh was no longer practical. She shut down her establishment in Monessen and opened another Edith M. Whitaker Funeral Home in the Hill District, on Fullerton Street. If the Hill had a "red light district," Fullerton was it, with its prostitutes who worked the speakeasies and the street corners at night. She couldn't charge anything close to the rates she had commanded on Bennett Street, but at least on the Hill there was a ready supply of customers in what by the late 1940s and early 1950s had become a virtually all-black section of the city.

Neither of my grandparents anticipated the devastating impact that their breakup would have on the Bennett Street business. For a decade, people had associated the Whitaker Funeral Home with both C.S. and Edith. Now that the two were separated, none of their friends or customers wanted to take sides, and instead they simply took their accounts and referrals elsewhere. As the phone stopped ringing, Granddad became obsessed with the belief that his clients were deserting him because they thought that he had wronged his children. He also felt hurt and outraged that his children all preferred to stay with Grandmother, even the daughters, who were his offspring and not hers.

He became determined to at least win Cleo back. Of all the children, she was the least judgmental; even after the breakup she always professed to love her parents equally. He told his youngest daughter, who was still in high school, that he would pay for her to go to college if she would come live with him. But she told him that she preferred to remain with her siblings and the woman she had known as her mother since the age of three.

Granddad was unforgiving. When Cleo graduated from Westinghouse, he refused to help her get another degree. "You made your decision, now you can go to college the best you can!" he said. She was forced to take secretarial work to pay for night school at Pitt, and for two years she gave up her studies to work full-time, which she was doing when she met the man she would marry: Eugene McCray, a trim, ebony-handsome member of the Baptist Youth League who was studying to be an engineer.

As the personal and financial stress mounted, my grandfather started to suffer from hypertension and other health problems. He couldn't keep his funeral business afloat and was forced to put the Bennett Street house up for sale. A local caterer, Hattie Green, purchased the imposing brick home he loved so much. Humiliated, he fled to Harrisburg, in the middle of the state. In his nursing home testament, he said he took a "church job" there. He didn't mention that he also worked as a butler and as a valet in a country club, tending to members' coats in the dining hall and shining shoes in the locker room.

Granddad's relationship with his namesake suffered the most as his marriage and business fell apart. Even in happier days, the two had never been close. My father had come along just as the undertaking business was taking off in Rankin, and Granddad was always busy with work. He could be tough on his son, taking off his belt to lash him when he misbehaved and demanding that he bring home good grades from school. But apart from that, he never gave him much personal attention. Although he loved fishing, he never took Junior along as so many fathers do; instead he went off on fishing trips with his pool hall buddies.

Few outside the family knew about the tense relationship, given the friendly face that my father presented to the world. He got along well with his three older sisters and had a wide circle of friends at school and church. On Sundays, he and his buddy Bobby Ayers and his brother would get dressed up to go to Bethany Baptist, looking sharp in their double-breasted suits and wide ties and broad-rimmed fedoras. Afterward, they'd ride the streetcars around town or take in a movie. They played poker at each other's houses and listened to Bobby's big band records. In one picture of the three friends taken when they were in their early teens, my father leans cockily against Bobby's brother with his elbow, wearing pressed blue jeans and a sleeveless A-shirt as though he had already anticipated the James Dean look that would become all the rage a few years later.

He was always popular at school, with the white kids as well as the black students. Unbeknownst to anyone in his family, he briefly developed a special friendship with one student in particular. She was an Italian girl named Julie who had been in his home room since the third grade. In the seventh grade, when he was twelve, they began to rendezvous secretly at the movies on Saturday afternoons.

It was 1947, and even in integrated Homewood, they knew better than to show interest in each other in public. They devised a code to arrange their trysts. When Julie saw my father in the school hallway, she began talking loudly to her friends about a picture that was playing in the local theaters. That was the signal to meet her at that movie on Saturday. They usually chose the Highland theater over the fancier Belmar down the street, because the tickets were cheaper and the lighting was dim and there were no ushers patrolling the aisles.

My father never knew exactly when Julie would show up, so he would buy a ticket in the morning and wait inside the dark theater, sometimes watching the same picture two or three times. On some Saturdays, she never showed up at all. But when the plan worked, Julie would enter the theater and look for an empty row in an unlit area. After waiting several minutes, he would quietly move to sit next to her. Keeping his eyes locked forward on the screen, he would touch her fingers, then slowly gather her hand in his. They would sit there for the rest of movie, never speaking or taking their physical contact any further.

For all their precautions, my father occasionally saw other children and parents whom he knew from the neighborhood at the Highland who could have easily detected him with the white girl and made a public fuss. If they didn't, he was convinced, it was because the idea of their interracial puppy love simply seemed too improbable for anyone to notice it.

Once they graduated to eighth grade, he and Julie stopped meeting and she acted as though she didn't know him. My father felt hurt and bewildered, particularly when he saw her with other boys. Had she completely forgotten, he wondered, or had she succumbed to the prevailing prejudices of the day?

Then, five years later, when they were seniors, Julie came up to him out of the blue and asked if he would perform a duet with her to fulfill their home room "performance requirement." She proposed that they sing "Prisoner of Love," by Frankie Lane, the teenage heart-throb. They were both nervous and off-key as they rehearsed. Yet on the day of the performance, she sang confidently. The last refrain of the song contains the line "too weak to break the chains that bind us." But instead she changed the phrase to "too weak to *make* the chains that bind us," and she looked straight at him when she sang the words.

"That was as close to open verbal acknowledgment as we ever came," he wrote decades later in a personal essay that he thought of submitting to a magazine. "Sometimes I have thought the thrill and anguish of taboo unleashed in me a taste for forbidden fruit. Nonetheless, to these furtive childhood intimations of love in the dark, I do attribute a steadfast and unwavering stance. I reserve to my own discretion, regardless of the reception or other consequences, the color or ethnicity of any girl I might find to love."

It was in his early teens that he began to defy Granddad for the first time. The feuding started with his announcement that he no longer wanted to be called Junior. It was childish and demeaning, he told his family. He had no desire to go by Cleophaus, either. So he settled on the shortest nickname he could think of: Syl, short for his middle name, Sylvester. He declared to his relatives and friends that he would answer only to Syl Whitaker. For months, his mother and sisters and old friends continued to slip and refer to him as Junior out of force of habit, and Granddad persisted out of prideful pique. My father pretended that he didn't hear any of them until, finally, his silence forced everyone to address him by his chosen name.

During the Monessen years, when he was in junior high, Grandmother started recruiting him as an ally in her battles with his father. She had long complained about C.S.'s infidelities to the older girls, Gertrude and Della. As an only child, she had no siblings to talk with, and she never knew which of her lady friends might be carrying on with her husband behind her back. She felt she could only trust her children, and she enlisted them as confidantes. Now she started to unburden herself to her son as well, and to even use him as a spy. When she returned home from Monessen, she would ask him what he had seen while she was gone and which other women had been in and out of Undertaker Whitaker's downstairs office.

The troubles at home broke out into the open as he was entering high school. When Grandmother asked for the divorce, my father was her champion. He confronted Granddad about the other women and told him how much he had hurt his mother. Furious, his father fired back that it was none of his business. "Don't you dare speak to me that way!" he thundered. They fought angrily and repeatedly until Grandmother took the kids and moved from Bennett Street. A bitter chill fell over their relationship until Granddad sold the house and moved to Harrisburg. After that, my father rarely spoke to his father and barely acknowledged his existence. If people asked what the "C" in C.S. Whitaker Jr. stood for, he refused to tell them.

Once he was living in the new house in Homewood, he began to think of himself as the man of the family. He didn't want to be a financial strain on his mother, so he looked for a part-time job that he could do after school. A Jewish drugstore owner in the neighborhood hired him to make home deliveries and perform odd jobs. As they got to know him, the pharmacist and his wife were impressed by how bright and well-spoken he was.

"What kind of grades do you get in school?" the pharmacist's wife inquired.

My father wasn't much on homework at the time. Ever since his parents' breakup, he had been spending hours after school playing pinball at a local arcade.

"Mostly Bs," he responded.

Other white people might have thought that was quite impressive for a colored boy attending a mostly white school, but the drugstore owner and his wife saw something special in Syl Whitaker. They told him that they thought he could be an A student if he applied himself.

He began to work harder in school, and his grades shot up. Then, in his sophomore year, the Bible school teacher at Bethany Baptist told him about the Quaker work camp in Ithaca that changed his life. When he returned to Pittsburgh in the fall, he was a different person. He gave up pinball and hung out less and less with old friends from the Baptist Youth League and the Westinghouse swim team. Instead he spent his time with adult Quakers from the Ellsworth Street Meeting House and the American Friends Service Committee. They paid for him to go to the work camp in Kentucky the next summer and on a youth trip to Berlin when he was a senior. And when it came time for him to think about college, they encouraged him to visit Swarthmore, the venerable Quaker school outside Philadelphia.

In his senior year, the guidance counselor at Westinghouse called him to his office and gave him a list that contained only all-black schools: Howard, Morehouse, Fisk, Lincoln.

"I already know where I'm going to college," my father informed him. "I've been to Swarthmore, and they've offered me a full scholarship."

"Swarthmore?" the counselor asked. "How did you find out about Swarthmore?"

When my father got home that evening, he was full of indignation as he told his mother the story. Why wasn't he supposed to know about Swarthmore? Did the counselor think he wasn't good enough for it? Were they hanging "Whites Only" signs on colleges too?

By the time June came, he was all too happy to accept his high-school diploma and leave Westinghouse. He sat for his graduation picture in the kind of smart outfit that pleased his mother, with a checked tie and a pocket square and his hair parted neatly on the left, then he packed his work camp blue jeans and khakis and traveled east to begin a new life at college.

Once her children were no longer at home, Grandmother briefly remarried. Her new husband was named Jack Taylor and he was a constable for the courts, a job that consisted mostly of serving subpoenas. He was a handsome fellow who got along well with her children, but she soon tired of his fits of jealousy. Being friendly with people was part of her job as an undertaker, yet every time Taylor saw her talking or laughing with another man, he would fly into a rage. After months of fighting, she divorced the constable as well.

In the fall of 1958, two years after my parents married, Granddad suffered a heart attack in Harrisburg. Grandmother went to visit him in the hospital; she returned on weekends for several months while he was convalescing, then helped move him back to Pittsburgh. For a while she thought that he would never work again, but he was determined to once again "put my shoulders to the wheel," as he wrote in a rare letter to my parents. He surprised everyone by getting well enough to take a job with Menzie Dairy, where he pitched their account to stores and restaurants and quickly became a top earner. He took a second job selling televisions door-to-door and pulled in commissions of up to three hundred dollars a month. He might not have been the rich and respected entrepreneur he once was, but he could still work as hard as anyone and he hadn't lost his salesman's touch.

Grandmother was reminded of his impressive willpower and constitution and found herself enjoying his company. Soon they were courting again like young sweethearts. Her exhusband was a welcome relief after Taylor and his insecurities. "At least I know C.S.'s faults," she told her friends. Then one day, after nine years of divorce, he asked her to marry him again, and she said yes.

According to Cleo, the news cut my father to the quick. He

couldn't believe that Grandmother was taking Granddad back after all the cheating and after turning him and his sisters against him. He must have felt humiliated too, as though his mother was putting him back in his place after making him feel like the man of the house. It was bad enough that he had been physically and psychologically abused by his father; now he felt emotionally betrayed by his beloved mother as well.

C.S. and Edith Whitaker remarried and moved into the funeral home she had opened at 325 Climax Street in Belzhoover. Several years later, he suffered the stroke that would take away all movement in half of his body. He lost the one thing that had kept him going for fifty years, his capacity to work, and he spent the last two decades of his life dependent on family members and nurses, being shuttled back and forth between Climax Street and the St. Barnabas home. Yet even then, he and my father still quarreled. Once when they were together, my uncle Gene saw them off in a corner, talking angrily, and noticed that my father was crying.

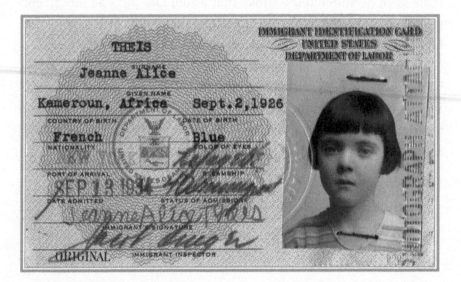

IMMIGRANT IDENTIFICATION CARD
UNITED STATES
DEPARTMENT OF LABOR

THEIS
SURNAME

Jeanne Alice
GIVEN NAME

Kameroun, Africa   Sept.2,1926
COUNTRY OF BIRTH   DATE OF BIRTH

French   Blue
NATIONALITY   COLOR OF EYES

PORT OF ARRIVAL   SS STEAMSHIP

SEP 13 1934
DATE ADMITTED   STATUS OF ADMISSION

IMMIGRANT'S SIGNATURE

ORIGINAL   IMMIGRANT INSPECTOR

3

As for my mother's story, the surprise was how she ended up in Swarthmore in the first place. I thought that her parents had been introduced to the Enders family through church contacts, or that Uncle Bob and Aunt Abbie were Good Samaritans who had advertised their willingness to take in refugee children during World War II. But that wasn't it at all. It happened because two seven-year-old girls became pen pals.

My mother and Trudy Enders first met when they were just a year old. Both Trudy's father and my mother's mother, whose maiden name was Dager, came from Wooster, Ohio. Or at least that's where they would retreat to when their parents, who were all Protestant missionaries, weren't living abroad spreading the faith and doing good works. The Enders family was always stationed in India; the Dagers, in Africa. When they returned to Wooster for sabbaticals, they put their offspring in a school for missionary children commonly called "the Incubator," or "the Inky" as it was known. ("The Incubator for monkey eggs," it was also called, since there were so many babies there who had been born in colonial jungles.) Uncle Bob and Grandmaman had known each other in "the Inky" when they were young, and that's where their two first-born children played together when both families were visiting Wooster in the year 1927.

My maternal great-grandparents, the Reverend William Cross Dager and his wife, Sarah, had first gone to West Africa in 1899 to help build the Presbyterian mission in Cameroon. In the mid-1920s, their daughter Mildred returned to work there and met Edouard Theis, a young French pastor who had been offered a position teaching languages in the mission after the country was put under French mandate. He came from Paris and had done his religious studies there before traveling to New York to take courses at the Union Theological Seminary. To earn extra money, he offered French lessons, and for a while he tutored the Rockefeller children. A half-century later, when he was watching TV with my mother during a visit to America, a news bulletin reported that Nelson Rockefeller had died. Grandpapa sighed and commented, "Ah, Nelson was so young. . . ."

Edouard Theis and Mildred Dager were married in Cameroon in December 1925 and quickly conceived their first daughter, Jeanne Alice Theis, who was born nine months later on September 2, 1926. When she became pregnant again, he hoped for a boy, but it was another girl and then another and then another, until my mother had seven younger sisters. The first, Jacqueline, was born while the family was still in Wooster. In 1928, they joined the Protestant mission in Madagascar, the island nation off the southeastern tip of Africa, where Grandpapa taught French, Greek, and Latin to future Malagasy pastors. There four more daughters were born: Louise, the twins Marguerite and Francoise, and Cecile. Then in 1934, eleven days after my mother's seventh birthday, they returned to Ohio again, and in the photo on her immigrant identification card she sports a pageboy haircut and has the pensive look of an already experienced world traveler.

In Wooster, she discovered Trudy Enders again, and this time, at age seven, they became fast friends. They were only a few days apart in age, both thin and tall, although Trudy had a more angular face and long hair that she wore in a braid. She was as chatty and forthright as my mother was reserved, and yet the two got along famously, whether playing games or talking about their families and hobbies. When Trudy went back to Swarthmore, they wrote to each other, and the letters and postcards continued after the Theis family moved back to the south of France, where Grandpapa took over a parish in a small village called Vezenobres.

A medieval walled town, Vezenobres had few modern conveniences. Water had to be fetched from a public fountain and heated on kitchen stoves fueled with coal. But Grandpapa was determined that his daughters wash at least once a week, so he devised a contraption that would allow them to bathe together. He cemented a wooden bucket on a slant to the wall of one of the rooms of the stone house, over a hole in the floor that opened onto a sewer outside. The girls all huddled under the bucket together, and after the hot water poured over them it flowed into the street, so all the townspeople knew when they were taking their weekly shower. They called it *"la piscine des Theis,"* the "Theis swimming pool," my mother wrote to Trudy.

From the beginning, my mother had always been *"la fille sage,"* the responsible one. Most of her earliest memories involved looking after her younger sisters. In Madagascar, she took Jacqueline to play with the other European children and the little Malagasy natives around the mission school. Rain pelted down every day at noon and kids scurried naked around the compound. Grandmaman taught them with a correspondence course called the Calvert System, and my mother especially enjoyed an "easy reader" about Greek myths. When the other girls arrived, she and Jacqueline became mother's helpers, assisting with the care of the younger sisters.

She had always been shy, though, and once they settled in Vezenobres she developed a pronounced stutter. By the time she was ten, it was severe enough that her parents dispatched her to Paris for treatment. She boarded with her father's mother, whom she called *"Bonne Maman."* A housekeeper took her for walks in the Parc Monceau and

showed her the right-wing newspaper *Gringoire* with its nasty cari-
catures of the Socialist prime minister Leon Blum. Later she moved
in with her father's older sister, *Tante* Alice, and her husband, *Oncle*
Louise, who owned a textile factory and was rich enough to afford two
live-in servants. Doctors prescribed breathing exercises and made her
blow bubbles into a tube of water. They lectured her to *"parler avec le
bec"*—to speak with the front of the mouth. After a year of treatment
she didn't stammer so badly anymore, but she still talked slowly.

When she rejoined her family, she and Jacqueline commuted
by train to a *lycée des filles* eight miles from Vezenobres, leaving at
five o'clock in the morning and often not returning until nightfall.
Because of her year in Paris, she was put in the same grade as her
younger sibling, who sometimes infuriated her by finishing her sentences for her. But she felt nothing but protectiveness toward her
other sisters. The twins, Marguerite and Francoise, were sweet and
inseparable. Cecile, the sixth, was bright and talkative. The third
Theis daughter, Louise, was the prettiest, with delicate skin and
perfectly symmetrical features, and she had a sunny nature and a
self-deprecating laugh. Her only flaw, as far as her parents were concerned, was her thumb sucking. When she was an infant in Madagascar, they wrapped her arms in sleeves made out of cardboard, but
that strange contraption and years of other stratagems failed to make
any difference. Up until the age of nine, Louise still stuck her thumb
in her mouth in moments of stress.

As the oldest child, my mother had intense and specific feelings
about her parents. For "Mother," as she called Grandmaman, it was a
mixture of admiration and irritation at her old-fashioned ideas about
child-rearing. She saw how gentle her mother was with the babies
and how patient she was as she taught the girls household chores.
Yet she disliked how strict Mother could be, particularly in matters of
eating; if the girls left food on their plates at dinner, she would serve it
to them again the next day.

For "Daddy," as she called her father, she felt nothing but adora-
tion. Despite his solemn duties, he was the entertaining parent, the

one who accompanied his daughters on walks and took them swimming and bicycling and taught them the silly songs he loved. He had high expectations for their schoolwork and sometimes lost his temper with them, but she always sensed that he regretted it. Decades later, her sisters gave her a diary that he kept in Madagascar in which he reproached himself for getting cross with his girls.

In that same notebook, Grandpapa listed his "projects for the future." He complained about the conservative strictures of the colonial government and the Protestant missionary hierarchy, and he yearned to join "the real battle" for "non-violence and a just social and international order" in Europe. He dreamed of creating a school where students could learn those values while studying for their baccalaureate exams. As fortune would have it, he was given the opportunity to fulfill both his ambitions when, in 1938, he was contacted by an old divinity school classmate named André Trocmé. Trocmé had accepted a parish in a Protestant village in the mountains of central France called Le Chambon-sur-Lignon, and he invited his old friend to come there to be his assistant pastor and to build the secondary school he had always imagined.

Grandpapa leapt at the offer, in part because he hoped that preaching alongside the charismatic Trocmé and teaching young Protestants would allow him to play a role in standing up to the Nazi menace that was looming across Europe. As it turned out, that desire would be tested sooner than he ever imagined. A year after the Theis family moved to Le Chambon, German troops stormed over the border into Poland. On September 3, 1939, the day after my mother's thirteenth birthday, townspeople gathered around shortwave radios to listen to Neville Chamberlain declare war. In a weary voice, the British prime minister admitted that his efforts to negotiate peace with Hitler had failed and that Britain and France had no choice but to retaliate.

"His actions show convincingly that there is no chance of hoping that this man will give up his practice of using force to gain his will," the British prime minister said over the crackling airwaves from

Number 10 Downing Street. "He can only be stopped by force. . . . We and France are today, in fulfillment of our obligations, going to the aid of Poland, who is so bravely resisting this wicked and unprovoked attack against her. . . . And now that we have resolved to finish it, I know that you will play your part with calmness and with courage."

Within weeks, Theis family relatives began moving south to the little village in the central mountains. One of Grandpapa's younger sisters, *Tante* Jeanne, the concert pianist, arrived with her children. Soon the other, *Tante* Genevieve, came too, and my mother remembers her two aunts playing Cesar Franck's sonata for violin and piano to keep everyone distracted from their worries. French Jews and refugees from the Spanish Civil War streamed into the area, many of them staying at a YMCA camp outside Le Chambon before finding families to put them up in town.

The idea of sending my mother and her sisters to America came later, after Marshal Pétain signed the armistice in June 1940. Grandpapa had heard the Nazis banned higher education for girls in the occupied countries and he didn't want to see that happen to his daughters. Although the Vichy authorities weren't allowing French citizens to leave, he thought an exception might be made for his children, since their mother was a U.S. citizen. Their seventh daughter, Marianne, was too young to travel, and Grandmaman was still pregnant with the eighth, later named Denise, but they resolved to send the six older ones to America. They contacted the Dager family to determine which relatives and acquaintances in Ohio might be able to take their daughters until the war was over.

But when my mother wrote Trudy Enders to tell her that she might be coming back to Wooster, her friend had a different idea. She beseeched her parents to let Jeanne Theis come live with them in Pennsylvania. A year earlier, the Theis family had invited Trudy to study at Grandpapa's school, the Le College Cévenol, for a summer, but that plan had been postponed when the war broke out. Now the least the Enders could do, she urged her parents, was to return the favor. As it happened, they were already lodging two young European refugees: Richard and Jennet Adrian, the teenage son and daughter of Edgar Adrian, a British scientist who had won the Nobel Prize in 1932 for discovering the presence of electricity in nerve cells. Trudy's mother, Abbie, loved having children around, and her father, Bob, was happy to do anything that would help the war effort. So they agreed, and it was arranged for my mother to go to Swarthmore.

How *les filles* Theis would get to America remained a quandary. After all, Edouard and Mildred Theis weren't the only parents desperate to get their children out of Europe. Then, through church contacts, they heard of a woman who was organizing a boat trip to New York for refugee children. Her name was Martha Sharp, and she was married to a Unitarian minister from Wellesley Hills, Massachusetts. After the Nazis occupied Czechoslovakia in 1939, the Sharps had traveled there to secure exit papers for refugees. A year later, they came back to Europe and obtained safe passage for writers and intellectuals under the auspices of a new organization called the Unitarian Universalist Service Committee. Now Mrs. Sharp was looking for children who had an American connection and could get State Department visas.

Grandpapa wrote to Mrs. Sharp to get his daughters on the list and Grandmaman traveled to Vichy to seek permission from the French authorities. After several months, they received the good news: The six Theis sisters were among the twenty-seven refugees chosen to accompany Martha Sharp to America. It was a motley group. Several were young Jews who had been freed from concentration camps in France. An English brother and sister, Clement and Mercedes Brown, came all the way from Paris, walking four hundred miles with their mother to the departure point in Marseilles. Two Russian sisters named Vakar made it onto the list only at the last minute, when their father ran into Mrs. Sharp's secretary on the street and pleaded with her to take his daughters.

In late November, Grandpapa and Grandmaman accompanied my mother and her five sisters to Marseilles, where the group was asked to assemble. The mood in the port city was frightening. The girls had grown used to the eerie quiet of curfew in Le Chambon, but in Marseilles there was a constant drone of Italian planes flying overhead. They got their travel papers stamped and proceeded to a rendezvous point with all the documents they had been instructed to assemble: vaccination certificates, U.S and French visas, and identification bracelets for the girls to wear on their wrists.

When they arrived, Mrs. Sharp informed them that the plans had changed. They were to set sail from Lisbon, but at the last minute authorities there had demanded that the names of all the children be forwarded to them and that visas be issued in Portugal. Days passed as they awaited word that the final travel documents would be approved. The parents were on edge, demanding to know when their children would leave. Rumors flew around the city that the Germans might reach southern France by the end of the week. At last, an associate of Madame Sharp's, Monsieur Okounieff, confirmed a departure date: November 26. He notified the parents that they should bring the children to the Hotel Terminus at ten past four in the morning with their baggage, nametags, and food for breakfast. "Please don't give them any candy," he added.

At the station, the children were issued ribbons to mark their luggage and beige berets to make them stand out in crowds. Monsieur Okounieff explained that they would move in pairs at all times. He divided them according to height, and since my mother, at fourteen, was among the tallest, she was placed with the older girls, not with her little sisters.

Only Louise cried as the six Theis girls kissed their parents on both cheeks and said their goodbyes. My mother remembers feeling strangely numb. She reminded herself of what one of the grownups had said in Le Chambon: In times of war, you have to make difficult choices. Besides, she knew, Daddy had important, dangerous work to do.

The compartments on the first train they took out of Marseilles had lace curtains and cushions on the seats. To pass the time, two girls played a counting game. One stayed inside the compartment and the other stood in the corridor as they watched for animals out the windows. A four-legged animal was worth four points; a white horse, ten; a flock of sheep, one hundred; if they passed a cemetery, they had to start over again from zero. In the restaurant car, there was rationed food the children hadn't tasted for months: real coffee with milk and toast with jam and butter. Before long, they had to change trains, and the rest of the day was exhausting. In all, they took seven different trains, buses, or cars before reaching Barcelona late at night.

The next day, Mrs. Sharp and the other chaperones took the children to a museum and a cathedral. They proceeded to Madrid, where they walked around the rainy capital while waiting for a train to Lisbon that left at ten in the evening. At the Portuguese frontier, a border patrol officer stamped their passports before a customs officer began inspecting their luggage.

"How many children have you, Madame?" the customs officer asked Martha Sharp as he rifled through a suitcase full of games and toys.

The passport officer laughed. "Madame has twenty-seven children!"

The customs official shook his head in bewilderment. "My God, if Madame has twenty-seven children, she has enough trouble and needs all these things for them to play with!"

When they neared Lisbon, the adults discovered another mixup. Believing the group would be delayed, the travel company had canceled their reservations. Now there were only a few seats left on the ship setting sail on November 29. It was decided that Mrs. Sharp would leave with two of the youngest children, and the rest would wait for another vessel scheduled to leave on December 13. "The travel company played a dirty trick on us!" one of the chaperones explained to the Vakar sisters.

Mrs. Sharp left behind her suitcase full of games and toys, and the chaperones did their best to make the next fourteen days pass quickly. They took the children to visit a castle and Vasco de Gama's ship and taught them English songs like "Row, row, row your boat" and "It's a long way to Tipperary." My mother had never seen so much white marble, and the warmth of Lisbon was delightful after the bitter cold in Le Chambon.

At last December 13 arrived, and the group boarded a ship called the U.S.S. *Excambion.* As it pulled out of port and headed toward the Azores, the seas were calm. Once the boat reached the Atlantic, the waves became so rough that the windows in the portholes shook and dishes in the dining cabin shattered. The captain announced that an extra day would be required to finish the voyage. Many of the children became seasick, but for my mother, it wasn't the turbulence but the sight of other children vomiting and fainting that made her feel ill, so she spent as much time as possible on deck.

The children slept on mattresses on the floor of a big ballroom in the center of the ship and amused themselves by detaching tea tables that were secured to the walls and riding them around the ballroom as the ship pitched and rolled. Hearing the noise, a steward put a stop to their little game, but he made up for it by pulling a handful of treats from a cupboard.

"This is called 'gum,' and this is called 'chocolate,'" he explained. "I will give you some if you say 'please.'"

"Please! Please!" the children squealed.

The steward handed out the candy. "Now say, 'thank you,'" he said.

"Thank you! Thank you!" they recited in unison.

For children who had become accustomed to severe rationing, the provisions onboard were nothing short of sumptuous. In the morning, a steward appeared in the ballroom with a big basket of fruit and walked among the mattresses, asking the children to pick what they liked. Breakfast was served on tables for four in the dining room, and they could order eggs, bacon, ham, and toast from a menu. Boullion and crackers were given out midmorning, tea and cookies in the afternoon. One of the Vakar sisters remembered feeling that they had a choice of "all the drinks that exist in the world."

At other times, the risks of the voyage were palpable. When my mother went on deck, she could see the ship lights flickering all through the day as well as the night. It was a signal to the U-boats, since a Nazi submarine had already sunk at least one evacuee boat despite German assurances that they would not attack vessels carrying refugees.

On the evening of December 22, the ship docked in Bermuda, and the next morning it sailed to New York. On Ellis Island, passport officials inspected papers and nurses administered vaccination shots. At last, the *Excambion* pulled into New York harbor. As the boat moored, *les filles* Theis lined up along the railing of the deck, their cheeks flushed bright red under the matching beige berets. A newspaper photographer captured the moment, and the next day a picture of my mother and her five younger sisters appeared in the pages of the *New York Times.*

Abbie and Trudy Enders were there on the dock to greet the girls and take them to Swarthmore to celebrate Christmas. Under a tree in the living room of the Enders house were twelve boxes, each containing a pair of roller skates: six for the Theis sisters, two for the Adrian children from Cambridge, two for Trudy and her younger brother Allen, and two for visiting cousins. Then her sisters left for Ohio, and my mother settled down to life as part of the Enders family.

She enrolled in Swarthmore High School, where she was so far ahead in math and Latin that Dr. Enders teasingly nicknamed her "Jeannius." But she quickly learned that in America it wasn't fashionable to be too brainy, so the first time she got a C, in chemistry, she bragged about it to her classmates. After the wartime restrictions in France, she was amazed to rediscover the comfort and freedom of the United States. She could take her own bath every day, although Trudy, remembering her letters from France, wanted to learn how to take a sponge bath. She even attended her first dance, but not before she wrote to her parents for permission.

Still, the war in Europe never seemed far away, even in sleepy Swarthmore. Uncle Bob brought the news to the dinner table, his spiky eyebrows rising and lowering with outrage under the unruly mop of hair that made him look like a wiry prophet. Aunt Abbie would watch with her warm, lively eyes and shake her braided head and try to reassure the children that things would turn out all right. At one point, Dr. Enders was recruited by the OSS to do intelligence work in South Asia because of his family missionary experience in India. Briefly called up to the Burmese theater, he got lost at sea for three days before being rescued by the British navy.

But then slowly the Nazis and their collaborators started to shut down mail routes between America and Europe, so my mother only discovered what was happening to her father, what kind of danger he was in, in fits and starts. In 1943, a relative from Wooster sent her a short newspaper clipping from a religious journal reporting that André Trocmé, Edouard Theis, and an associate from Le Chambon named Roger Darsissac had been taken to a Vichy internment camp for several months. Several months later, when my mother wasn't home, there was a knock on the door of the Enders house. Trudy opened it and came face-to-face with a small female stranger who said she had a letter for Jeanne Theis. When my mother got home and opened it, it was a message from her father, written from a jail cell in Switzerland. Yet even then he didn't tell her the whole story of his wartime adventures, no doubt for fear that his mail was being searched.

When historians later studied Le Chambon and analyzed why the townspeople were capable of what they did during World War II, they started with the physical setting of the town. Perched on a plateau at the top of the Massif Central mountains, it is verdant and refreshing enough in the summer to attract tourists and convalescents. Yet in the winter, it turns witheringly cold. An icy wind called *la burle* settles in for the duration. A local expression—*"Neuf mois d'hiver, trois mois de misere"*—captures the yearly cycle of toiling during three warm months to make enough money to survive nine months of winter. The brutal conditions breed toughness and fatalism into the long-suffering townsfolk. *"Que voulez-vous?"* is the stoic response of Chambonnais to hardship, according to Philip Hallie, an American scholar who wrote a book titled *Lest Innocent Blood Be Shed,* about the heroism of Le Chambon during the war. What do you expect?

Centuries of religious persecution made the villagers suspicious of official authority. From the early days of the Reformation, the Cévennes became a refuge for French Protestants and the site of some of the worst horrors perpetrated against them. Their temples and places of worship were banned and destroyed. In 1529, one of Le Chambon's first pastors, Laurent Chazot, was burned alive. The atrocities eventually ceased after the French Revolution, but the locals never shed their distrust of the Catholic Church or the French state. As far as they were concerned, the word of their pastors was to be obeyed before any orders from political or military leaders.

The head pastor, André Trocmé, was a warm, passionate man whose small round spectacles added to his air of intensity. He delivered fiery sermons from *la chaire,* the wooden pulpit of the town's plain stone Protestant temple. Grandpapa shared Trocmé's height but not his extroverted personality. The first time he was called upon to preach while his partner was away, he sat in the pews at the back of the temple until congregants realized who he was and invited him to climb up to the pulpit. But together the two ministers preached a compelling gospel, that faith must be accompanied by compassionate deeds. Their favorite Bible passage was the Sermon on the Mount, in which Jesus tells his followers that the key to eternal life is to "love the Lord your God with all your heart . . . and your neighbor as yourself."

They began to put those words into action after Marshal Pétain proclaimed a new "state" in the south of France in July 1940. The Vichy authorities ordered schools throughout the area to fly the French flag and decreed that children were to assemble before class to greet it with the straight-armed Nazi salute. Appalled, Trocmé and Grandpapa vowed that nothing of the sort would happen at Le College Cévenol. They conferred with the headmaster of the primary school in town, Roger Darsissac. The three agreed to fly the flag in the public school's courtyard but not to compel any of the students there or at the secondary academy to salute. After a couple of months, no one in either school was obeying the order from Vichy, and a spirit of subversion began to spread.

Jewish refugees and partisans from the Spanish Civil War had made their way to Le Chambon even before 1940, the year my mother and her sisters left for America. In the following years, two events accelerated the influx and turned the town into a true "city of refuge." American Quakers who were assisting concentration camp prisoners in southern France agreed to send children who they could get released to Le Chambon for safekeeping. Then the Gestapo and Vichy police stepped up their roundups of French Jews. In July 1942, a violent two-day *rafle* in and around Paris sent tens of thousands of Jews to the death camp in Auschwitz and caused thousands more who escaped the deportation to flee toward the south.

Over the next three years, five hundred or more Jewish children and other refugees at a time hid among Le Chambon's two thousand peasants and seven hundred villagers. Some blended in with the students at Le College Cévenol. Others squatted in cellars and attics around town. Still others lodged with farmers in the countryside, huddling in barns or crouching under floorboards when Vichy or SS troops were in the vicinity. In all, thousands of refugees passed through the tiny village and its surrounding hillsides for days or weeks or even months.

Trocmé kept the underground railroad running with the help of thirteen parishioners he called *"les responsables."* Ostensibly, these villagers met with him for weekly Bible study at the presbytery and passed along the lessons to townsfolk who couldn't make it to church. Their secret role was to arrange for hiding places. When the authorities arrived, they were "responsible" for spreading the word quickly and activating what the townspeople called "the disappearance of the Jews."

One summer Saturday in 1942, the chief of police of the Haute-Loire drove into the village square to confront Trocmé, arriving in a black sedan and surrounded by police motorcycles and several buses.

"Pastor, we know in detail the suspect activities to which you are devoted," the police chief said, according to Hallie's account. "You are hiding in this commune a certain number of Jews, whose names I know. I have an order to lead these people to the prefecture . . ."

"Even if I had such a list, I would not pass it on to you," Trocmé replied defiantly. "I am their pastor, their shepherd. It is not the role of a shepherd to betray the sheep confided to his keeping."

Returning to the presbytery, Trocmé summoned the town boy scouts and told them to fan out and warn those in hiding. The next day, the Vichy officers were still in the square when Trocmé and Grandpapa arrived at the temple to preach. As soon as the service was over, the police began an intensive two-day search through the town and the surrounding farms. They knocked on doors, demanded to see ID cards, and searched attics and cellars. In the end they found only two people to arrest. An Austrian Jew named Steckler was led away in one of the buses, as townspeople passed food to him through the window. Another woman was taken away and, according to Grandpapa, later perished in the Nazi death camps.

When the Germans troops occupied southern France, they established a local garrison in the nearby city of Le Puy. The SS began to make periodic sweeps, but each time they came away empty-handed. They may have suspected that a sympathetic spy within their ranks was warning the villagers in advance, and they may have been right. Sometimes the telephone would ring at the presbytery the day before an attempted rousting. "*Attention! Attention!*" an unidentified voice would whisper. "*Tomorrow morning!*"

The Nazis pressured the Vichy authorities to get tougher with the town leaders. On the night of February 13, 1943, a Saturday, the chief of police of the Haute-Loire, a Monsieur Silvani, drove into Le Chambon with one of his lieutenants. Pounding on the door of the presbytery, they demanded to see Trocmé. The pastor was out visiting parishioners, but as soon as he returned he was put under arrest. Trocmé's enterprising wife, Magda, offered the policemen dinner, allowing time for the news to circulate and for townspeople to arrive with food and supplies for their pastor to take to prison. The policemen escorted Trocmé to their car, then drove to arrest Grandpapa, then to the primary school to sweep up Darsissac.

The three men were taken by train to Limoges, a city on the next mountain, and detained at the local police station. On Sunday morning, when Trocmé and Grandpapa would normally be conducting services, they were driven into a valley in a bus with shuttered windows. It passed through two barbed-wire fences, under a watchtower manned by guards with machine guns, and into the internment camp at Saint-Paul d'Eyjeaux.

In one of the camp's long wooden barracks, guards took photos and fingerprints and issued bracelets with prisoner ID numbers. The three men were relieved of most of their personal possessions, and their noses were measured to determine if they were Jews. All Trocmé kept was a small roll of toilet paper that one of the Chambon parishioners slipped him at the presbytery, and when he pulled it out of his pocket later, he founded verses from the Bible scribbled on the sheets.

Conditions at Saint-Paul d'Eyjeaux were not as infernal as the death camps of Eastern Europe, but they were bleak. The three men spent their days in a group of thirty prisoners answering roll calls, doing menial labor, and subsisting on meager rations. Their only consolation was that one prisoner had snuck a radio into the barracks and hidden it in a large jar. At night, the men huddled around the hidden device to learn the news of the war. It was while listening to a BBC broadcast that the prisoners learned the Germans had surrendered to the Russians at Stalingrad, and they quietly cheered the news.

After several weeks at Saint-Paul d'Eyjeaux, the three men asked the prison authorities if they could conduct religious services. Seeing no apparent harm, the camp director let them use a blackboard and a room in one of the barracks. The first night, fewer than twenty other prisoners joined in as Trocmé delivered a sermon and Grandpapa wrote prayers and hymns on the blackboard. The next night, twice as many came. Before long, so many inmates wanted to worship that some had to stand outside in the courtyard and listen through the barracks windows.

After more than a month of captivity, the three men were summoned to see the camp director. By this time, they had heard about the Nazi camps where prisoners were sent for extermination, and they feared the worst. Instead, the director informed them that they would be released on condition that they sign an oath "to respect the persona of our leader, Marshal Pétain."

When Grandpapa pointed out the second part of the pledge to Trocmé, the senior pastor put down his pen.

"We cannot sign this oath," he said. "It is contrary to our conscience."

The astounded director erupted with anger. Why would they decline to pledge loyalty to Pétain? Weren't they patriots? How could they be so foolish? But the two pastors wouldn't budge. Darsissac eventually signed the oaths and was set free, but Trocmé and Grandpapa were sent back to the barracks. As they trudged across the camp courtyard, Grandpapa wondered if he had signed his own death warrant.

The next morning, the clergymen were called to the director's office again. The office of Pierre Laval, Pétain's deputy, had phoned to order them released with no conditions. As the pastors packed their bags, they pondered what might have led to their sudden liberation. Had someone powerful intervened? After Stalingrad, was Laval hedging his bets? Was he making a gesture that might impress the Americans and the Free French forces under DeGaulle? They never learned the answer, but at least they were free.

When the two pastors stepped off the train at Le Chambon, dozens of villagers were there to greet them. They opened a path for the men to walk through, but no one made a sound. Decades later, one of those townspeople told Grandpapa that they suspected that there were Gestapo spies in the crowd, and they didn't want to give them any cause to arrest the leaders again.

Grandpapa knew he was no longer safe in Le Chambon; more

than a month in an internment camp had made that clear. He went underground to join the Cimade, a resistance group that helped Jews escape from occupied France over dangerous mountain trails into neutral Switzerland. At one point the Swiss authorities arrested him and kept him in jail for several days, but then he was released. He didn't return to Le Chambon until September 1944, after the Vichy regime fell and Allied forces had liberated southern France.

My mother had just turned eighteen. After living with the Enders while she finished high school, she had enrolled at Swarthmore College at the age of sixteen and was now in her junior year. Apart from the brief clipping about his stay in the internment camp and the letter she had received from the Swiss jail telling her to inform his sisters and the Dager family that he was alive and well, she didn't learn the full extent of her father's heroism until 1945, when the fighting was over and he came to the United States to make a speaking tour and to raise money for Le College Cévenol.

He gave a lecture at the Swarthmore Meeting house, and the audience sat in hushed silence as he recounted the story of wartime Le Chambon. My mother could see people with tears in their eyes, and she never felt more proud to be her father's daughter. Once the fighting was over and she graduated from college at nineteen, she returned to France to study at La Sorbonne and spend summers helping to build a permanent campus for Le College Cévenol alongside other work campers. Even after returning to America to get a master's degree in French literature at Bryn Mawr, she wasn't entirely sure whether she would stay or return to live closer to her family in France until two of her favorite college professors, Edith Philips and Hal March, wrote to invite her to join the Swarthmore faculty in 1951.

Although the Enders were happy to have my mother so close again, there was one thing that concerned Uncle Bob about his Jeannius. When Grandpapa had visited America after the war, she had dropped everything to help edit and translate his speeches, and he hadn't appeared to show her much gratitude. He had also persisted in correcting her grammar when they spoke French, and Dr. Enders wondered whether that habit might have had something to do with her childhood stammer and her self-conscious way of talking. Just as later he would be wary of my father because of his hatred for Granddad, Uncle Bob had the opposite worry about my mother: that perhaps she revered her Daddy a little too much.

4

"Did you tell him?"

My mother looked away, too embarrassed to meet Trudy's gaze. "No."

"Jeanne, you must tell him. What if Syl doesn't make it to the hospital in time? What if the baby is born and the doctor doesn't know? There could be quite a scene."

Since my mother didn't drive, Trudy Enders was taking her to the obstetrician. Like her father, she wasn't one for beating around the bush.

"Well, if you don't tell him the next time, I will," she warned.

"Yes, all right," my mother said.

When she emerged from the next checkup, her swollen belly predicting a delivery that was just weeks away, Trudy asked again.

"Well?"

"I told him," my mother said.

Her friend's eyes gaped with curiosity. "*How* did you tell him?"

"I asked if the hospital in Lower Merion was segregated."

"And what did he say?"

"He said it wasn't but that he could arrange for me to be in an all-white room if I preferred."

Trudy's eyes widened even more, in wonder that a doctor would actually say such a thing, in the Philadelphia suburbs, in the summer of 1957.

"And what did you tell him?"

My mother produced one of her shy giggles. "I told him that that wasn't exactly the problem. I explained that my husband was a graduate student at Princeton, and that he was black."

Luckily, my father did make it to the hospital for my birth, which took place on the seventh of September, a Saturday. He brought along a camera that took color photographs, a luxury that my parents couldn't afford but that he insisted on buying anyway. He was somehow convinced that I would be born with very light skin, like my mother, but as the days and weeks progressed I would become darker, like him, and he wanted to record the transformation.

As it was, I came out of the womb purple and quite fussy. Everyone assumed that it was because of the long delivery, which lasted through the early evening and only ended at eight o'clock at night. It wasn't until later that X-rays revealed that I had cracked my collarbone emerging from my mother's body. When I learned that, I thought it remarkable that I didn't appear even more miserable in those first few days, and I viewed it as an early sign of the capacity for stoicism that I would have to rely on later.

My parents had decided to call me Mark. My mother wanted a biblical name and one that would be common in both English and French. As for my father, he just wanted it to be as far as it could possibly be from his name: Cleophaus Sylvester. He had always hated the name Cleophaus. He hated it because it was his father's name, and he hated his father. He hated it because it was so similar to Cleo, his older sister's name. And he hated it because he thought of it as a slave name, which it was. As far as my father was concerned, it was enough of a reminder of slavery that the family name was Whitaker, which he later explained to me was a contraction of "white acre"—what they called freed cotton pickers who were so anonymous that no one even knew the names of their owners.

When my mother was released from the hospital, my father drove us home to their little apartment on North Chester Road in Swarthmore. When she wasn't teaching, she nursed me and changed me and sang lullabies to put me to sleep. He helped out too, although he was gone several days a week to Princeton, where he rented a room in an attic for the nights he spent there. He was doing well in his graduate courses and had already charmed several members of the Politics Department faculty, but he found the atmosphere stressful. There was little of the love of learning for learning's sake that had made Swarthmore so stimulating; most of his classmates seemed interested only in getting ahead, in who would receive grants and assistant teaching positions. The year before, my parents had attended a reception for new doctoral candidates and met a young professor who put his finger on the Princeton mentality. "A lot of people in this room are probably surprised to see that you are a mixed couple," the man said, "but this is a place that likes nonconformism as long as you do good work. Yes, people here approve of nonconformists who succeed; they only disapprove of those who don't."

My father couldn't wait to finish his required courses and get to work on his doctoral thesis. He had set his sights on becoming an expert in Africa and planned to write a dissertation on the transformation from imperial rule to nationalism in Nigeria, the most populous country on the continent. He had received a grant from the Ford Foundation, which he planned to use to study British colonial documents for six months, then spend a year doing research in the field. My mother had arranged to take a sabbatical from Swarthmore so that she and I could go with him. And so at the end of May, several months before my first birthday, the three of us set out on our first great family adventure: a year-long trip to England and Africa.

In her letters home, my mother recounted the going-away party that my father's college roommate Michael DeLaszlo and his wife, Barbara, threw at their tiny apartment on Riverside Drive in New York City. She said that her energy flagged halfway through and that she felt badly about not keeping up her end of the conversation with all their other fascinating friends. She wrote that my father was exhausted from his Princeton exams as well but that he still managed to be the life of the party. I imagine him telling stories and expounding on his theories but also listening intently, because that was the real secret of his charm: how he made *you* feel interesting. He would nod and murmur agreement, then chuckle at what you said, and then at what he said, so that you came away with a memory of both deep conversation and laughter. Of course, that talent wasn't surprising if you knew that he grew up around undertakers, who were always comforting mourners and courting new business. It was almost second nature. But like his first name, his upbringing in Pittsburgh was something that most people he met as an adult knew nothing about.

My mother had brought a blanket for me to sleep on and tried to put me to bed in the DeLaszlos' bathtub. But I was too excited by all the adult conversation, so she rolled the blanket up into a makeshift travel bed and let me lie in the corner of the living room. As they came over to admire me, everyone agreed that I looked quite jolly for a nine-month-old and that I was the very spitting image of Syl.

The next day we set sail on the SS *Liberte* for Le Havre. My father always liked status symbols, so he must have loved the ship's pedigree. The Germans had built it in 1929, one of the first 50,000-ton vessels that could cross the Atlantic in five days, and after the war it was awarded to the French, who turned it into a commercial liner. The ship had appeared in movies like *The French Line* with Jane Russell and *Sabrina* with Humphrey Bogart and Audrey Hepburn. On board, my parents passed the time with my father's favorite Princeton professor, H.H. Wilson, an expert on American and British politics, with a gravelly voice and a weatherbeaten face. "Hube," as he was nicknamed, was recovering from his wife's suicide, in a state of what was referred to at the time as "menopausal depression." He wanted to get away from Princeton and was taking a year's leave to study the effect of television on British politics, and so, hoping it would distract him, my father had invited his mentor to travel with us.

It's not clear whether they were commiserating or celebrating, but they must have had a fair amount to drink. Several months later, the transport company, Hostage (a rather disconcerting name for that line of business), sent my father an extra bill for all the liquor they consumed during the trip. In a letter to my mother while she was in France that summer, he described himself as "much chagrined with Hostage's query about the Champagne. Groan." That's all he said on the matter, and apparently neither one of them had any sense of what a dark harbinger that "Groan" would be.

Once we arrived in England, we spent several days staying with Wilson in downtown London, then moved to a flat in Wimbledon, the home of the famous tennis tournament. It was on the third floor of a row house, "close enough to spit on the Centre Court," my father wrote to the DeLaszlos. My mother, who found English architecture "ghastly," described it as "one of the ugliest houses, for outward appearance, I have ever seen." But the apartment had two pleasantly furnished rooms, a bath, a kitchen, and a small alcove where I slept. It cost only four and a half guineas per month, which is all they could afford. My father welcomed "the priceless factor of our landlady, who is unbritishly friendly and helpful" and seemed unfazed by renting to a black man with a white wife and a small brown baby. The neighborhood, on the other hand, he found "a little too bowler hat for me—but good with Mark."

In the mornings, he took the underground to Russell Square, where he had managed to arrange for a large, sunny office at the Institute of Commonwealth Studies. He was also studying Hausa, the language of northern Nigeria. The State Department had hired a tutor at the London School of Oriental and African Studies to teach two of its aides, and he had talked his way into the class. He described the tutor as a milquetoast and was offended when he wouldn't accept an invitation to dinner at Wimbledon. He suspected unspoken racism, but my mother offered a more charitable interpretation: Perhaps in England it "simply wasn't done" to invite people to dinner because they might feel obliged to return the favor.

As usual, he made friends wherever he went, so the flat was always full of entertaining guests. Two acquaintances of Hube Wilson's, a South African editor for the Compass News Service named Neil Tyfield and his wife, Mary, became enchanted with my father, and he was thrilled when they accepted his invitation for Thanksgiving dinner. Wilson came over too, and he engaged my mother in a heated argument over the motives of the Tories and American conservatives. Hube accused them all of cynical self-interest; my mother thought some might actually believe what they said. Through Quaker contacts in London, my father met a left-wing British writer named Reginald Reynolds, who showed up with his wife and put everyone in stitches by describing how he was going to achieve publishing immortality by writing a series of books all beginning "I Was Wrong . . ." Everyone roared as he rattled off the titles: "Number One: 'I Was Wrong About India'! Number Two: 'I Was Wrong About Africa'! Number Three: 'I Was Wrong About Atomic Weapons'! And so on . . ."

Another night, my father brought home two new African friends, a visiting professor from a university in northern Nigeria named Hussaini Adamu and one of his associates. He had told my mother about how fascinated he was by the way they dressed, in long robes and skullcaps, and how convinced they were that their tribal homeland already had a form of government that was superior to anything that Britain or America could offer. Wanting to impress them, my mother cooked what she thought of as a properly elegant English meal with a rib roast. But at the dinner table, they just picked at the beef. Afterward, my father talked to them and discovered that they were used to African stews, with cut-up meat and spices. When she heard that, my mother slapped her palm to her head and said that if she had known, she would have made them a French stew, because that's what she had grown up eating too!

According to my mother's letters, I was completely under my

father's spell. I wasn't walking yet but I could almost stand on my own, and I had figured out how to bid him goodbye when he went to work. "He has finally really learned to wave and makes a great ceremony every morning of scooting his eating chair to the kitchen door so he can wave to 'dada' as he goes down the stairs," she wrote. "He even waves when he sees Syl's briefcase or coat."

She was supposed to be working on her thesis too, on French poetry, but she found it far more diverting to spend time with her husband or, while he was working, to take me shopping or walking in the park. She was delighted that I seemed to have inherited the Whitaker side's conviviality. One day we were at the shopping mall and a party of riders on horseback passed by carrying crops and wearing formal habits and hard bowler hats. They stared straight ahead as though they were part of the Queen's guard, but I waved and whooped at them until one of the riders broke out in a broad smile. "I think Mark, like Syl, has a fundamentally happy and open temperament," she wrote, "which will probably be quite resistant to sobering influences. We trust he won't have to meet anything too sobering."

Shared amusement and exasperation at the ways of the Brits and my infant high jinks brought my parents closer together than ever. They would shoo me away as I tried to commandeer their typewriter and chase after me when I attempted to play with the gas fixtures. When they put me in my crib, I rocked so vigorously that it slid across the floor. Finally our kindly British landlady informed my parents that the neighbors were complaining. Not knowing what else to do, my father went out and bought a hammer and nails and bolted the crib to the floor.

When my mother took me to visit her family in France for a week, my father wrote to tell her how much he missed us. "Since I now have to make the rounds in Wimbledon for myself," he said, "I enjoy the accolades usually bestowed on you: but how does one answer to 'Mark is lovely, isn't he?'" He said he had just read *Lord of the Flies* and was dying to discuss the meaning of the allegorical tale of British schoolboys who turn savage on a desert island. It was "the best thing

I've encountered in a long time," he wrote. "Golding would seem to be profoundly conscious of sin—sin without theological definition or relief. . . . You have to read this as soon as you get back. . . . I want very much to talk to someone about it." He signed off affectionately: "Stay very well, my darling. And don't let them steal the boy up there. Love, Syl."

In anticipation of the rough African outback, he had purchased a used Land Rover, paid for with funds that he borrowed from Michael DeLaszlo and promised to pay back when he sold the vehicle at the end of his travels. One weekend, we drove to visit Michael's father, Dr. Henry DeLaszlo, a rich British chemist and drug manufacturer who lived in a country estate in Surrey with his second wife and their young child, Stephen. On the way home, my parents passed judgment on the distant style of British upper-class child-rearing and the way Dr. DeLaszlo seemed to want to control their friend Michael's life, implicitly agreeing that they would never inflict that fate on me.

On another weekend my father made an excursion to visit Swarthmore grads who were "up" at Oxford. He watched a production of *Love's Labour's Lost* on the lawn of St. Johns College and ate at a country inn. But he left feeling glad that he hadn't tried to blaze any new racial trails by going the Oxbridge route after college. "The whole thing was a little too creaky for me," he wrote, "and I have the suspicion that one develops habits there ill-suited for anything but ultra academia—in the words of Lucky Jim, 'shedding pseudo light on non-problems.'"

My parents' old nemesis, the president of Swarthmore, happened to be visiting the university, but my father gave him a wide berth. "Horrible dictu, Courtney Smith arrived the same day," he wrote, "and if Oxford worked a salutary effect on him or not, I was determined not to be the witness."

By December, he had almost finished his documentary research and was more than ready to take us to the open spaces and warmth of Nigeria. The leafy British summer had long since given way to the cold, damp days of fall and winter. The skies were low and dark, and the fireplaces in our apartment burned all day long. When a dinner with the Hausa teacher and his wife was finally arranged in town, my mother found them "the most depressing people I ever met," and my father had to drive the Land Rover back to Wimbledon in fog so thick that he could see nothing but the taillights of the car directly in front of him. When we got to our little walkup, all the fires had gone out and the fog had invaded every corner of the flat.

My mother had just discovered that she was pregnant again, with a due date in late July, but she was determined to stay with him in Africa for as long as possible. They packed our belongings and the drugs friends had shipped from America: Diodoquine for dysentery, Promoquine for malaria, Halazone as an antiseptic. We went to the doctor for our shots, and I apparently took mine without crying or complaint, although several days later my mother reported that I "exacted revenge" by pulling down half of the wallpaper in my alcove in Wimbledon.

In a final letter to the DeLaszlos before our departure, my father combined a hint of wistfulness about Britain with mounting anxiety about what lay ahead in Nigeria. He also couldn't help showing off for Michael with the kind of pun the two former roommates liked to volley back and forth. "Although my anti-romance with the Isle is well known to you," he wrote, "I must confess that we will leave with mixed feelings, prompted less by thoughts pro-English as by blanks and question marks African. A womb in hand is worth two in the bush."

On New Year's Day, 1959, my mother loaded me into the Land Rover and my father drove us to the British Channel ferry. After crossing, we went to visit Grandpapa and Grandmaman in Le Chambon for several days. From there we proceeded to Marseilles, where he shipped the car and our baggage ahead to Cotonou, in Benin. We took boats that stopped in Majorca, Algiers, and Casablanca, retrieved the car in Benin, and drove to Lagos, Nigeria's largest city. Next we went to Ibadan, the center of the western region, and stayed there for several days while my father interviewed local politicians. Finally we drove to Kaduna, the capital of the north, traveling along rugged, unpaved roads that gave way to tarred highways only at the end of the trip. For the next four months, we moved with my father from town to town as he cajoled for housing at every stop.

Another thing my parents had in common was food—they both loved to eat and to cook—so they were fascinated to sample the local delicacies. They ate groundnut stew and palm nuts stew with fufu, a peppery yam paste. To wash it down, they drank local beer that was usually warm because so few of the lodgings had refrigeration. Concerned that my one-year-old's constitution wasn't ready for such spicy fare, my mother fed me chicken and rice made with preboiled water, when she could get me to sit still. I was walking now, and weathered family photographs show me merrily running around naked at the rest houses where we stayed.

In a letter to his benefactors at the Ford Foundation, my father described how his work was going. He had devised a questionnaire called a "Comparative Leadership Recruitment Profile" to study the tribal backgrounds of local politicians. Once the House of Assembly convened in Kaduna in mid-February, he parked himself every morning in the Members Lounge, buttonholing lawmakers in white skullcaps and robes and posing questions from the form. "There are 151 elected members of the House, and I was successful in completing my questionnaire for almost a hundred of these," he noted.

As usual, he didn't stop there. He quizzed the Nigerians about their personal stories and kibbitzed about everything under the sun. As he put it in the funding report: "I find that interviewing for biographical data in this way is a good introduction to people, and I had some good talks with members of the House on other matters of interest."

One day in April, my parents took me to see a *sallah,* the colorful pageant that marks the end of Ramadan fasting in the Muslim north. It was in a small city with mud walls and a whitewashed entrance called Kazaure, in an emirate by the same name. They had awoken me at three o'clock in the morning, and I got sick to my stomach before we set out. Yet once we arrived in Kazaure, my mother described us all as mesmerized by the three-hour ritual. It had everything from stampeding horses to meandering camels to gun salutes with flintlock Hausa hunting rifles. There were drummers in grass skirts, trumpeters in red-and-green harlequin costumes, and guards in suits of armor. When the emir finally appeared in a dark red gown and a sculpted round helmet, courtiers lofted an immense multicolored umbrella above his head and two clowns circled around him. One rode a donkey and had the word "*Sarki*" written on his chest; my father translated that it was Hausa for "chief" or "lord." The other clown was dwarflike and wore a short tunic and cap and carried a staff with ribbons on it. When he saw my father's camera, he stopped to dance in front of us.

We were in Kazaure at the invitation of Hussaini Adamu, the visiting African professor whom my father had met in London. He hadn't returned yet, but he sent instructions for my mother to meet his wife. According to the Islamic customs of that part of the country, she lived with the other women of the emirate in *purdah*, separated from the men in a compound within the village. If I had been any older, I would not have been permitted to enter, but since I was not yet two my mother was able to bring me along. While we were there she snapped a picture that I discovered when I began collecting family photographs, of me alongside a beautiful Nigerian woman with her dark skin and braided hair, holding a tiny baby in her arms.

Although Kazaure was "real bush," as their steward put it, my parents managed to rent a spacious rest house with a beautiful view of the surrounding countryside. They slept outside on the porch to the light of a kerosene lamp, marveling at the sense of peace that they had found in this tiny corner of northern Nigeria.

But when we returned to Kano, the only place my father could find was a tiny apartment in a concrete compound. It had two small rooms, no indoor water, and a putrid outdoor latrine. They had to cook on the porch, and it was so hot they couldn't get to sleep. There was also no place to keep dangerous things out of my reach, and I kept wandering into adjoining apartments because they all looked the same. "He had desperate weeping spells at being restricted and reprimanded so much, and all of us are worn to a frazzle," my mother wrote to the Enders. "After that and a disastrous night and a half in a hotel we had to come to the conclusion that if he isn't given enough free space our nice little boy can be a veritable hellion."

By May, she was visibly pregnant, her legs so swollen that the garters the DeLaszlos had sent from America no longer fit. The rough roads and heat became increasingly hard for her to take. She liked her British-trained African obstetrician and thought her ideas about sedation and length of hospital stay sounded quite sensible, but she found my father's need to travel and the difficulties of finding housing too much. So my parents decided that she should take me to her parents in France and have the new baby there.

"This was a decision arrived at most reluctantly as I hate the idea of Syl not being on hand and not being able to see his child for six months," she wrote sadly. My father must have felt forlorn about the separation too; as a going-away gift, he managed to talk the wealthiest merchant in northern Nigeria into letting us house-sit in a comfortable villa he owned. We stayed there for several weeks before May 21, the last day the airline would allow someone in my mother's condition to fly.

When we arrived at my grandparents' in the French mountains, she fell into her usual habit of helping Grandpapa with his papers and sermons, even with a baby already kicking inside. "Daddy wants me to work in his office this afternoon," she reported in one letter to my father, saying how relieved she was to have her sisters and their children around to keep me distracted. Her letters reported that I took a particular liking to my cousin Anna, who was just six months younger than me. She had curly brown hair and big brown eyes, and I followed her around with my head lowered and my hands behind my back, as if stalking her like some animal I had observed in Africa. When my cousin Myriam arrived, I followed her as she made the rounds at bedtime, to be kissed by the whole family, and I squirmed with delight when she kissed me too.

My mother was particularly delighted to see how Grandpapa doted on me. He taught me how to puff up my lips and blow out, and he read me funny headlines from the satirical political newspaper *Le Canard Enchainé*, as though I could understand what they meant. Once he was listening to a speech by the conservative politician Michel Debré on the radio, and he turned to share his thoughts with me.

"That's Mother Michel, *mon vieux*," he said, using the derisive nickname Debré's critics had given him. "He's completely off track."

"Um-papa!" I replied sweetly.

My brother finally arrived on July 27, 1959. For months my parents had jokingly referred to the unborn fetus as "Berkeley," after Berkeley Place, where my father took language lessons in London. But they had officially decided to call him Paul, another biblical name that was common in two languages and would never be mistaken for Cleophaus or Sylvester. The delivery was long and difficult, requiring the help of a doctor and a midwife, and upon his arrival, everyone discovered why: Paul weighed eleven pounds. The local obstetrician pronounced him the biggest baby he had ever seen.

Unlike me, he had no amber-colored skin or dark curly hair to suggest his black heritage. As my mother described him, "He looked like John Bull . . . very pinked-skinned, with quite light brown hair, and blond eyebrows, blue eyes and a turned-up nose." Because he was so big, she required two incisions, one to get his head out and a second one for his shoulders, and afterward she was required to stay in bed for two weeks while the stitches healed. She wrote my father that I was quite shy when Grandmaman brought me to see my baby brother when he was just two hours old, but after that I cheerfully returned the next day, bouncing up the hospital stairs and knocking on the door of her room to announce my arrival.

My father was thrilled to receive the telegram when it finally made it to the African bush several weeks later. Unfortunately, he had to put off any thoughts of celebrating due to a bad case of dysentery, the result of drinking water that a local doctor described as the worst in West Africa. "Pexl born, 5 kilos," the message read. Making the conversion into pounds, he concluded that the weight must have been as much of an error as the name.

When it came time to fly back to America, my mother discovered that she had lost her reentry permit, and she wrote him frantically about her trips to the American consulate in Lyons and then all the way to the embassy in Paris to secure the papers that finally allowed us to leave. Back in Swarthmore, she resumed teaching and adjusted to caring for two young sons, but she ached for my father and wrote him several letters a week. In one she enclosed a picture she thought would amuse him, of me sitting on her lap and looking like I was reading a copy of the journal *Foreign Affairs*.

Often she didn't hear back for weeks at a time, because her letters took so long to catch up to him in the bush, and she fretted terribly. "Darling, the days do drag when I don't hear from you because I can't help worrying and waiting anxiously from mail to mail," she wrote. When his letters did arrive, she savored his accounts of his travels but became even more worried for his safety. After he described fording a five-hundred-yard-wide stream, she told him to be careful because it reminded her of how Dr. Livingston's son had drowned in the Susquehanna River. In another letter, she warned him not to drive alone at night if he was too tired, because that's how Albert Camus had died. When the French government tested its first atomic bomb in northern Africa, she imagined him driving through radioactive dust that had drifted south over Nigeria.

Gradually he became more and more homesick too and wrote her of his melancholy. "I wish there was some concrete way to help your loneliness," she replied. He was anxious about the slowness and difficulty of his research, so much so that one of his best friends among the graduate students at Princeton, Dick Sklar, felt compelled to send a note of reassurance. "Try to relax a bit," Sklar wrote. "I can appreciate how tough things must be for you now but you needn't be reminded that on balance your ledger is mainly credit and it's just a matter of putting up with it for 6 months or so and returning with a solid accomplishment."

To his mentor Hube Wilson, he confessed his concern that out of sight, he would also be out of mind in the jockeying for favor among the doctoral candidates in politics. "My reaction is that you haven't anything to worry about re: the Department," Wilson wrote back in a letter posted to Zaria. "You are still considered handsome, charming, youthful, vigorous and altogether promising. . . . Stay sweet and keep swinging." Then he signed off using an obscure term for Greek Orthodox prayer that was their inside-joke word for academic toil: "Yours in *Hesychasm,* Hubie."

From the start of their voyages, my parents had struggled with money. They had thought that her sabbatical pay and his Ford Foundation grant would be enough to fund most of the trip, but they had badly miscalculated. Not only did they have to borrow money from Michael DeLaszlo to buy the Land Rover, but they had to ask him for additional loans for boat tickets and other expenses, and their communications were full of sheepish excuses. "I hope you did not think it too rude of us not to apologize for our check bouncing," my mother wrote after one repayment didn't clear the bank, "and it was certainly nice of you not to complain about it. We don't know quite when we'll be able to repay you, but we will eventually. And in the meantime we are very contrite."

Yet in spite of their debts, toward the end of his year in Africa my father became obsessed with buying a new car. He wrote my mother to propose that he purchase a French model that he could drive while on his way back and ship to the United States, thereby saving import taxes. "I have no objections at all to your plans for the car, if it is workable," she responded compliantly, only ruling out one French automaker that she still didn't forgive for continuing to produce cars during the Nazi occupation. "I would prefer it though if you didn't buy a Simca," she wrote, "the politics of the company is most reactionary, detestable." In the end, he chose a Peugeot, because he had seen an advertisement in the *New Yorker* magazine listing it, at a little more that $2,200 at the time, as the cheapest of the seven best-built cars in the world. My mother posted him the downpayment, and the rest he funded with the proceeds from the Land Rover sale that he was supposed to repay to Michael DeLaszlo.

As his return drew near, she described how impatient I also was to see him. I had started calling other men "Daddy," alarming his college roommate Knowles Dougherty with all my attention during one visit. I became fixated with cars, no doubt because I associated them with his driving us across Europe and Africa. On a visit to Pittsburgh, I frightened my mother by wandering out of the funeral parlor to gaze at the vehicles parked on Climax Street. I picked up telephone receivers and chimed, "Hello, Daddy!" I pointed at photos of him and announced, "Picture, Daddy!" I marched around the Swarthmore apartment announcing, "Coming home soon, Daddy! Daddy coming, see Mark! Daddy, coming big boat! This, Daddy's house!"

My mother still didn't drive, so Michael DeLaszlo brought his station wagon down to Swarthmore and chauffeured us to New York City to await his arrival. Grandmother Edith came from Pittsburgh and stayed with Aunt Cleo and Uncle Gene in Queens. Hostage, the transport company, dispensed only one ticket to the pier, so on Tuesday, February 17, two days after his twenty-fifth birthday, my mother went down to New York harbor by herself to welcome back the husband she so desperately missed.

At the DeLaszlos', they celebrated his return with store-bought cake and fish mousse, his favorite, which my mother had made from scratch. He regaled everyone with his tales of Nigeria and his opinions of the new Gaullist government in Paris, which he had honed while visiting her relatives in France on his way home. Then he picked up the new green Peugeot and drove us back to Swarthmore, where he finally grew acquainted with his second son and we became a family of four.

For the next year and a half, we resumed life in the big blue-gray apartment building on North Chester Road. My mother taught and my father began writing his dissertation and I played with the other faculty brats in the spacious yard outside while my brother grew into a toddler. At the end of the day, they caught up with each other over cigarettes and a glass of sherry before we sat down to one of my mother's French meals. Everyone I spoke with remembers mostly happy memories from this period—except, that is, for two rather unforgettable incidents.

In one, my parents were taking my brother and me for a drive. They had put Paul in the front seat of the Peugeot but then got distracted by a heated discussion over something or other. Paul started playing with the stick shift and put the gear in neutral. The car, which was at the top of a steep driveway that sloped toward North Chester Road, started rolling downhill. My father made a mad dash for it and managed to jump into the front seat and slam on the brakes just in time to keep the vehicle from careening into oncoming traffic.

In the other incident, the DeLaszlos had come down from Manhattan to visit for the weekend. It was Sunday morning, and the adults were in the kitchen of our third-floor apartment eating and smoking and debating the columns in the *New York Times*. I was perched on the windowsill, doing my best to entertain Alexander DeLaszlo, their first child, who was one year old.

All of a sudden the screen gave way and I fell out the window. Fortunately there was a big bush planted just below our apartment, and it broke my fall. I rolled over onto the ground on my back, stunned but not badly hurt. Looking up, I saw my father racing down the outdoor staircase, his dark brown arms and legs pumping under pale yellow pajamas.

"Mark! Mark!" he yelled. "My God, are you all right?"

A doctor was summoned to examine me and assured my parents that I didn't have a head injury or any broken limbs. Then he attended to my mother, who was still trembling with fright.

It is the first conscious memory that I have retained from my childhood. When I reminded my father of the fall decades later, the same look of pained relief I saw in his eyes that morning came back all over again. "I thought I was going to find a bag of bones," he said solemnly.

5

This is what I remembered about the year we moved to Princeton, when I was four.

I remembered that we lived in a big modern building with a view of a lake. We had an apartment filled with Danish Modern furniture, and my parents would throw parties. Before being put to bed, I would walk around in my pajamas, the kinds with the feet at the bottom, and pluck Fritos and stuffed olives from the snack trays. Later on, when I learned the term "sweet tooth," I would think that I must have been born with a "salt tooth."

I remembered that Aunt Cleo and Uncle Gene were invited to one of the parties but that they didn't show up until the next morning. "We had a little slippage!" Cleo announced cheerfully as my father opened the door. I could see from his disapproving frown that he was not amused with his older sister.

I remembered that on New Year's Eve, my parents went out for the evening and hired our favorite babysitter to stay with Paul and me.

He was a tall high-school student named John Lithgow, who lived in another faculty apartment upstairs. He was extremely friendly and spoke in a loud voice. I had no idea then that he wanted to become an actor, but I wasn't surprised a few years later when my mother showed me a rave review of a performance he gave in a student production at Harvard or, after that, when I saw him in movies and TV and on the Broadway stage.

John read us a bedtime story and tucked us in. When I woke up in the morning and padded out to the living room in my footed pajamas, he was still sitting on the couch.

"Where are Mommy and Daddy?" I asked.

"They're not back." He yawned. "They called. They'll be home soon."

For the next hour, I waited anxiously by the door for the sound of a key in the lock. Finally my parents came in, making apologies for getting home so late. As they hugged me, I smelled cigarette smoke and the odors on their breath that I associated with the parties with the olives and the Fritos.

I remembered the day my mother came in to talk to my nursery school teacher. The teacher was concerned because I had started to cry in class. It wasn't because of anything I had done, or anything that had been done to me, she said. I would get very upset at naptime, when other kids wouldn't lie still on their cots and the teacher would take out a wooden paddle to spank them. They would start crying, and that would make me cry.

I remembered that afterward, my mother told me that there was nothing wrong with sympathizing with other children's suffering, but that I had to learn not to show my emotions so easily in public.

This is what I didn't know at the time.

We had moved to Princeton because my father had been offered a teaching-assistant position by the Politics Department. He saw it as a stepping-stone toward securing a tenure-track offer, and he told my mother that he had no choice but to take it. Because she barely knew how to drive—she had learned just enough in Swarthmore to take me to nursery school—and Paul and I were so young, they decided that it wasn't practical for her to commute. So she resigned her tenured position in the Swarthmore French Department and accepted a temporary teaching-assistant job at the university in New Jersey.

When they got there, she discovered that people in Princeton drank much more heavily than my parents were used to. Because of its Quaker roots, Swarthmore was a dry town; liquor could be served only in private homes, and usually it was wine or sherry or beer. But here, there were cocktail parties every weekend, where hard liquor flowed freely. During the week, my father would stay out late at the bar at the Annex, a restaurant where Hube Wilson held court every night with his favorite graduate students. When he got home, she could tell that he had been drinking, usually Scotch or gin.

The atmosphere within the faculty was different too. If she thought some of the professors at Swarthmore were overly cynical and "too-too faddish and witty" for her taste, it was nothing compared with Princeton. There, the trendier faculty members prided themselves on not just their rejection of the fuddy-duddy bourgeois morality of early 1960s America, but on a willingness to act on their "liberated" worldview.

Specifically, there was a professor and his wife, Gina, who had an "open marriage," and they encouraged their friends to join in the fun. My mother learned this after discovering that my father had become part of this "lively group," as she would later put it in a letter to Barbara DeLaszlo. Before that, she had known that my father was friendly with Gina, who had once come to visit us in Swarthmore before they moved. I had a vague recollection of that visit, because she brought her children, and one of them was blind, and I remembered that. But it was only when they got to Princeton that my mother discovered that my father and Gina were having an affair.

When she confronted him about it, he didn't deny it.

"It's just the way I am," he said.

She was crushed. How could he so easily disregard their wedding vows, let alone the Quaker values that she thought they shared in common? When she had so admired his good-hearted commitment to racial integration, the idea that he would become the first black member of an open marriage club was hardly what she had in mind! And what made it even more humiliating was that, under the circumstances, the entire group must have known what was going on.

Just as galling, she was convinced that he wasn't betraying her merely out of love for another woman, or even lust. He was also ingratiating himself with his mentor Hube Wilson, who, while still single after his first wife's suicide, was an active participant in the mate-swapping scene.

"You're more loyal to Hube Wilson than you are to me!" she protested, and he did nothing to try to persuade her otherwise.

He started suggesting that she change her appearance. Why couldn't she wear lipstick, or put on high heels rather than the French espadrilles she favored? But that only upset her more. Was that really why he was having an affair, just because she wore espadrilles? Why wasn't he happy with her the way she was, the way she had been when he fell in love with her and caused her to fall in love with him? And did he want her to alter her looks for him or for the others too? Was this some kind of invitation to join in his licentious group, since at the very least he should have known her well enough to realize that *that* was the last thing she would ever do?

But for the life of her, she couldn't put her angry questions into words. Mostly she felt powerless to do anything about her unhappiness, and when his philandering and flirtations upset her she just broke down crying. She needed to talk to someone, so she confided in Barbara DeLaszlo, but that conversation ended in uncontrollable tears as well.

Looking back on it a few years later, she would blame herself in a letter to her friends for "treating things as if they weren't real for much too long, particularly that horrid year in Princeton—when Barbara told me that she could see why I didn't feel at home there I shouldn't have wept I should have gotten into the car and driven away. Then I wouldn't have the nightmare of that particular night to haunt my memory."

When I asked both of them what "the nightmare of that particular night" referred to, neither could remember. Was it a particularly nasty fight with my father in which unforgivable things were said? Was it a scene at a cocktail party, where my father flirted with his mistress or made a suggestion that my mother might be available to one of his colleagues? For women of their ages, my mother in her mideighties and Barbara in her midseventies, they had remarkable recall, but both had erased that particular episode from their memories.

At the time, my mother never contemplated walking out. It wasn't something that a person of her devout upbringing would do, nor something she wanted to inflict on her children. When he received an offer of a professorship at UCLA that year, she hoped the change of scenery might repair the damage. He had just turned twenty-seven years old and hadn't even finished his doctoral thesis, yet he was being asked to join one of the most distinguished African studies faculties in the country. He argued that it was another offer that he couldn't turn down, and she figured that life in California could hardly be worse for them than it had been in Princeton. And so in the summer of 1962, my parents loaded up the Peugeot and drove Paul and me across the country to yet another new home in Los Angeles.

On the way, we stopped in Pittsburgh, and Grandmother Edith took a picture of the four of us sitting on the big brown couch in her living room. My brother and I are both wearing striped shirts and shorts and Keds sneakers. I am sitting between my parents, and they are both looking at me with amusement, while Paul is on the other side of my mother, gazing at the camera—a tableau that must have pretty well captured the family dynamic viewed from his perspective. My father has on tennis whites that make his skin, already darker than usual from being outside in the summer sun, even blacker. Had he just come from playing a match? Was he dressing for the good life in California? I was never able to pin down that detail.

On the rest of the trip across the country, we stayed in highway motels, where my father would approach the suspicious desk clerks while my mother stood by nervously clutching the hands of her sleepy little sons. They made detours to show Paul and me the Grand Canyon and the Boulder Dam, then swung north to the Bay Area and Golden State Park before driving south to Los Angeles. My mother fell in love with the beauty of San Francisco, but as we were touring the city Paul pulled an alarm bell on the street while no one was looking. Wary of how police would treat an interracial couple even in supposedly enlightened Northern California, my father instructed us all to hurry away before the cops showed up.

Getting settled in L.A. involved a lot more stress than they had bargained for. We moved three times in the first year into temporary housing: first a cheap rental apartment in Westwood; then another one in Santa Monica; then a house-sit in Malibu that my father finally wangled because he wanted to be near the beach. He was anxious about his teaching duties and figuring out the institutional politics of UCLA while still working on his doctoral thesis, which wasn't finished yet. And my mother had to juggle taking care of two young boys with working too, because they couldn't afford for her to stay at home.

The chairman of my father's department had arranged for her to substitute for a semester at Beverly Hills High School, replacing a teacher who was taking a semester off to try to kick a tranquilizer habit. She discovered that many of the teachers at Beverly Hills High took tranquilizers, and she quickly saw why. The kids and parents were far more competitive and mean-spirited than any she had encountered at Swarthmore or Princeton. Students came to her to report their classmates for cheating. She started to monitor them more closely and caught one copying during a test. When she confronted him, he blew up at her. Then he told his parents, who instead of getting angry at their son complained to the principal about my mother. The boy had his sights set on MIT, and they protested that he couldn't afford to have a black mark on his record. Eventually the former tranquilizer addict returned, and my mother had to look for substitute teaching jobs at other schools around the city.

It all left her confused and deflated. She realized how much she missed the security and stimulation of the tenured job she had given up at Swarthmore. Then, in the middle of the year, the Princeton couple with the open marriage suddenly showed up in town. My father announced that he wanted to see Gina again, and my mother was heartbroken.

That summer, he had made plans to travel back to Nigeria to do more research for the dissertation. Before he left, he told her that he wanted to separate when he got back.

Despite all their unhappiness, she was still stunned. For someone of her religious background, wedding vows made under oath to God were to be honored, no matter how difficult things got. She also knew how hard it would be on Paul and me, and she pleaded with him to reconsider, for our sakes if nothing else. But his mind was made up, and he told her coldly that he would brook no further discussion on the matter.

She took us back to Swarthmore for the summer, not sure whether or not we would return to California. My father wrote her from Africa, but he seemed more concerned with finishing the last chapter of his thesis than the emotional turmoil he had inflicted on the entire family. My mother had told her father about the separation, and Grandpapa had written his son-in-law in Nigeria to ask for an explanation. "His distress was disturbing to me naturally," my father reported, "but as I say I had anticipated all this and was able to put aside answering and thinking too much about it for the sake of continuing with the conclusion."

He complained that Grandmother Edith had thrown his work offtrack with her own distress over the news about the breakup.

"The next morning I received a bitter and unfair letter from my Mother," he wrote, "and I spent the rest of the weekend trying to conquer my anger and depression and finally working out the poison that letter injected into my system by writing a reply. I have recently had quite a bit of talk of irresponsibility directed at me but my Mother's letter is something of a specimen in that department. Be that as it may I am now at work on the conclusion again, I made good progress yesterday, and the resolve to finish it quickly has mercifully returned."

He even continued to send my mother chapters of the dissertation to edit and, amazingly, she kept helping him, even when he lost the index cards containing all the information for the bibliography and started suggesting that she was the one who had misplaced them. ("I have an image in my head of taking them out, explaining how they were to be used and leaving them in your hands," he wrote.) Meanwhile, he sent letters to Paul and me that gave no hint of the trouble our parents were having, except to suggest that he didn't know when or where he would see us again.

"My dear sons," began a letter that arrived in late June. "It has been a long time since I saw you last. I have missed you very much. It won't be long now and I will be back and can see you again. I look forward to seeing you more than anything I can think of. I'm not sure whether I'll see you in New York or California, but that doesn't matter. The important thing is that it won't be long now. Stay the very good boys you are. Love, Daddy."

In the fall, my mother decided to take us back to Los Angeles after all. Abbie Enders, among others, had convinced her that she should try again to save the marriage. My parents went into counseling, but they got nowhere. In the sessions, he was terse and accusatory, suddenly showing "very unpleasant tendencies to the nth degree in his dealings with me," as she put it in a letter to the DeLaszlos.

"You said marriage was a constant commitment, but you've withdrawn that commitment!" he said bitterly.

That's exactly how I feel! she thought.

But she couldn't bring herself to say it out loud. Despite her growing fury, she found herself defending him in the sessions. *Why do I lie like a trooper in Syl's favor?* she asked herself. Was it to protect his ego in front of the doctor? Why was her resistance to saying anything against him greater than her resistance to blaming herself? "The man," as she called the therapist, tried to console her that my father was angrier with himself and with his mother than he was with her; but that didn't make any sense to her.

She wrote letters to a Quaker psychiatrist whom she had known in Philadelphia. He had lived in Pittsburgh and had met my father at the Ellsworth Meeting when he was in high school. "I have not heard Syl's side, so I should not judge," the doctor wrote back, "[but] it sounds to me, from your side of the story, that the problem comes from his not accepting the responsibilities of marriage and fatherhood. However, as often happens, it is the wife and mother who suffers most. Because she gets the symptoms, she is the one who sees the doctor, when the chief trouble is the husband, who is immature in some ways, though perhaps mature in other ways."

That diagnosis captured the situation in a nutshell, yet she still had trouble accepting it. Had she misjudged Syl that badly? And if she had, wasn't that her fault? Shouldn't she have foreseen that he might not be ready to be a good husband and father and that something like this might happen to her and her boys?

They agreed to the usual visitation rules: My brother and I would live with her but he would take us on the weekends. On Fridays, he would show up in the circular driveway of University Elementary School, known by its initials, U.E.S., where I was in first grade. Paul would already be in the backseat, and he would drive us to his apartment. For lunch he cooked us "cheese dreams," English muffins covered with tomato slices and melted cheddar; for supper, he treated us to hamburgers and orange soda at our favorite diner. He took us to the UCLA courts and introduced us to tennis. Paul was still too young to do anything but watch, but he bought me a racket and sneakers and a little white tennis outfit and taught me how to return a ball over the net.

One Friday in November, instead of arriving at U.E.S. at the end of the school day, he burst into my first-grade classroom in the middle of the afternoon. He looked very emotional and asked my teacher to excuse me. "Someone shot President Kennedy," he told me when we got into his car.

We drove to pick up Paul, who was staying with a babysitter while my mother worked. He took us to his apartment and turned on his small black-and-white TV set. For the rest of the weekend, the three of us sat in front of the wooden box. We watched the footage of the motorcade in Dallas over and over again and the scenes of people weeping all across the country. I looked over at my father and saw tears in his eyes too. On Sunday morning, we watched as the man they said had killed the president was brought into a police station in handcuffs. Suddenly there was a popping sound and the TV reporter announced excitedly that JFK's assassin had been shot too. Barely six, I didn't understand exactly what all these events meant, but I knew that they were significant and I was proud that my father wanted to share them with us.

By comparison, life during the week with my mother was lonely and scary. We had moved into a rental at 2014 North Beverly Glen Boulevard, a steep, winding road where cars whizzed around the corner all day long. Unlike the friendly college towns we were used to, here it was impossible to go outside and find playmates in the neighborhood. One day, I went exploring in the woody hills behind our apartment and got into a tearful panic when I couldn't find my way home.

Without my father around, my mother had to drive everywhere herself, which completely unnerved her. When Michael DeLaszlo had first tried to give her driving lessons in Swarthmore, it had been a disaster; he took her to an open field to practice, but she kept barreling toward a tree. In Los Angeles, the speedy highway traffic threw her for a loop. She shouted at Paul and me to sit still as we fought in the backseat. Once she swerved around and slapped us both—the only time I can remember her hitting us. Another time, she got so upset that she pulled the car over to the side of the Santa Monica Freeway and wept. My father had let her keep the Peugeot, but one day she stopped at a red light and the car behind smashed into her. She suffered whiplash and spent weeks going to doctors and driving a strange loaner car while she negotiated with the woman's insurance company.

She continued to live temp job to temp job. Eventually she landed part-time work at Los Angeles State, a community college, but her applications for full-time positions at UCLA and colleges back East were all rebuffed. "To say that your candidacy is an interesting one would be an understatement," read one reply from the chairman of the French Department at Smith. "There is no doubt that you are a very strong candidate for an assistant professorship. The difficulty at Smith at this time is that we have no opening at this rank."

Finding babysitters to take care of Paul and me while she was working became an endless ordeal. One young black girl didn't have a clue about how to handle restless boys, and she talked openly in front of us about how lucky we were to have light skin and how dark-skinned Negroes couldn't be trusted. A second sitter quit after several weeks to undergo an operation. Eventually she found a nice young woman with young children who was married to a graduate student at UCLA and who took us in after school. But she worried constantly about the toll all the disruption was taking on us.

She told her therapist that I was having nightmares that she had been kidnapped. At U.E.S. the teachers reported that I was having weeping fits in class. A group of aggressive boys had begun to taunt me until I cried, and yet I kept following them around, seemingly inviting more abuse. Was I imitating scenes I had witnessed between her and Syl? she worried. Typically, she intellectualized the situation; remembering a book she had read by Carl Jung, she wondered if my attraction to the little bullies had anything to do with his theories about the "interplay of opposites."

Even my mercurial flights of fancy concerned her. Why did I come home from school one day saying that I wanted to be a tennis player and the next day a traffic policeman? When I badgered her to take me to the World's Fair in New York, she said she would try. But "Mark also expressed the desire to visit the Ed Sullivan show—and there I put my foot down," she reported to the DeLaszlos. She wanted badly to introduce me to finer art and culture and to find nicer friends for me to play with outside of school, but she was too drained to do anything about it and didn't know where to start.

For a while, she held out hope that things might get better after my father finished his dissertation. Once the damn thing was submitted, he might come back to her. But then he turned it in and the cold war between them didn't thaw in the least. Gradually, she came to accept that reconciliation wasn't in the cards. She felt tired all the time, bone tired. Realizing that it was a sign of depression didn't make things any easier. The whole mess reminded her of one of the nineteenth-century French novels she taught at the community college, where every chapter brought another nasty turn of the screw.

With no visible way out of her predicament, she sought solace in books and the teachings she had grown up with in her father's church. A work called *The Inner World of Choice*, by a Jungian psychologist who also believed in God, was a particular comfort. "I've got to trust that some way there will be a way out," she wrote in one of her letters. "I guess this is faith, 'Though I go through the valley of the shadow of death.' . . . Of course, I can tell myself that other people have much worse troubles, and feel very ashamed. But, everybody should be able to live according to their best capacities—and it is hard to have been brought up to believe this, and to have known this in experience for a while, and to find one's self just surviving. It is comforting to realize that one can hope that such conditions will not necessarily be permanent, that many people have known the slough of despond, that life is not always necessarily onwards and upwards—but that the downward spiral need not last forever."

Finally they went through the grim motions of divorce. When it was finally granted, the grounds were listed as "mental cruelty" on the part of the defendant, Jeanne Theis Whitaker, against the plaintiff, C.S. Whitaker Jr. It was a complete lie, and they both knew it. If anything, he was the one who had been mentally cruel to her. But in those days, there was no such thing as no-fault divorce in California. My mother refused to be the one to ask for a divorce, even on the factual grounds of adultery, because she wasn't the one who wanted out of the marriage. But at that point she was desperate for the agony to be over. So when he pressured her to accept the blame for the whole thing, she agreed on the condition that he allow her to take Paul and me back to the East Coast.

She didn't know what she would do there, but she told herself that anything would be better than sticking it out in L.A. Her sister Jackie had said that she could get a job at Friends Central, a high school in Philadelphia, paying $4,500 a year. She still believed she could do better than that, but she wouldn't know until she got back to a place where she could feel safe and sane and not perpetually on the verge of losing her mind.

"I just do not want to start roaming the country with these two kids, but I guess that's exactly what I'll have to do," she wrote Barbara DeLaszlo. "The moral of this story is never let your husband leave you until you are well settled in life; but then again, yours probably wouldn't."

I remembered that she took Paul and me back to Swarthmore the next year, and that I attended second grade there. My French grandparents were living in the nearby town of Westtown for the year, where Grandpapa had taken a temporary teaching position at the Friends boarding school; we would visit them on the weekend, and my mother seemed relieved to have their company and support. During the week, she taught part-time at Lincoln, a black college near Philadelphia. Then one day she sat my brother and me down and told us that we were going to move again, to Massachusetts. A former Swarthmore dean named Bill Prentice had become president of a women's college called Wheaton, in a small town called Norton, and hearing about her predicament he had written to offer her an assistant professorship in the French Department.

I wasn't happy about the news. Returning to Swarthmore for second grade had reunited me with old friends I had made as a toddler on North Chester Road. Now I would have to say goodbye to my pals and start all over in yet another new town. I wasn't even eight yet, and it was the fifth time we had moved to a new place just as the school year was beginning.

My only consolation was that my father had invited Paul and me to spend the summer with him in California. On my last week of school in Swarthmore, the teachers divided the second-grade class into teams of White and Garnet, the school colors. We engaged in two days of footraces and beanbag contests and tugs-of-war. I won four first prizes and my Garnet team took home the overall team award, and I proudly packed the five gold ribbons in my luggage to show off to my daddy.

He had persuaded Aunt Della, the middle of his three sisters, to accompany us to L.A. on a Greyhound bus. My mother drove us to our grandmother's house in Pittsburgh, and Della took us the rest of the way. When we got to California, we were thrilled to discover that he had moved to a yellowish bungalow in a neighborhood called Venice. It was right by the ocean, so close that you could walk out the front door and right onto a wide, sandy beach.

Everything about that summer is still fresh and exciting in my mind. My father took Paul and me fishing on the Venice pier, teaching us how to bait a hook and waiting patiently until each of us pulled up a catch. Dodging the foamy waves, he showed us how to dig for sand crabs. We walked down the boardwalk to Pacific Ocean Park, where we went on the roller coasters and an airplane ride and ate cotton candy. Paul remembered another ride that spun us around and that my father told us about "centrifugal force." He took us to play tennis at the university like old times and introduced us to hand-ball on a court down on the boardwalk. Exhausted but blissful, I fell asleep at nights to the soothing rhythm of the ocean tide.

One weekend, he drove us in a rented convertible up the Pacific Coast Highway to Monterey, the top down the whole way. We must have stayed in someone's house, because I remember that it had a re-cord player. He recalled how excited I had been to watch the Beatles on the *Ed Sullivan Show* at his apartment when we lived in L.A., and he played us their new album, *Meet the Beatles*. He taught us how to do the twist, and the three of us danced to "I Saw Her Standing There."

The apartment in Venice was always full of his friends and stu-dents. Two of his favorite doctoral candidates were a young married couple named Gerald and Tammara Bender, or Jerry and Tammy for short. Paul and I playfully christened them "Terry and Jammy." They taught us the lyrics to "Heart of My Heart," and I can still see them sitting with my father on the front patio of his bungalow, smoking cig-arettes and drinking cocktails as people in shorts and sandals passed by. My father cooked for everyone, dishes that were a mix of African stews, French casseroles, and black soul food. As we ate, he told his stories and elaborated on his latest theories and chuckled at his own wry comments.

One day, Hube Wilson arrived for a visit. He had a new wife named Cora, who had been one of his graduate students, and they had driven all the way across country in a Volkswagen bus. As they stepped out of the vehicle, I recall thinking that he looked like a British movie star, with his mane of slicked-back hair and lined face tanned a nutty brown. Cora was small and vivacious, with short-cropped dark locks. When they opened the back door of the VW, the biggest dog I had ever seen jumped out and hungrily sniffed the wet, salty air. His name was Andy, and it was the first time I had ever seen a full-grown golden labrador retriever.

The whole summer felt like one big adventure, so different from the quiet, serious life we had settled into with our mother. As August wore on and the time for us to leave approached, I starting thinking about what I wanted to say to my father, and finally I screwed up the courage to do it.

"Can I stay here and live with you?" I said.

There was a long silence.

"Hmmm," he said finally.

Then there was another silence.

"Hmmm," he muttered again.

I kept waiting for an answer, getting more self-conscious by the second. Why didn't he say anything? Was he so surprised that I wanted to live with him?

"I don't think your mother would agree to that," he said at last. "Besides, it would be too hard on her. She needs you, Mark. Paul needs you too."

I nodded glumly and told him that I understood. Part of me was proud that he viewed me as such a grownup and so necessary to my mother and brother. But I also felt rejected and suddenly very mad at the world.

During the three-day ride back to Pittsburgh with Aunt Della, I got madder and madder. All I could think about was another long trip to a new home where I won't know anyone. Another birthday in a town where I wouldn't have any friends to invite to my party. I was mad at my father for being so selfish. I was mad at my mother for whatever she had done to drive him away. I was mad at Paul, because we had been a happy family before he came along. I was mad at Aunt Della for pretending that everything was wonderful when it wasn't, and I was mad at the weird smell of the Greyhound that was starting to nauseate me and that would make me hate traveling on buses for the rest of my life. But most of all, I was mad at myself, because deep down I was sure that I was to blame for what had happened to my parents. And once my mother picked us up in Pittsburgh and we drove the last six hundred miles to Massachusetts in her used Rambler wagon, I turned that anger on myself. I started to eat compulsively and I slowly but surely became obese.

6

When we first moved to Massachusetts, he called from time to time. "It's your Dad!" my mother would shout out, no longer calling him "Daddy." My brother and I would go to the rotary phone in our little apartment on the edge of the Wheaton campus and each say a quick hello and answer a few questions. Then she would close the kitchen door, and when I listened from the other side I could tell from her tense whispers that they were arguing.

Eventually the phone calls stopped, and all we had to connect us to him was Pittsburgh. Grandmother Edith was still eager to see her grandsons, and my mother wanted us to feel like part of the Whitaker family, so every Christmas we would get in the Rambler and make another 1,200-mile-roundtrip journey. We would visit Aunt Cleo and Uncle Gene in Queens and the Enders in Swarthmore and my aunt Jackie and her family in Philadelphia and then drive across the state on the Pennsylvania Turnpike. Paul and I sang songs and played car-spotting games to make the hours go more quickly, and at night my mother put down the backseat of the Rambler so we could sleep.

Finally a string of tunnels and the sulfurous smell from the steel plants told us that we were approaching Pittsburgh. We drove into the grimy heart of the city, over the rivers that converged in its center and up through the Liberty tubes to Belzhoover, where at last we pulled up to the big gray house at the top of a hill with the funny address of 325 Climax Street and a sign on the lawn that read "Edith M. Whitaker Funeral Home."

Grandmother lived above the family store, which was eerie if you were her grandsons and her business was burying people. During the long drive across the state, Paul and I would speculate about whether there would be a body in the first-floor parlor when we arrived. We played odds-and-evens to decide who would look first. As we entered the downstairs lobby, sometimes the parlor door to our left was shut. Sometimes it was open, but there was only a closed casket in sight. But on some visits, the door was open and the casket lid was lifted all the way up and we could detect the outline of a chalky brown head inside. As soon as I saw the corpse, I averted my eyes and scurried up to the second floor.

"Come here and give me some sugar!" Grandmother would command from the top of the big wooden staircase, instantly causing any trepidation to melt away. She would pull my brother and me to her huge, soft bosom and smother us with lipstick and the scent of perfume. Then she would push us back for an inspection. "My, my, you boys have gotten so big!" she'd exclaim. "But my Lord you need a haircut!"

It didn't matter that we already sported crew cuts. The next day, she would take us to the barbershop down the street. As we sat waiting for our turn in the barber chair, we'd take in a scene that would be familiar to anyone who has seen the plays of August Wilson, the Pittsburgh writer who set all his dramas in the Hill District on the other side of the river. Black men smelling of pomade and aftershave wandered in and out of the shop, some settling into the red barber chairs for a haircut or a straight-razor shave with lather and hot towels, others dawdling on folding chairs along the wall as they leafed through copies of *Ebony* and *Jet* and traded jokes and gossip about the neighborhood and the local sports teams.

"You boys look like you could use some chittlins!" Grandmother would say as soon as we arrived, telling us to dump our bags in the attic so we could go to the kitchen and eat. She began preparing her specialty days before, scrubbing the pig intestines over the kitchen sink and stewing them slowly in vinegar in a big steel pot. She served them up on flowered yellow china with fried chicken and collard greens, salty and greasy with ham hocks. She made biscuits from scratch, not from a Bisquick box like we did at home. "And I know what you'll want for breakfast!" she would announce, pointing to her prized waffle iron.

Grandmother was one of the first people I thought of as overweight, until I stopped being more than just husky myself. But there was something I would have described as very sensual about her, if I had known at that age exactly what that meant. Sometimes at night, I caught a glimpse of her stripping down to her white girdle and could see the voluptuous rolls of smooth, light-colored skin she kept restrained underneath. Her face was beautiful: round, with elegant eyebrows arched over wide-set eyes. I could see why everyone talked about what a catch she was in her youth.

She was a mesmerizing talker. Her house was always full of black folk from the neighborhood: mourners who came upstairs after the viewings, friends who dropped by to drink coffee or to play bridge. She seemed to know exactly what to say to all of them. "It was a mercy, really," she would murmur, holding the hands of her grieving customers. "He led a *good* life, and now he's going home. . . ."

I listened as she bargained over the phone with the Cadillac dealer who rented her a hearse for burial days. I didn't understand what a "notary public" was, but I saw her counseling neighbors about their financial and legal woes as she pressed a stamp on their documents. On Christmas Eve, she made her special eggnog with ice cream and bourbon and let Paul and me have a sip or two. She kept us entertained with her stories as she played her collection of records that included Ella and Basie but also her favorite white musicians, Trini Lopez and Barbra Streisand.

According to my mother, the gift for gab ran in the family. My great-grandmother, who was called Gram, had only gone as far as the third grade, but she had a photographic memory and a wonderful way of talking. Her daughter inherited the trait, and she was always pulling out funny expressions I had never heard anywhere else. "You better come over here or I'll jump down your throat and dance on your gizzard!" she scolded if she thought I wasn't minding her.

During one summer visit, she bought me an ice cream cone on the street on a very hot day. As soon as I started licking, she grabbed the cone out of my hand and helped herself. "Child, you need drip insurance!" she said.

On Sundays, she would take us to church, which I remember for the rhythmic gospel music and the fiery Baptist sermons and the fancy hats she and all the other ladies wore. Afterward, we would go to an outdoor picnic at her cousin Ernestine's, or to visit Aunt Gertrude, my father's oldest sister, and her husband, Robert, and their children, Mayotis, Loretta, Theresa, Bobby, and Leslie. On visiting day, she would take us to see Granddad at the St. Barnabas nursing home, and sometimes she would help fold his crippled body into the car so he could come back with us to the funeral home for a longer visit. Once I remember we were eating breakfast in the kitchen, and he pointed to the waffle iron from his wheelchair. In the slow, thick way he had of talking ever since his stroke, he said that he had come up with the idea for a machine that would make waffles before anyone had ever heard of it, but that he never bothered to do anything about it because in those days white people would never buy a product invented by a black man.

I loved visiting Pittsburgh, except for one chore. When the garbage can in the kitchen got full, Grandmother would instruct me to take it downstairs to the weedy concrete yard in the back of the house. That meant navigating a narrow wooden staircase that led down to a first-floor landing with a back door to the embalming room.

Sometimes I nudged it ajar by accident and caught a glimpse of the hospital table where Grandmother's assistant laid out the bodies and needled them full of formaldehyde. I never saw more than that, but for years I had nightmares that one day I would be taking out the garbage and come face-to-face with a stiff, naked corpse.

During all those years of holiday visits, Grandmother Edith was also corresponding with my mother, and their letters paint a very different picture from the one I had as a child: not of a mother and a grandmother, but of two working women reeling from the blows that life had dealt them. One year, Grandmother confessed to my mother that she had had only three or four "cases," as she called her burial orders. To make ends meet, she had to sell Avon cosmetics door to door. "I am so sick of selling Avon I could die (smile)," she wrote. By the mid-1960s, as white flight and foreign competition in the steel industry started to eat away at Pittsburgh's economy, she contemplated selling her business altogether. She put out job feelers with Reverend Gray at Bethany Baptist and at the city's Poverty Program, but the only referral she got was for a position as a nursing assistant at the veterans hospital. She said that after working with dead people her whole life she needed that job "like a hole in the head" and joked: "I'd soon be ready for the booby hatch if I worked all day around more sick—particularly the chronically ill."

She would always send Paul and me money for our birthdays—usually ten dollars, sometimes twenty—but once she admitted that "if Gertrude hadn't sent me $10.00 (without my asking for it) we would not have eaten this weekend." She often felt like she was ready "to throw in the sponge," but after Granddad's stroke she had to keep working, despite the chronic arthritis that made her fill her knees with cortisone. Through it all, she carried on with her patented blend of plaintiveness and wisecracks. She wrote my mother that she "cried all day" after a water line broke in the funeral home and she received an unexpected plumbing bill of $275. "Honestly, Jeanne, I hate to see a new day come," she said. "Why I am having it so hard, when I try *so hard,* I can't figure out. But I was born on Saturday, and I guess that's it." Again and again, she followed her latest tale of misery with a funny line, like "I'm just too pooped to pop" or "No one here has hit the numbers lately."

Hearing that my mother had scraped together enough money to buy a small black-and-white TV set, she wrote: "I am happy about the T.V. just hope the boys appreciate your sacrifice, and after the novelty wears off, they will go outside for air! (smile) . . . I hope you never have to break up and move again. It worries me that I can't help you in *no way.* Maybe some day this struggle will all end. Would you let me live with you part-time—I could be your baby sitter, asst. cook, housekeeper?"

My mother appreciated the letters, not just because they were good for a much-needed laugh but also because it made her feel a little bit better about her own financial woes. I knew from listening behind the kitchen door that my parents were arguing over child-support payments, but it wasn't until I read the letters between the two of them that I learned the sordid details.

He was supposed to send $150 a month, but he kept falling behind and blaming everything under the sun. He blamed the IRS for not sending his tax refund back in time. He blamed a "Freudian slip" when he shorted one check by fifty dollars. He blamed the student protesters at Berkeley in the late 1960s for making it political impossible for Clark Kerr, the chancellor of the University of California, to push harder with the state legislature for faculty raises. He cited the debt he was still paying off to Michael DeLaszlo for the loans that piled up during their trip to England and Nigeria. He even suggested that *she* forgive $500 *he* owed her so that he could use it to repay Michael. Meanwhile, he kept describing the places to which he was traveling: Bloomington, Indiana . . . East Lansing, Michigan . . . Denver . . . Dakar . . . If he was so poor, she wondered, who was paying for all those trips?

Yet despite being a deadbeat dad, as he would have been called a few decades later, he still felt free to offer opinions about his sons. My mother had told him that I was doing well in the Norton schools, but that she was worried that they weren't challenging enough and that I was getting As too easily. "I don't believe that the relative advantages Mark now has in relation to his Norton peers will do him any harm," he wrote back. "A foundation of confidence and the habit of excelling is a better one than the school of hard knocks and self-doubt. When the time of struggle and tougher competition comes, he'll know and value the rewards of effort rather than having to imagine them with the taste of defeat in his mouth. That's a very anti-Darwinian view, too bad, but then it never seems to have occurred to Darwin that human satisfaction may be the pre-condition of survival as much as the other way round."

When I read that, I thought it sounded very impressive, referencing Darwin and all; but wasn't it just a highly intellectualized way of reassuring himself that I would turn out all right without having him around?

He also wanted to commiserate about personal matters. He told her how torn up he was about the death of Hube Wilson's second wife, Cora, when she was three months pregnant, after a swift and lethal bout of cancer. "If you are so moved, a note to Hube would I know be welcome," he wrote. "He has nothing but good-will toward you." My mother couldn't remember whether she sent a condolence note or not, but he clearly had no clue how she really felt about Hube Wilson. She didn't believe that his old professor had acted with good will toward her in the least; she thought that he had taken sides with him after the divorce, and she was still angry about the way he had encouraged my father's drinking and philandering.

After another year of missed payments and rationalizations, she decided that she had had enough and she stopped asking him for money. From then on, she relied on her meager assistant professor's salary to raise Paul and me. It was only $6,000 a year when she started at Wheaton, and she never received the kind of raises that her colleagues got because she didn't have a doctorate. It was all she could do to afford our little one-floor apartment and the smallest, cheapest cars she could find: first the Rambler, then later a used Pinto and an AMC Gremlin. One year, she had to explain to Paul and me that she didn't have enough money to buy us Christmas presents. She promised to make it up to us the next year by letting us choose any gift that we wanted, as long as she could buy it secondhand. When the time came, Paul asked for a piano, and she managed to find a dilapidated, out-of-tune wall model she could afford. But then she told me she had no money left to buy what I wanted, a secondhand encyclopedia.

Getting to know new people in a new town was torture for her, but she did find a few friends that she could confide in. One was the other new professor in the French Department, a German immigrant named Eva Gerstel. As a child, Eva had gone into hiding from the Nazis with her Jewish father and Catholic mother, then moved to Texas after the war. She had majored in French at Rice University and also specialized in modern poetry. My mother was overjoyed to find someone with whom she had so much in common but was crestfallen a few years later when Eva returned to Germany to marry her fiancé. When she left, she gave us her cat, who was named Golo, after Golo Mann, the son of Thomas Mann.

There were also a few old Swarthmore acquaintances around, which came as a relief. One was Jean Kudo, who had taken French classes from my mother when she was an undergraduate. She had married a Wheaton English professor named Dick Pearce, and they became supportive friends. Another was a poli-sci prof named Dan Lewin, who had graduated from Swarthmore a year ahead of my father and also gotten his doctorate at Princeton. But Lewin was a depressive who was never sure where he stood at Wheaton, and shortly before he came up for tenure he committed suicide in the mistaken belief that it would be denied.

For all three of us, the first few years in Norton were a grim time. My mother's mind was a horror chamber of regret and self-recrimination, and often she was too lost down its dark corridors to keep company with Paul and me. At night, she would come from teaching and shut the door to her bedroom and smoke and drink alone. One day I returned home from school at three o'clock in the afternoon to find her sitting at the kitchen table next to an empty bottle of wine. Her eyes were glassy and she was muttering under her breath about Miss Mandel, an older colleague in the French Department who upset her by tormenting their students. When she got together with faculty friends, she poured out her heart as they poured her more cocktails. One night I awoke to the sound of her returning from a dinner at the Pearces', and when I peeked out of my bedroom to make sure she was all right, she was undressing in the hallway, too inebriated to realize where she was.

She was grateful that I was doing well in school but alarmed by how heavy I was getting, and she was even more worried about Paul, who was acting out in school. With what little money she had, she paid for him to see a child psychiatrist. She briefly went to therapy herself, but the doctor she found was too quiet and inscrutable for her taste. She desperately wanted more assertive help in coping with her depression, and she unburdened herself in letters to the Quaker psychiatrist in Philadelphia who had treated her when we returned to Swarthmore, and his kindly but worried response captured what rough emotional shape she was still in.

"What bothers me the most, I suppose, is that you still blame yourself and speak of 'the mess I have made of my life,'" he wrote back to her. "You could say, you know, 'the mess Syl made of my life'—tho perhaps you could have handled it better if you had been all-seeing and all-knowing. . . . The acute edge of your suffering and confusion has worn off, I suspect, but the character traits are still there. Most notably, the one of blaming yourself first. . . . As I used to keep telling you, you are a fine person who deserves to enjoy life and has a lot to contribute to the world."

On some days, when my mother took my brother to his appointments at Mass mental health, I would tag along. On the way back, I would ask her to stop at Dunkin' Donuts. She would pull into a store off

Route 128 and hand me a few dollars and I would go inside and pick out a dozen assorted jellies, creams, and crullers. I dug into them as soon as I got back in the Rambler, and by the time we were home the entire box of doughnuts was empty.

I had always been a bit chubby as a young child, but once we moved to Norton I started eating around the clock. After school I headed straight for Fonseca's, a little convenience store near the campus. With coins I picked up around the house when my mother wasn't looking, I bought Yodels and Ring Dings and Yankee Doodles. On nights when she made dinner, I helped myself to third and fourth servings of her favorite French dishes: a boiled meat and potato stew called *pot-au-feu* and artichokes whose leaves I loaded up with her homemade mayonnaise. I craved a rich custard with sour cherries called *clafoutis* that she served for dessert and that I would finish off for breakfast the next morning. On evenings when she taught, I volunteered to cook for my brother and concocted meals of towering tuna-melt sandwiches and instant mashed potatoes made from flakes in a box and huge bowls of ice cream smothered in chocolate syrup that we ate on TV trays as we sat glued to our favorite sitcoms.

I was always fairly tall for my age, and I played baseball and threw footballs with my friends after school, so it took a while for everyone to realize how fat I was getting. I began shopping for oversized clothes and flinched when family photos came back from the drugstore. In Little League, I changed my position to catcher so my growing gut wouldn't be so visible. During one game I fell over an opposing player who was sliding home and broke his leg. The boy's father was the home plate umpire, which made the experience all the more humiliating. On days when I wasn't playing, I went to the ballpark and sat in the stands munching on a big bag of candy that I would finish off by the end of the game. In a not-so-subtle sign of her concern, my mother bought a scale and put it in the bathroom, and by the time I entered junior high the dial jumped past two hundred pounds.

The weight gain wasn't the only sign of my unhappiness. At times, Paul and I were able to find respite from our misery by playing together in our little yard or putting on skits that we would dream up during our long car rides. But much of the time we fought ferociously, tearing at each other's bodies and hair so savagely that my mother gave up on having us share a bedroom and sacrificed her little study so that we could be separated. During one pitched battle while she was away teaching, Paul pulled a bread knife out of a kitchen drawer and threatened to kill me. He only put it away when I picked up the phone and pretended to call the police.

When her friends expressed dismay at our public battles, she would throw up her hands and say that, as one of eight sisters, she knew nothing about raising boys. But because she never remarried or dated other men after divorcing, we didn't have a man around to teach us how to behave. My only male role models were Dick Pearce, a sixth-grade teacher named Mr. Trivett, and my elementary school principal, Mr. Holbert. He was a rolypoly man with glasses and pale skin who came from a black Portuguese community in Rhode Island. Most students were afraid of him, because he kept a huge wooden measuring stick in his desk that he called "the Golden Ruler" and used to discipline troublemakers. But Mr. Holbert always winked and smiled when he saw me in the hallway, and I took it as a secret signal that we had a special bond and that he was looking out for me.

I was light-skinned enough that most of my classmates didn't know. They might have suspected that I came from some kind of exotic background, because my hair was so curly, but since apart from Mr. Holbert there were no other black people in Norton it probably never occurred to them that I might be mixed race.

Did I not want them to know? I'm not sure. I do remember one time, in the fifth grade, when my homeroom teacher made us practice public speaking in front of the class. She wrote down questions on little note cards and asked each of us to pick one from the deck. The first card I pulled read: "What does your father do?" I quickly shuffled it back in with the other cards and selected another topic. But I don't think it was my father's color that embarrassed me. What I dreaded was being forced to explain why he lived in California and not in Norton like the fathers of all my friends.

It wasn't until 1967, shortly before I turned ten, that I saw him again in the flesh. Out of the blue, he called to announce that he was planning to come east for part of the summer and that he wanted Paul and me to spend a week with him on Cape Cod. I was excited to hear his voice again and to imagine being near the beach like we had been that summer in Venice. And sure enough, in early August, he appeared at our house in a big blue car and drove us to a motel in Truro, near the very tip of the Cape. But instead of being alone with him, we discovered that a tall blond lady and her two children were staying in the room next door, and it became clear that they were more than just friends.

"She's the daughter of the owner of the *New York Post*," he told me in a tone that suggested that I should be impressed.

We all went sightseeing and ate picnics together, but his lady friend seemed a little tense, and I couldn't wait for her and her kids to leave so Paul and I could have him to ourselves. Once it was just the three of us, he took us to a drive-in movie, and I remember how beautiful the night sky was and how thrilling I thought it was to watch the big outdoor screen. One day we were sitting in the motel room and I noticed that he was leafing through a copy of *Newsweek* magazine. "Their coverage of civil rights is quite good," he said, and that was enough to persuade me to ask my mother for a subscription for my tenth birthday.

For years one more memory stuck with me from that Cape Cod visit. It was the image of my father kissing another woman—not the publisher's daughter—on the lips. The second one had long brown hair, and he was saying goodbye to her. I didn't remember more that that, except that I found it very confusing to see my father kissing two different women, and I wondered which of them was his girlfriend.

The next time we saw him was a year and a half later, over Christmas vacation in 1968, when he showed up at Grandmother Edith's house in Pittsburgh while we were visiting for the holiday. He was with yet another woman, white like the others, with an athletic figure and long straight black hair and the sporty name of Sally. They stayed in the back bedroom on the second floor of the funeral home, while my mother and brother and I roomed in the attic upstairs. I was eleven years old and was beginning to become aware of what went on between men and women, and I remember thinking how strange and awkward it was to have my father and his girlfriend sleeping together in the same house as my mother. He announced that he was going to make the chitterlings for Christmas dinner, and Paul and I watched as he cleaned the intestines in the kitchen sink. But then Grandmother's stove broke down and he couldn't cook them, and for the big holiday meal I think we ate a precooked turkey from the store.

When he left Pittsburgh, I had no idea when I might see him again. But then several months later, in the spring of 1969, he phoned us with big news. He was leaving UCLA and moving back to the East Coast. Princeton University had asked him to start its first African-American studies program, and he was also going to be a fellow of something called the Woodrow Wilson School. I had no clue what all those positions involved, but for the first time I got a sense of him as somebody very important in his profession. And after five years of separation, I finally allowed myself to hope that he might become a part of my life again.

7

His best friend in the world, I discovered, the man he described as
the brother he never had, was someone I met as an infant but never
saw again. He was Hussaini Adamu, the Nigerian professor who
came to our flat for the ill-fated roast beef dinner the year we lived in
Wimbledon. At the time, Adamu was on leave from his position in the
Department of Islamic Studies in Kano. The next year, he returned to
Africa and became one of my father's "informants"—the name anthro-
pologists give to locals who help them decipher a foreign culture. He
was two years older, portly and slightly shorter, with pitch-black skin,
big round eyes, and a trim beard. Like my father, he loved to talk,
and his gapped teeth flashed easily with laughter. Whenever they saw
each other, they would converse for hours, often well into the night.
They sometimes disagreed but they never got cross with one another,
and for the rest of his life, he was the one friend with whom my father
would never have a falling out.

Adamu was never seen in Western clothes and, for all anyone
knew, he didn't own any. He dressed in long white Muslim robes,

and on his head he wore a traditional Hausa skullcap. His father also happened to be the emir of Kazaure, the man we had watched in the *sallah* pageant at the end of Ramadan when I was a toddler. Under centuries-old tradition passed down to the Hausa tribes from the Fulani Muslims, that meant Hussaini was in line to become emir himself one day.

As he explained the custom to my father, each emir was required to take four wives. The first was almost always a member of the royal family, often a first cousin. For his next wives, the ruler could choose from among all the women in the kingdom. When he died, his throne didn't simply pass to his first-born son; a council of elders chose his successor from among all his male children. Unlike the kingdoms of Europe, where pure nepotism often produced wayward heirs, this system made it more likely that new emirs would be capable, and it also increased the incentive to marry into the royal line for families that weren't already related.

As my father learned more about the emirate structure, he began to grasp its paradoxical power. What might look to Western eyes like a backward system of feudalism and polygamy was actually a remarkably durable form of government. The fact that each emirate was relatively small—there were dozens strewn across northern Nigeria— only strengthened the sense of loyalty and cultural pride within each kingdom.

Once Adamu became his boon companion, my father was treated to the trappings of royal authority himself. Because his friend was in direct line of succession to the throne, fellow Nigerians were required to greet him with a deep, exaggerated bow, in which they thrust out their arms and lowered themselves to the ground.

"*Rankadada!*" they would shout in a ritual chant of respect. "*Rankadada!*"

When people saw how close my father was to Hussaini, they began to offer him the royal greeting as well.

"*Rankadada! Rankadada!*"

During the year my father spent traveling across northern Nigeria as a graduate student, he came to see that new Western forms of government weren't sweeping away the old ways of Africa. Instead, they were being co-opted. Chatting up the lawmakers in the Members Lounge at the Kaduna Assembly, he was struck by how many also held positions in the feudal hierarchy. In Hausa, there was a term for the traditional practice of seeking high office: *neman sarautu*. There was another word for gift-giving, or what Westerners might view as bribes: *talakawa*. Neither had disappeared under the British; colonialism just offered a new way to play the old games. Running for parliamentary office enhanced a man's status within the emirate. Colonial jobs in tax collection, the police, and the courts offered ways to buy off non-Muslims. Sometimes secular winds even hardened the feudal order, pushing kingdoms that had fought for centuries to make peace in order to protect their power and patronage.

Along with Adamu, my father was also heavily influenced by another kindred spirit he got to know that year. At the time, Michael Garfield Smith was perhaps the world's leading colored anthropologist, a descendant of British colonial officers whose mother, a mixed-race Jamaican nurse, had died in childbirth. Smith's early research also focused on northern Nigeria, and he had written a book showing how the emirate of Zazzau had retained its feudal character throughout the colonial era. As far as Smith was concerned, that was all to the good: He believed that Western democracies filled people's heads with unattainable dreams and that a society where everyone knew their place was more sustainable and realistic. As they compared notes, my father found himself agreeing about the power of tradition but disagreeing about its immutability. What he saw, in his journeys and interviews, was a feudal system that was enveloping the forces of colonialism and nationalism rather than being washed away by them. He coined a phrase for it: a "manipulative response" to political change.

When he returned to America, he started parlaying his insights into a reputation as an exciting new voice in African studies. There was so much talk about his doctoral thesis, which he called "The

Politics of Tradition: A Study of Continuity and Change in Northern Nigeria," that he was invited to expand it into a book before it was even finished. As a teaching assistant at Princeton and then as a faculty member at UCLA, he became a big draw at academic conferences, where audiences marveled at the originality and subtlety of his insights, particularly coming from a young black scholar.

Unlike most of his colleagues in the field, he wasn't satisfied to merely present empirical research that showed how Nigeria worked. He aspired to join the rarified, and exclusively white, club of theorists who offered more universal propositions about how political change takes place. In the mid-1960s, he published an article that hit the world of African studies like a mortar shell. It took aim at the prevailing school of "modernization" theorists who argued that the Western forces of democracy and free-market capitalism would inevitably sweep away the old ways of the developing world. My father attacked these scholars for seeing change as following only a "eurythmic" pattern—moving forward toward a more Western future, or backward toward the tribal past. Instead he proposed a new model of "dysrythmic change," in which tradition feeds off modernism and vice versa—almost like the polyrhythmic pattern of African drums, although he never would have used that metaphor for fear of trivializing his insights.

In the decorous jargon of academia, he all but accused the leading white American experts of patronizing the people of the Third World. He wrote that "today's student of 'modernization' has inferred what in effect is a hypothesis about how non-Western people generally will react to the kind of institutions yielded by change in the West. To reject this hypothesis is to discard the notion of 'modernization.' To do so in light of its pervasive influence and deep intellectual roots must at first appear foolhardy; certainly to dismiss it simply on the grounds of cultural relativism seems lame and unpersuasive. To challenge the concept at the roots, however, seems to me essential if social scientists are to come to grips with important realities in at least parts of the non-Western world."

At UCLA, his graduate students were thrilled with his ballsy brilliance. His personality and lifestyle excited them even more. He was a star professor who was only a few years older than they were, tall and handsome and black, for heaven's sake, with a warm laugh and a dimpled smile. He lived in a cool bungalow apartment on the beach, in the funky neighborhood of Venice with its Beats and hippies. He loved the ocean and invited his students to take walks on the sand at sunset. He reveled in discovering out-of-the-way restaurants and shops in the neighborhood, bragging joyously about his "finds." He befriended and bargained with merchants as though he was in an African bazaar. He threw lively dinner parties where he mixed drinks and served delicious French and African dishes that he cooked himself. He loved all kinds of music—folk, jazz, classical—and played his eclectic collection of records through speakers that he had assembled from parts. He even made his own furniture, a coffee table and a credenza. He was a wonderful raconteur and liked nothing better than to engage his students and colleagues in discussion about everything from politics and philosophy to the latest movies.

One day in January 1966, a young white graduate student named Barbara Callaway arrived at his mustard-colored bungalow on the beach. She had heard about a seminar that he was giving and had asked for permission to audit. She knocked and he opened the door. He was wearing casual slacks with a green crew-neck sweater over a buttoned-down shirt.

"You must be Barbara!" he said.

In that instant, she fell in love.

Barbara Callaway was an all-American beauty, with long brown hair, smiling eyes, and a voluptuous figure. She grew up in Arizona, attended Trinity University in Texas, and enrolled in an elite graduate program in African studies run jointly by Harvard, MIT, and Boston University. When she finished her course work in Boston, she applied for a grant to study Ibo, the tongue of southeastern Nigeria. UCLA had the best Ibo instruction in the country, so she decided to head west while she wrote her dissertation.

She had first become interested in Africa as a teenager, through her church in Tucson. Every year her pastor, Dr. Glenn McGee, exchanged pulpits for a week with another Presbyterian minister from New York City named Jim Robinson. When Dr. Robinson came to Arizona, he spoke in his sermons about a program he had created called Crossroads Africa. Every year, he took college students to the continent during school holidays to build housing and do other good works. It sounded fascinating, Barbara thought, so she applied and spent a summer traveling to Nigeria as part of a group of ten American students. She became enthralled with the country and its people and made several lifelong friends, including a black girl from Georgia named Lillian Miles, who would later marry a brave young leader of the civil rights movement, John Lewis.

When she moved to Los Angeles, Barbara rented an apartment in Brentwood and took a teaching position at Mount St. Mary's College, a Catholic school for girls. She heard about a UCLA graduate seminar called "African Politics," taught by a dynamic young professor named C.S. Whitaker Jr., and she phoned him to inquire if she could sit in.

As she sat listening to my father in his beachside bungalow, she became captivated by his intellect and charm. He was so smart, she thought, and so handsome! Was he interested in white women? He appeared so at ease with all his students, and seemed particularly flirtatious with her. She began to fantasize about what they might be like as a couple, but she told herself that it wasn't practical, at least not then. In April, she planned to travel to Nigeria for six months, to do more research for her thesis and to witness firsthand the crisis that was tearing the country apart.

By the winter of 1966, Nigeria was in turmoil. When the British had granted the country independence six years earlier, they had left behind a federalist constitution that kept the country divided along ethnic and geographical lines. The feudal emirates of the north, populated by the Hausa people and the Fulani Muslims who had come to rule them, remained semiautonomous. The south, which was mostly Christian, was split between the Yoruba in the west and the Ibos in the east. Sir Abubakar Tafawa Balewa, a British-educated colonial official, was elected prime minister, but he had little power and spent most of his time mediating among the tribal factions.

By the middle of the decade, a group of leftist Ibo military officers who had trained at the Sandhurst academy in England decided that Balewa needed to be overthrown and that Nigeria should be united as a socialist state. On January 15, 1966, they staged a bloody coup. The president and twenty-nine other top political leaders were killed. Six days later, Balewa's body was found dumped on the side of a road outside Lagos. Another victim was Sir Ahmadu Bello, the premier of the northern region and the sardauna of Sokoto, the highest religious post in the Muslim north.

As Barbara arrived in Nigeria in April 1966, the Ibo officers were struggling to establish a new government, but the hellish logistics of the vast and fragmented country overwhelmed them. In July, military officers from the north mounted a countercoup, ousting the Sandhurst graduates and declaring a "federal military government." A Christian military officer from central Nigeria was declared the new leader: Lt. Col. Yakubu Gowon, or "Jack" for short. Soon Hausa were slaughtering Ibos in the north by the tens of thousands. In the east, Ibos retaliated by killing Muslims. A military summit to negotiate a truce was organized, but among Ibos there was a growing move to secede from Nigeria and form a new country.

Barbara believed passionately in the Ibo cause, and when she got back to California in the fall she threw herself into raising awareness of their plight. She gave talks in local churches and rotary clubs around Los Angeles and helped collect money to send to relief workers. She described how the military government had shut off supply lines and left the Ibos to starve, the first signs of what would later be labeled genocide when the Ibos tried to create an independent state called Biafra.

When she reentered my father's life, she was eager to hear what he thought about the brewing civil war. To her surprise, he was quite judgmental of the Ibos. He argued that the Sandhurst officers who staged the initial coup were naive. "They underestimated the wound to northern pride," he said. "This wasn't just about power or *talakawai*. The Hausa are very easily offended." Besides, he reminded her, their job as scholars was not to take sides but to study the conflict objectively.

As they debated Nigeria's future, Barbara felt more and more drawn to him. Although they disagreed, she was impressed with the thoughtfulness of his analysis and flattered that he took her so seriously. Do I have to choose between a man and a cause? she asked herself, and she realized that she didn't want to. So on that first night in January, when he moved to kiss her, she didn't resist. And when he invited her to spend the night at the bungalow, she didn't refuse.

Once they were a couple, my father began to share some of his other passions with her. He took her to play tennis and encouraged her to sign up for lessons. She helped him shop for a new car, a green Mercury Cougar convertible that they both fell in love with. It was a 1966 model that the dealer was trying to clear off the lot before the 1967 models arrived, so he got a break on the price. The way he crowed about it, she thought he enjoyed getting a "steal" almost as much as the Cougar itself.

The more time she spent with him, the more Barbara was touched by his emotional vulnerability. He confided in her about his last great love and how painful the breakup had been. She was a prominent Los Angeles woman—indeed, a *very* prominent woman—named Adele Leopold. Her exhusband, Fred Leopold, was a powerful lawyer who had been elected mayor of Beverly Hills. Her mother was Dorothy Schiff, the legendary publisher of the *New York Post* and *grande dame* of Manhattan society.

My father had met Mrs. Leopold at the home of his friends Maury and Adrienne Hall. Maury was a fellow graduate student from Princeton who had moved out to Los Angeles, invested in land, and made a killing as a real estate developer. His wife, Adrienne, grew up in Beverly Hills, the daughter of a Jewish dry-cleaning magnate. They threw fancy parties at their swanky home with a pool out back in the San Ysidro Hills, and one evening they introduced their friend Syl to a vivacious socialite who immediately started flirting with him. Within weeks, they began an intense affair.

Like my mother, Adele Leopold was almost a decade older than he was, but in every other way she couldn't have been more different. If my father had tired of my mother's prudishness and yearned for more glamour, Adele certainly provided it. She was blond and willowy and worldly, a true Brearley girl from Manhattan. She dressed elegantly and mixed as easily with local politicians and the Hollywood crowd as with brains from UCLA. They would go out to restaurants, and people would stare, and he would tell her gallantly that it was only because she was so beautiful. She introduced him to her teenage children from a previous marriage, and he won them over with his encouraging advice about college. They flew to New York, where Mrs. Schiff hosted a lavish reception at the Regency Hotel to introduce him to her society friends. In his mind, it was all but an engagement party.

Adele didn't see things quite that way. She may have been in love with my father, but she had already been married twice and was in no rush to wed another man who was almost a decade younger. She put off his insistent questions about marriage and, increasingly alarmed by his obsession, started making excuses not to see him. My father confided his anguish over the fading romance to Adrienne Hall, and she interceded with Adele. "Well, I'm sad that Syl is sad," said the divorcée, but she didn't appear terribly torn up herself. Of course, Adrienne never told any of this to my father, for fear of further wounding his pride.

"I felt used in the end," he told Barbara. "Very used. And I can't figure out how I let myself get in so deep!" His soft eyes were filled with hurt, and that just made her fall for him even harder.

She was even more moved by my father's sorrow over losing Paul and me. He told her the story of his marriage to the French professor he met at college, and how it ended in a bitter divorce, and how she had taken his boys away from him. They had come back to visit one summer, and it had been wonderful, but then they left and the pain of separation was worse than ever. He missed us every day, he said as his eyes misted up. He claimed that he had moved to the beach partly as therapy, to help him get over losing us.

"So why don't you call them more often?" she asked. "Why don't you invite them here for another visit?"

He insisted that it was his exwife's fault. She was angry and didn't want us to have contact with him.

Barbara had never met my mother, but based on everything she had heard she found that hard to believe. My father had mentioned Pastor Theis and his acts of bravery during World War II, and from growing up in Dr. McGee's church she sensed the kind of values he must have instilled.

One day, she called my aunt Cleo in Queens to ask what she knew about the situation.

"That's crazy!" Cleo told her. "Jeanne would never keep those boys from Syl! She wants them to see their father. She takes them to Pittsburgh every year so that they can be part of the family."

That night, Barbara told my father what Cleo had said.

He hit the roof. "Well, damn Cleo and her disloyalty!" he shouted.

His jolt of fury startled her. What did any of this have to do with Cleo? she wondered. Why did he view it as disloyal for his sister to talk that way about his children? And why did he seem so mad at his exwife? Was he fending off his own sense of guilt about the divorce? Was it even worse now that he had been dumped by Adele and experienced the kind of pain that my mother must have felt? She couldn't figure it out, but his anger was frightening to behold, so she let it drop.

By coincidence, or perhaps not, shortly after that argument they started talking about going east for the summer. A Boston friend had offered Barbara the use of her house overlooking Quincy Bay for a couple of months, and she thought it would be an ideal place to work on her still unfinished doctoral thesis. When she told my father, he proposed that she drive to Philadelphia in her blue Nash Rambler and that they meet there and travel together to Boston. While she was writing, he could spend some time with his sons on Cape Cod.

That July, Barbara drove the Nash Rambler across the country, and when they got to Boston, he took the car and said he would be back in a few days. She didn't hear from him for almost two weeks. She had no idea where he was, let alone that in addition to seeing Paul and me he had arranged a rendezvous with Adele Leopold to see if they could make another go of it.

Finally, on the second Sunday after he had left, the Rambler pulled into the driveway of the house in Quincy. My father got out of the car along with my brother and me. Barbara guessed that I must be the heavy one with glasses and that Paul was the smaller one with a touch of blond in his hair.

"I lost the key!" he explained sheepishly. "I hot-wired the engine, but I have to keep it running or it will stall out again. Mark's baseball bat and mitt are in the trunk and I can't get them out."

He asked Barbara if she would take the Rambler to a garage and get a new key made. He had called my mother and convinced her to drive us back to the Cape. As usual, they both went along with his wishes, and once Barbara had the new key she drove the Rambler back to the motel near the ocean where we were staying. Keeping the car, my father drove her to a bus station and put her on a Greyhound back to Boston. "I'll see you in a few days, sweetie," he said as I looked on, storing away the hazy memory of the mysterious second woman who kissed my father on Cape Cod.

In graduate school, Barbara had taken courses with a black professor at Boston University named Adelaide Cromwell Hill. She was a legendary character around BU, a small woman with a blunt manner and a townhouse full of African art. Barbara had remained friends with Adelaide, and shortly after the car key incident she told her what had happened.

"You did *what*?" Professor Hill said. "You got that key made for him and drove that car all the way to Cape Cod? What are you, his servant?"

Barbara shrugged ruefully. "I don't know why," she said. She felt embarrassed but also grateful to her old professor, since it was the first time anyone had ever gotten mad at Syl on her behalf.

• • •

It was during the next school year, after they returned to L.A., that Barbara decided my father had a drinking problem. From the time they met, he had always enjoyed a few Scotches at night. The cocktails mellowed him out and made him less antsy or angry if he had had a bad day. But after the second or third drink, he would put the bottle of Chivas Regal away. Some nights, when they were attending an evening lecture or a movie on campus, he didn't drink at all. But now he seemed unable to stop. As soon as he had one drink it would lead to another and another until the entire bottle of Chivas was empty. It was deceptive, because he was such a sweet drunk. He never got angry or abusive, and he could still carry on a conversation. But Barbara saw how much he was putting away and how it slowed his speech and took the sharp edge off his wit and conversation.

Most days, he managed to will himself through a demanding schedule of meetings and classes. But for the first time, he started to miss events and had to invent excuses for his absences. When they had first met, he was still churning out academic papers and lectures to maintain his star status in African studies; now he wasn't writing anymore.

He no longer wanted to socialize with people who didn't drink. The two of them had always enjoyed hosting dinner parties where liquor and wine flowed plentifully. Barbara herself liked a cocktail or two, or preferably a few glasses of Chablis, and so did most of their friends. Yet occasionally someone would demur, explaining that they had a paper to write or a class to teach in the morning. "Well, they're not invited back!" my father would say as soon as they left the apartment.

It became a particularly touchy subject with Barbara's friends Emily and Lamar. Lamar liked to drink, but Emily didn't. After several dinners where she turned her glass over on the table, my father declared her banned. "Emily's not welcome anymore!" he said. "No more Lamar and Emily!"

It took a while, but other friends began to worry too. At a party at Maury and Adrienne Hall's house one day, the discussion in the kitchen turned to whether Syl was becoming an alcoholic. Maury defended his old friend, saying that he didn't think the situation was out of hand.

Suddenly there was a loud splashing sound outside, and Maury rushed to see what had happened. "Syl fell into the pool!" he reported when he got back. "Maybe he does have a problem. . . ."

From then on, Adrienne Hall stopped inviting my father and Barbara to her home. She and Maury still came to the beach, and they would meet them for dinner at a restaurant, but it became clear that Adrienne didn't want to deal with the prospect of a drowning or a lawsuit.

Syl needed help, Barbara decided. She didn't know much about Alcoholics Anonymous, but she decided to investigate. She found a class for relatives and friends who wanted to understand alcoholism and help get their loved ones into AA.

"So now you're a know-it-all because you've gone to a few Al-Anon meetings?" he taunted her when she talked about the class.

Finally he agreed to attend an AA meeting, at a community center in Santa Monica, but he returned full of disdain.

"You're supposed to stand up and say that you have no control over booze," he said. "Well, that's just not true in my case!"

Barbara still adored everything about him when he was sober, so it never occurred to her to leave him. Besides, she was making plans to return to Africa again, this time to spend a year in Ghana on a Fulbright Fellowship. He toyed with the possibility that he would take a sabbatical and go with her but concluded that it was impossible now that he was helping to run the university. A year earlier, a fellow political scientist named Chuck Young had become UCLA's chancellor and named his friend C.S. Whitaker Jr. as associate dean of the graduate school, putting him in charge of all the social science and humanities departments as well as the schools of business and engineering and all of UCLA's museums.

It was a remarkable position for a black man still barely in his thirties, but then again, Chuck Young was just a few years older himself.

He had become head of the university almost by accident, when the former chancellor left and a temporary replacement was needed. Unlike my father, Young wasn't even a full professor yet, so a battlefield promotion had to be quickly arranged. But Young immediately fit the part, with his Hollywood good looks and cool demeanor.

In the spring, when the lease on her apartment in Brentwood was up, my father suggested that Barbara move in with him at the beach.

"Okay, but I'm still going to Ghana," she said.

"That's fine," he replied. "You should go."

She lived with him until she left for Africa, and for those three months, it felt like the Venice bungalow was "their place." Or almost their place, since he still put limits on what she could bring with her. She filled the closets with her clothes, but he insisted that she put her artwork and favorite furniture from Hong Kong into storage.

Before she left in the summer, she urged him one more time to go to AA while she was gone.

"I'll try," he promised.

As usual, he wasn't much of a letter writer. Barbara received only two pieces of mail from him during the year she was in Ghana. The first one arrived in late January, and it shook her to the core.

While she was gone, my father had been pulled into a nasty dispute among black students at UCLA. The "brothers" and "sisters" on campus had started to take sides in the Black Power battles that were raging in the wake of Martin Luther King Jr.'s assassination. Some had joined the Black Panthers, the militant antigovernment group that had become famous for its uniform of dark sunglasses, black berets, and leather jackets. Others embraced an organization called US, or United Slaves, that preached a black separatist agenda. The US students favored native African garb, greeted each other in Swahili, and derided the Panthers for mouthing the rhetoric of Marx and Herbert Marcuse rather than the wisdom of Mother Africa.

The local leader of the Panthers was a street activist and part-time UCLA student named Alprentice Carter, better known by his nickname, "Bunchy." He came from inner-city L.A. and had belonged to a street gang called the Slauson Renegades as a teenager. Convicted of armed robbery, he had been introduced to the writings of Malcolm X and converted to the Nation of Islam as an inmate in Soledad prison. After he got out, he had met Huey Newton, the founder of the Panthers, who encouraged Bunchy to join the party and form a chapter in Southern California.

Bunchy had enrolled in UCLA's "High Potential Program," for city kids who couldn't qualify for regular admission, and begun to recruit for the Panthers on campus. One conscript was a grad student named Geronimo Pratt, who later served as the party's minister of defense. Another was a beautiful, light-skinned sister named Elaine Brown. A native of north Philadephia, she had moved to L.A. to become a songwriter and supported herself working as a cocktail waitress at a strip club. Later, in the 1970s, she would become involved with Huey Newton and take his place as the head of the Panthers after he was sentenced for murder and fled to Cuba.

A black student named Clyde "Imamu" Halisi led the US faction on campus. He was a disciple of the movement's founder, Ron Karenga. The fourteenth son of a chicken farmer from Maryland, Ronald McKinley Everett moved to California in the 1950s to attend Los Angeles College and later enrolled in a doctoral program at UCLA. He dropped out of the university in 1965 to establish US, which he proclaimed also stood for "us black people." He changed his last name to *"Karenga,"* the world for "nationalist" in Swahili. He demanded that followers call him *"maulana,"* for "our master," and invented a black alternative to Christmas called *"Kwanza."* He urged his disciples to follow "the Seven-fold path of Blackness . . . Think Black, Talk Black, Act Black, Create Black, Buy Black, Vote Black, and Live Black."

Observing the growing militancy and rivalries among the black students on campus, my father was filled with dismay. As a Quaker, he was appalled at the Panthers and their calls for armed struggle against the government and the "pigs." As a political scientist, he thought their talk of revolution was grandiose and silly. He also looked askance at Karenga and his separatist, pan-African rhetoric. He understood Africa well enough to know how ridiculous it was to think that American blacks could resettle there. His old friend Dick Sklar, now a fellow Africanist at UCLA, spoke highly of Halisi, but my father thought Imamu and Bunchy and the other loudmouths on both sides were all on ego trips.

He also didn't think much of the adviser for the black students. In the fall, a group of undergraduates had petitioned to form a Black Student Union, and when they learned that the university required faculty supervision they approached Al Cannon, a psychiatrist at the UCLA Medical School and the only other tenured black at the university.

My father believed that Cannon was badly miscast. As an administrative matter, he disapproved of someone from the medical school meddling in undergraduate affairs. He also objected to the notion that only a black adviser was acceptable. Wasn't that a form of reverse racism on the part of the black students? And wasn't it patronizing of the university to cave in to their demands? From what he knew of Cannon, he also didn't think the man was equipped to deal with the rough characters who were starting to throw their weight around at UCLA.

He went to his friend the chancellor with his concerns. But Chuck Young wasn't about to tell the black students that they couldn't have a black adviser. If my father didn't approve of Al Cannon, Young suggested, why didn't he volunteer to advise the group himself?

My father didn't like that solution either. While he was friendly with many black students on campus, he knew what the militants on both sides said about him behind his back. He was a member of the university administration, so in their eyes he was by definition a sell-out and a toady. Being publicly denounced as an Uncle Tom, he told the chancellor, was not what he signed up for when he agreed to become an associate dean. Still, Chuck Young would not take no for an answer, and he made it clear that he was counting on my father to keep an eye on the black students.

By the beginning of spring semester, their disputes had reached a boiling point. Bunchy Carter was talking about running for the presidency of the Black Student Union, and Halisi and his US followers were warning of a Panther coup. In a bid to make peace, Al Cannon encouraged the union to hold a meeting to allow both sides to air their grievances.

On Friday, January 17, more than 150 black students gathered in the first-floor lunchroom at Campbell Hall. US supporters were identifiable by their Karenga-inspired outfits: shaved heads, sunglasses, and dashiki tunics. Some of the Panthers were in their usual black leather outfits, others not. John Huggins, Bunchy Carter's top lieutenant, wore combat boots and a used gray suit, with a .44 Magnum pistol hidden inside his jacket.

Elaine Brown showed up midway through the meeting and found it a boring affair. The midday sun streamed in through floor-to-ceiling windows and caused her to yawn. Huggins whispered in her ear that he was hungry and urged her to call for an adjournment. The motion was accepted, and the meeting ended at twenty to three in the afternoon.

In the hallway outside the lunchroom, a US follower named Harold "Tawala" Jones came up to Brown. He had an eyeliner mustache penciled over his lip, she recalled in the account of their exchange in her memoir, *Taste of Power: A Black Woman's Story.*

"You need to watch what you say, Sister," he said.

She brushed him off and went to rejoin Carter and Huggins and the rest of the Panther contingent.

"What did that nigger say to you?" Carter asked her angrily.

"Nothing really, Bunchy," she said.

"Don't let another nigger talk crazy to you!" he said. "Do you understand?"

"Yes, Bunchy, I do," she said.

She started up a stairwell on her way to another meeting as Carter and Huggins rushed into the cafeteria to find her harasser. When they caught up with Jones, they started kicking and punching him.

Hearing the commotion, a US member named Claude Hubert, also known as "Chochezi," ran into the lunchroom. He pulled a pistol from under his dashiki and shot Huggins in the lower back, right through his gray suit jacket. Then he pumped several bullets into Bunchy Carter's broad chest.

As he fell to the ground, Huggins reached for his .44 Magnum and fired off several shots. He missed his assailant but clipped another US follower, Larry "Watani" Stiner, in the shoulder. Bloody but still able to run, Stiner fled the scene with the shooter and two other militants. Other students who hadn't left the meeting yet screamed and scrambled for safety. One jumped out of the lunchroom window; the rest raced into the hallway and away from Campbell Hall. When the police arrived several minutes later, the lunchroom was empty except for the bodies of Carter and Huggins, lying in a pool of blood in the middle of the floor, their fingers touching.

The police never found the killers. Witnesses said that they saw four men run from the building and that one of them held a shiny object, but no one could say who they were and no weapons were found at the scene.

Worried that the Panthers might retaliate for the shooting, dozens of Los Angeles police officers swooped down later that afternoon on the house where Huggins lived at 806 West Century Boulevard in South-Central. They confiscated handguns, rifles, shotguns, and a homemade bomb and arrested seventeen Black Panther Party members, including one who had just arrived at the house carrying a paper bag filled with blasting powder.

Halfway around the world in Ghana, Barbara Callaway felt stricken as she read and reread my father's account of the "shootout" at UCLA. How awful for Syl! she thought. How unfair that he should have been dragged into this horrendous mess! In his letter, my father vented his anger at everyone involved, particularly Al Cannon. "This never would have happened if Al Cannon had stayed out of it," he wrote. "I hold him responsible, and I will hold him responsible for the rest of my life!"

As she absorbed the dreadful news, Barbara shared my father's outrage. But she also worried that his fury at Cannon might be masking his own sense of responsibility. After all, Chuck Young had told him to take charge of the crisis, so the killings had happened on his watch.

She wrote back to tell him how shocked and sorry she was. She didn't say what she was also thinking: Don't take it out on yourself!

My father's second letter arrived in Ghana several months later. He said he was writing to let Barbara know that he was leaving UCLA. Princeton University, his graduate school alma mater, had offered him a position he couldn't refuse: as director of a new African-American studies department, with a tenured joint appointment at the Woodrow Wilson School. He had even negotiated to take a sabbatical leave, fully paid by Princeton, before he began, and he planned to spend the next year fulfilling his lifelong dream of traveling around the world.

He also reported that he was engaged. Barbara was startled to read the name. She knew the woman in question, who was named Sally, only vaguely as a Stanford graduate who had also come to UCLA to study an African language: Wolof, the native tongue of Senegal. Barbara didn't know that Syl and Sally were that close, let alone that they had become a couple while she was in Ghana. Now he was writing to say that Sally was moving to Princeton with him and that they planned to get married.

Heartbroken and completely mystified, Barbara returned to Los Angeles over the summer. Another letter had been forwarded to her from her old address in Brentwood. It was from the landlord of my father's apartment in Venice, saying that he had left without taking his things. Would she be kind enough to pack up his stuff so the place could be rented again? the landlord asked.

When Barbara opened the door to the mustard-colored bungalow by the beach, it was still full of my father's furniture. Ashtrays piled with stale cigarette butts and empty liquor bottles were everywhere. She opened the closets and found her clothes still hanging there. But the green Mercury Cougar was gone, and so was Syl.

8

The Christmas message he sent us that year came from Uganda and was enclosed in a card made from the bark of a mutubo tree that had been beaten into a thin brown "cloth" by disabled natives in Kampala.

"My Dear Sons," he wrote. "This is to wish you both a fine Christmas. I will be spending my Christmas this year in Uganda with nice friends, but I will be thinking of the grand time I had last Christmas with you in Pittsburgh and wishing I could be in both places at once. This trip generally has been wonderful, but especially am I once again fascinated by Africa. It is not an easy place, in fact poverty and other handicaps are always evident. Yet I find a spirit among so many that I can only admire. Perhaps you'll come with me for a visit here someday. The King of Swaziland has agreed to my writing his biography, so chances are I'll return here in another 2 years to do the research. Take care and have a great day. Love, Daddy."

Finally he returned from his trip around the world, and my brother and I went to visit him during the last week of summer vacation before I entered the eighth grade. He had moved into an apartment near the Princeton campus with a double-height living room and big windows that flooded in light. African art was everywhere—colorful paintings, batik prints, witch-doctor masks, and large sun-weathered drums—and the walls were lined with wood-and-bracket bookshelves stacked with hundreds of volumes. When I asked if he could recommend one, he picked out a dog-eared paperback copy of *Catch 22*. I instantly fell in love with Yossarian's cock-eyed voice and felt proud that my father thought I was smart enough to grasp Heller's irony.

He showed us a fresh copy of his newly published book on Nigeria, *The Politics of Tradition*, explaining the pains that he had taken to choose the right shade of green for the cover. I leafed through the first few pages and came across the dedication: "For my mother, Edith McColes Whitaker." All of a sudden I was struck with a different perception of Grandmother, as the object of my father's devotion. His eyes were moist as he told us how long and hard he had worked on the book, and for the first time it occurred to me that he might be so remiss about sending letters because he found the act of writing so difficult.

He had a cool car, a green Mercury Cougar convertible, and he had grown his hair into a short Afro and wore colorful dashiki shirts around the apartment. He showed Paul and me how to "slap me five" and "slap me ten" and taught us the palm-thumb-fingers Black Power handshake. His girlfriend Sally, the one we had met in Pittsburgh, came over for dinner. He cooked a chicken dish with olives and served it with garlic bread, which I had never tasted before and pronounced especially delicious. We spent time with his new friend Conrad Snowden, another black faculty member who had a 'fro that was almost as big as the black cop's on *Mod Squad*. On the last day of the visit, we played touch football on the lawn outside the condo, my father and I against Conrad and Paul. I threw him a pass to score the winning touchdown, and when he ran over to slap me five, it was the happiest feeling I had had in years.

Inspired by the visit, I returned to Norton and announced to my mother on the morning of my thirteenth birthday that I wanted to go on a diet. "I'm tired of being a fatso," were my exact words.

My mother told me that I should consult a doctor first. She took me to see a pediatrician with glasses and limp blond hair in Attleboro, a nearby town. Frowning and shaking his head at the scale, he told me that I was eighty pounds overweight. The easy thing would be to prescribe pills, he said, but he didn't believe in diet medication for children my age. Instead he said he was going to put me on a diet of 1,200 calories a day, and he handed me a chart with options for breakfast, lunch, and dinner.

"I see a lot of kids with your problem and most of them can't stay on a diet," he said as I left. "Usually they just gain the weight right back."

I was furious. *I'll show you!* I thought.

Over the next five months, I made a point of consuming even fewer calories than the snide doctor prescribed. Day after day, I stoically ate the same thing: a soft-boiled egg and unbuttered toast for breakfast; a roast-beef sandwich with mustard and an apple that I carried in a paper bag to school for lunch; and a piece of grilled chicken and my mother's lettuce salad for dinner. An extra teaspoon of her vinaigrette counted as my dessert.

Over the winter, I played backup center on the junior high basketball team, and during practice the coach made us run up and down four flights of stairs for twenty minutes. By the time we finished, our legs were burning and our jerseys were drenched. Between the Spartan meals and the sweaty exercise, I shed weight quickly, and by March I was down to my goal of 135 pounds. My mother gave me money to buy a pair of white jeans, and at school a dark-haired girl named Doreen started passing me notes. I summoned the courage to "pin" her and for the first time I had a girlfriend.

But even more than Doreen, I wanted to impress my dad. I couldn't wait to see him again and to show him the results of all my hard work and determination.

That winter, as I was losing eighty pounds, my mother finally gave up cigarettes. I always thought it was because my brother and I had nagged her for so long about her pack-a-day habit. But I had that wrong too: It was because of her parents.

With her seventh year on the Wheaton faculty approaching, she was eligible for a sabbatical, and she had decided to take Paul and me to live in France for a year. She wanted us to learn the language and to get to know the Theis family, and she longed to be close to her father and mother and sisters again. But she knew how much her smoking bothered Grandpapa and Grandmaman, so she resolved to stop. As part of the effort, she enrolled in yoga classes that were offered at the college at night, and the deep breathing reminded her of the exercises that the Paris doctors had given her to help cure her stutter when she was a child.

Wheaton allowed full-year leaves only at half-pay, which for my mother amounted to less than $5,000 at the time. So she began figuring out how we could survive in France on an even tighter budget than usual. Her sister Louise lived in Grenoble, in southeast France, in a housing project with two of her children. She was planning to move into a larger apartment in the neighborhood and offered to let my mother take over her tiny two-bedroom, which would make it possible for Paul and me to attend the local French public school for free. Louise also said that she would look for part-time work at the Université de Grenoble, and Grandpapa wrote to say that he would loan her money from his minister's pension.

The prospect of being reunited with her family wasn't the only fresh breeze that had begun to disperse the dark clouds over my mother's head. At Wheaton she had made two new friends who not only listened to her woes but helped her forget them with laughter. One was Renee Wells, a petite preschool teacher who had come to work in the Wheaton-run nursery school and moved into the apartment upstairs from us. She was recently divorced too, from a high-school gym instructor in Northern California, and they commiserated about their roguish exes. But she could also be as lighthearted as the sound of her name, which to my mother's amusement she pronounced "Reenee" instead of "Re-nay." And by training and temperament, she was wonderful with kids, and she delighted in spending time with Paul and me and giggling at our made-up songs and skits.

My brother had always been very musical, and when he turned eight my mother decided he should learn an instrument. She had heard that one of her French majors played the recorder. Gretchen Ellis was a tall junior from upstate New York who wore funky thrift-store clothes and thick auburn hair down past her waist. But when she showed up to teach Paul the little wooden flute, he wanted to teach her how to pick pockets instead. Their lessons quickly dissolved into silly games. She soon befriended me too, and would take me to hang out with her classmates at a student grill called the Cage, where I played Jimi Hendrix on the jukebox. And gradually she disarmed my mother, who found herself highly entertained by Gretchen's antics. ("Look, I'm a monkey!" she would cry as she jumped around our apartment and scratched her unshaven armpits.)

Not surprisingly, we discovered that she was rebelling against a cold, conservative upbringing. Her father was a dour, independently wealthy Princeton dropout who collected Oriental rugs, and her mother was a narrow-minded housewife. When Mrs. Ellis found out that her daughter had a teacher who had married a black man and given birth to two mixed-race sons, she wouldn't even utter her name. She referred to my mother as "that woman." Mr. Ellis wasn't thrilled either, until he read about my father in his alumni magazine and decided that a Princeton man couldn't be all bad, even if he was colored. As their friendship blossomed, my mother would sometimes say that she had adopted Gretchen as the daughter she never had. But Gretchen insisted that it was the other way around: *She* had adopted Jeanne Whitaker as the *mother* she never had.

As her mood brightened, my mother rediscovered her favorite pleasure: cooking. She started hosting dinners for her friends on a ping-pong table in the hallway of our galley-style apartment and taught herself how to make baguettes using the recipe in Julia Child's *Mastering the Art of French Cooking*. She would knead and shape the dough into long batons and place them on brick tiles laid out in our electric oven, then throw a red-hot skillet into a pan full of water just as the oven door closed, creating a dramatic gush of steam that fogged up the entire kitchen. On Sundays, she would proudly take her home-made bread to the potluck lunches that were held after services at the Friends Meeting in Providence.

That ritual too had become a refuge for her. Even during her gloomiest periods of depression, she had always insisted on taking my brother and me to Quaker Meeting. Every week, she would drive us to Providence and sit in silence on the spartan wooden benches as the sun streamed through the big windows overhead and Paul and I went upstairs to Sunday school. At first, she found it hard to get all the voices of doubt and regret out of her mind, but bit by bit she had rediscovered the spiritual peace that she had known in her youth, and it too slowly helped bring her back into the Light, as the Quakers would say.

Through the Meeting, she got involved with the American Friends Service Committee and its opposition to the Vietnam War. She volunteered for petition drives to end the draft, worried sick that Paul and I would be conscripted and die in combat. Like many members of the Wheaton faculty, she sympathized with students who had turned against the war. In May 1970, after four student protesters were killed by the Ohio National Guard at Kent State, the Wheaton girls joined hundreds of other student bodies in going on strike. It fizzled out quickly, however, and by June all of my mother's French majors took their exams and graduated.

Yet Kent State had another unforeseen impact on the college. The previous year, a member of the History Department had gone on leave, and as a substitute the chairman, Paul Helmreich, had hired a young woman who decided to teach a class on women's history. It proved so popular that when the professor on sabbatical returned, Helmreich asked the school's president, Bill Prentice, for permission to create a permanent course.

Prentice was on tense terms with the faculty at the time, due to the strike but also to an epidemic of sexual hanky-panky with students. Four members of the Class of 1969 had become involved with their professors and ended up wedding them after they graduated, breaking up several longstanding marriages. Another department chairman had been stripped of his position after getting a girl pregnant. In a testy mood, Prentice turned Helmreich down. But then the students found out about it and, emboldened by the Kent State protest, they went to the president to appeal. When he saw how passionate the girls seemed about the women's history course, he relented.

Although no one realized it at the time, it was the birth of the women's movement at Wheaton, a force that as 1970s went on would change the way the entire college viewed its mission, and the way my mother saw herself.

With spring break nearing, my mother contacted my father and arranged for Paul and me to visit him again in Princeton. He suggested that we arrive on a Sunday, and since she had a class to teach the next day, she told us that she would drive us as far as New York and put us on a train the rest of the way. When we got to Penn Station, she bought us two tickets, and half an hour later Paul and I got off at Princeton Junction and started looking around the little station for my father.

He was nowhere to seen.

A middle-aged white couple walked over to us.

"Do you remember me?" the man asked. "I'm Hube Wilson, an old friend of your dad's."

"Yes," I said. "We met you in California a long time ago."

"I remember it well," he said. "But I had a different wife then."

"I'm his new wife," the woman said, putting out her hand. "I knew you too when you both were little boys. My name is Gina."

I didn't remember her.

"Where's Dad?" I asked.

"He's under the weather," Hube said. "He asked us to pick you up. He'll be at home when you get there."

The Wilsons grabbed our duffel bags and took us to their car. It was an ordinary sedan, not the VW bus I remembered from Venice. They did their best to make small talk, remarking on how much we had grown and asking how we liked school. But it was awkward, and Hube no longer matched the matinee idol image I had of him in my mind. His hair had gone white and his face was etched with deep wrinkles.

When we arrived at the apartment, I noticed that the blinds were drawn. Hube rang the bell and we waited for over a minute before my father opened the door. He said hello and gave my brother and me a hug, but his embrace felt weak and he looked tired. It took several minutes before he said anything about my appearance.

"It looks like you've lost some weight, Mark," he said wanly.

Is that it? I thought, dejectedly. *Is that all you're going to say? I lost eighty pounds and you barely even noticed?*

He had prepared sandwiches and iced tea for lunch. The Wilsons stayed and chatted while Paul and I ate. My father smoked and drank coffee and didn't touch anything on his plate. When the Wilsons left, he told us that there wasn't much to do in Princeton on Sundays but that he had plans to take us sightseeing and to a movie the next day. He suggested that we might want to take a nap. I wasn't tired, so I browsed through the bookshelves in the living room to find something to read. I picked out *The Godfather,* by Mario Puzo, and quickly became engrossed by the opening scenes of the big wedding and the horse's head in the movie producer's bed.

For dinner, he reheated spaghetti he emptied from a plastic container in the refrigerator and made garlic bread in a toaster oven. "I remember how much you like garlic bread," he said. Paul and I got into our pajamas and climbed into the sofa bed that he had prepared in his upstairs study. He kissed us goodnight and went down the stairs.

I still wasn't sleepy, and as I lay awake thinking, I heard the front door open and close. *Where's Dad going?* I wondered. *Is it okay for Paul and me to be here by ourselves?* Then about twenty minutes later, I heard the door open again and the sound of my father's footsteps. Relieved that he was home, I drifted off.

Paul was sound asleep when I awoke the next morning. I listened for other noises but didn't hear any. I felt hungry, so I rose quietly and tiptoed downstairs to see if I could find something to eat.

The kitchen in his condo was small and modern, with a little eating counter and bar stool. I didn't know exactly what sizes liquor came in, but I could tell that the Beefeater bottle on the counter was the big kind. There was still some liquid left in it, but not much, only a tiny bit at the bottom. Next to it was a pumpkin pie. It was the store-bought variety in a tin shell, not like the pies my mother made from scratch for Thanksgiving. The center had been scooped out, as if by a scavenging animal. There were no slices, just an ugly hole in the middle.

I stood there for a long time, trying to figure out the meaning of what I saw in front of me. It reminded me of the still-life paintings in my mother's big books about French art, only with a gruesome twist. Had Dad done this? I wondered. Did he drink that whole bottle of gin? Was that why he went out at night, to go to a liquor store? And why would he eat the pie that way? Was he so drunk he couldn't even hold a knife and fork?

I heard Paul getting up. I didn't want him to see the sad tableau, so I hid the bottle and the pie in the back of the refrigerator. I made us toast for breakfast, and we sat around waiting for my father to wake up. Sometime after noon, I smelled cigarette smoke upstairs. Then there was the sound of a phone being dialed and my father talking in a low voice. At last he came downstairs, covered only by a terrycloth bathrobe.

"I'm sorry, boys," he said. "I have to leave. I've called your grandmother in Pittsburgh and she's going to come to take care of you."

"Where are you going?" I asked anxiously.

"Back to the hospital," he said. "I wanted to get well to spend time with you boys, but I'm sick again and have to go back."

He went back upstairs, and Paul and I sat there in the living room until sundown, dazed and disappointed, not knowing what to think about what was happening. The next day Grandmother Edith arrived, and a taxi came to take my father away. He must have been too proud to call my mother, because she only learned what had happened when Grandmother phoned her to make plans to meet at Aunt Cleo's.

On the train ride to New York, Grandmother Edith tried to keep our spirits up, but I could see how distraught she was.

"Do you know we're going to France next year?" I asked, hoping to say something that would make us both feel better.

"Yes, Jeanne told me," she said. "I think it will be a wonderful experience for you boys."

"And what about Dad?" I asked. "Do you think he'll be okay while we're gone?"

There was a long pause before she answered.

"I don't know, child," Grandmother said, "but I want you to pray for him."

9

Our year in France started in Luxembourg, the hub of Icelandic Air-lines, the cheapest carrier my mother could find. After landing there, we took a train to Strasbourg, the capital of Alsace, where my aunts Marianne and Marguerite lived. Marianne, one of the two babies who had stayed behind with my grandparents during the war, had grown to be even taller than my mother, five-feet-nine or so, with a long face and nose like their father's. She had alarmed Grandpapa by falling in love with a Catholic, a cheerful Alsatian named Jean-Paul Wendling, but Grandmaman had helped bring him around and now the two were married and about to move to Holland. I'll never forget my first breakfast in Marianne's kitchen: how delicious a real French baguette tasted when it was slathered with fresh butter and jam and dunked in a bowl full of coffee and warm milk.

I was surprised by Marguerite, because she seemed so unlike the other Theis sisters I had met. When we went to dinner at her house, she chain-smoked Gauloise cigarettes and talked a blue streak. My mother warned us that she wasn't as good a cook as her twin sister,

Francoise, because she was so busy at her job with the national train company, and it was the first time I saw how competitive the Theis sisters could get when it came to their kitchen skills. But I thought the dish of salt pork and potatoes and sauerkraut that she made in a pressure cooker tasted just fine. "One cannot visit Strasbourg without eating *choucroute!*" she said in her accented English.

It was only later that my mother told me Marguerite's sad personal story. She was one of the first sisters to get married, to a Protestant missionary like their father. His name was Bernard Kopp, and he was universally loved for his kindness and warm wit and gentle way with children. They had two sons, Michel and Emmanuel, the latter of whom went by the nickname "Manouche." But while they were doing missionary work in Cameroon and she was pregnant with their third son, Bernard met a tragic end. He was shopping in a store when a group of thugs barged in and started randomly firing at white people. He was shot at point-blank range and died soon after. Since then, Michel and Manouche had both grown up to be successful students with winning personalities, but their younger brother was moody and had some difficulty in school. Within the Theis family, everyone attributed the difference to the fact that the older boys had been exposed to their charismatic father, while the third one never was.

From Alsace we went to Paris, to spend Bastille Day with Gretchen Ellis. She had moved to France to work for Sweet Briar College's junior-year abroad program, and she was as funny and spontaneous as ever. She was living with a former roommate from Wheaton in a tiny apartment near the Quai de Grenelle, not far from the Seine, with a view of the Eiffel Tower out of a tiny bathroom window. On July 14, she took us to a festive *Bal des Pompiers* at the firemen's station in her neighborhood. After tiny, humdrum Norton, Paris seemed to Paul and me like the most exciting place in the world, with intoxicating sights and sounds and smells on every street corner. Although I was still eating sparingly for fear of gaining any weight back, I was fascinated by all the new food we were discovering. Gretchen introduced us to *crème fraiche,* which tasted like a cross between yogurt and sour cream, and served a sweet chestnut paste called *crème de marrons* out of a white tin can. "I call them 'creamed morons'!" Gretchen proclaimed, eliciting an involuntary giggle from my mother.

In America, I was used to my mother's cheap secondhand cars—the Rambler, the Pinto, the Gremlin—but I had never seen anything quite so flimsy as the Deux Chevaux. It was a tiny little car that we saw all across France with, as the name suggested, a two-horsepower engine, a body that looked like a big metal mousetrap, and all the comfort of a high-school bleacher. I took my first ride in one when we traveled south to see my grandparents and Grandpapa arrived in his gray Deux Chevaux to pick us up at the train station in Valence, a city in the Rhone Valley. He was wearing a black beret and the formal uniform I would discover he put on every day—a plain gray suit, a white shirt with a thin black tie, and huge black shoes—as though he might be called on to preach a sermon at any moment. From his visit to the States when I was seven, I had retained an image of him as tall and forbidding, but now he seemed frailer, with the stooped shoulders of a seventy-one-year-old and a kindly expression framed by enormous ears.

"*Alors, mes bonshommes!*" he said as he kissed Paul and me on both cheeks. "*Ca vous plait, la France?*"

The four of us got into the little car and we rattled our way up the winding mountain roads. In French that I could barely understand, my mother peppered her father with questions about the whereabouts of her sisters and nieces and nephews. The Deux Chevaux was barely going twenty miles an hour, as though Grandpapa was worried that he might veer into a ravine at any minute. *Now I know how Mom got to be such a slow driver!* I thought. Finally we saw arrowed signs marking off the kilometers to the village named Boffres where my grandparents lived in semiretirement. On the edge of town was a large stone house with big shuttered windows and a small, gated yard. It had once been the mayor's office, but Boffres and the surrounding towns had offered it to Grandpapa as a parsonage to entice him to move to the area and preach part-time in the local Protestant temples.

For the next year, the house in Boffres was the place where Paul and I would experience what it was like to belong to the huge extended Theis family. Over the summer and school holidays, aunts and uncles and dozens of our nineteen French cousins would converge from all corners of the country. We filled the drafty bedrooms on the second and third floors and gathered in the parlor at night to play Scrabble. At mealtimes, we crowded around the long table in the dining room. Grandmaman was not as talented a cook as her daughters, but everyone eagerly awaited the simple but satisfying menus that for decades she had served like clockwork on the same day every week.

Before we ate, we held hands and sang grace with an old Huguenot prayer:

> *Toi qui dispose de toute choses,*
> *Et nous les donnes chaque jour*
> *Recois O Pere! Notre priere*
> *De reconnaissance et d'amour.*

Translated, it went:

> *You who controls all things,*
> *And gives them to us every day,*
> *O Father please accept*
> *Our prayer of gratitude and love.*

From my junior-high classes in Norton, I knew that the French addressed people they didn't know well as "*vous*" and friends and family as "*tu*." I asked my mother why the mealtime prayer referred to God as "*Toi*," and she explained that it reflected the belief of French Protestants that every believer should have an intimate personal relationship with their Father.

I learned the French word for "gratitude" from that hymn, but it was embedded in my memory by something else that happened on that first visit to Boffres. One night, Grandmaman was circling the dining room encouraging everyone to take second helpings. Nervous about overeating, I summoned my spotty French and told her: *"No, merci. Je suis plein."*

Grandpapa coughed disapprovingly. I hadn't realized that the American phrase "I'm full" is considered very rude in France. *"Plein de reconnaisance!"* he bellowed. "You are full of gratitude!"

By this time, I knew a bit about what had happened in Le Chambon during the war, and I was struck by the contrast between the heroic Pastor Theis of those stories and the Grandpapa I was getting to know again. At times, I saw evidence of his serious side: when he closed his eyes and led the family in the *"Toi qui dispose"* grace before supper, or when he presided over a solemn Protestant service that we attended in Vincennes, a small town near Boffres. But mostly, I saw an impish streak that seemed at odds with the sober righteousness of the war narrative.

At mealtime, he rubbed his hands with glee as Grandmaman brought his favorite dishes to the table. He took childish delight in the funny headlines of *Le Canard Enchaîné* and our nightly board games. I forget how I learned this, but I discovered that he was a believer in nudism, and that in his youth he had vacationed at nudist colonies. He loved to make puns and to puncture hypocrisy and snobbism. One of his favorite stories was about a nouveau riche woman who belonged to his grandfather's parish in Paris and liked to complain about the indignities of modern life.

"Things were so much better in the seventeenth century!" she would sniff.

Finally his grandfather had heard enough. *"Madame,"* he told her, "in the seventeenth century you would have been a farmhand!"

It was no accident, I came to see, that all the French uncles I was getting to know had two things in common. Except for Jean-Paul, they were all Protestants, in a country where the tiny religious minority accounted for only two percent of the population. And like Grandpapa, they all had a sly, kidding sense of humor. Even my one

American uncle on the Theis side—Jack Gregory, an artist who married my aunt Jackie, the other sister who stayed in America after the war—was an incurable teaser and punster. Of them all, my mother also had the closest intellectual relationship with Grandpapa, as well as the strongest interest in his ideas about nonviolence. So I can I see why, when she first met my father, she was so smitten with what she perceived as his combination of scholarliness, pacifism, and sense of the ridiculous. And I can also see why, once their marriage fell apart, she never again found another man who she thought measured up to her daddy in those ways, particularly if another requirement was that he be attracted enough to her to penetrate her formidable shield of diffidence.

After a week in Boffres, Grandpapa drove us in the Deux Cheveaux farther up the mountain to Le Chambon-sur-Lignon, my mother's childhood home. She had bartered her services as a teacher to get Paul and me a free month of summer courses at Le College Cévenol, the school her father founded in the late 1930s. At the beginning, during the war, Cévenol classes had met in the local hotel and other public spaces around the village. After the war, largely on the strength of the town's wartime exploits, Grandpapa raised enough money to build a permanent campus. He secured a piece of land outside town, and local laborers and summer work campers put up concrete buildings and barracks-like dorms where girls roomed as well as studied alongside boys, a radical innovation at the time.

My mother was our French teacher for the month, which made the ordeal a bit easier but not much. Day after day, I confronted the realization that I wasn't remotely prepared to attend a school where no one spoke English. Listening to my relatives in Boffres was one thing; having to follow lessons, speak in class, and read textbooks in French was quite another. Hoping to build our vocabulary, she encouraged us to learn French poems by heart. The memorization worked—I can still recite a Charles Baudelaire poem called *"L'Homme et la Mer"* from memory—but we had no clue what all the words meant or how the grammar worked. She assigned the class *The Plague*, by Albert Camus, in the original, and I stayed up late into the night reading by flashlight as I labored to decipher each sentence.

"Why didn't you speak French to us when we were little?" I reproached her one day. "It would have made this a lot easier."

She sighed and said that she thought that speaking both French and English had contributed to her childhood stutter and that she didn't want to confuse us. Still, her pained look told me that she regretted it.

My struggles with the language made me see just how inadequate two years of junior-high French in Norton had been. My teacher in both seventh and eighth grade was a lecherous little man named Mr. Precourt. He would ask the pretty girls in class to write French words on the blackboard and then lean back in his chair to look up their dresses. We called him "Mr. Presex." By that age, I had become a bit of a class clown, no doubt to disguise self-consciousness about my weight, and I was particularly subversive in French class. One day, Mr. Precourt got upset with my antics and ordered me to leave the classroom and wait for him in the hallway. "You know, you've really gotten wise!" he reprimanded me in his thick New England accent. "And by 'wise,' I don't mean *wise*. I mean *smaahht*!"

I had officially stopped dieting in the spring, but I continued to worry about eating too much. At Cévenol, my fastidiousness tipped into full-blown anorexia. Unlike the food in Paris or Boffres, the offerings in the school's cold, dark dining hall were institutional and unappetizing, and I barely touched my plate at mealtimes. After several weeks at Le Chambon, I could see my rib cage and hip bones jutting out from my skin when I showered in the open-air stalls outside the dorm barracks.

Alarmed, my mother asked me to go to the nurse's office to weigh myself. The scale registered 50 kilos. "Mark, that's less than 110 pounds!" my mother said in a distressed voice. "You're starting to look like one of the children here during the war!"

After a frustrating month of summer classes at Le College

Cévenol, we traveled to Grenoble to start the school year. At first we stayed with Louise and her two youngest children, Myriam and Jean-Jacques, in their small apartment in the Village Olympique. It was a complex of gray cinder-block towers that had been erected to house athletes during the Winter Olympics of 1968, the year Jean-Claude Killy thrilled France by winning three gold medals in skiing. After the Games were over, mostly poor and lower-middle-class families moved in and the "village" began to look like just another dingy urban housing project.

Louise was divorced from a doctor named Daniel Hollard, who came from a prominent local Protestant family. Their two older children, Olivier and Catherine, lived with him and his girlfriend across town, although Olivier had dropped out of high school and joined a youth commune in Paris. Myriam, the little girl I had followed around for bedtime kisses as a toddler, was now a chatty thirteen-year-old with a round face and a ripening figure. Jean-Jacques, who was a year younger than Paul, was blond and wiry and hyperkinetic. The two fought like untamed animals, even more ferociously than my brother and I ever had. They screamed and slammed doors and pulled each other's hair. It made for a very stressful arrangement until Louise and my cousins moved to another apartment nearby and my mother took over the rent on their place.

In a photo snapped of me on the small balcony of that apartment, I am wearing maroon suede pants and sporting an unruly Afro. I am also alarmingly thin. Even after my mother's warning at Le Chambon, I couldn't bring myself to eat normally. In Grenoble, we didn't have a refrigerator and had to shop for food every day and keep perishables on the balcony, which didn't make things any easier. The one thing that prevented me from becoming even more emaciated was peanut butter. Although the French kind was oily and came in a big tin, it reminded me of home. Yet even that pleasure made me anxious, and I decided that I could justify it only by adding millet, a tasteless health-food grain that I had read about in one of my mother's Adele Davis cookbooks. So for months, the combination of peanut butter and millet became the only thing that kept me from keeling over.

In the beginning, going to school in the Village Olympique was torture. In Norton, I was accustomed to getting A grades without much effort or homework. Now I was confronted with much harder classes in a language that I was struggling to comprehend. The algebra in my grade level—*troisième*—was much more advanced than any math I learned in junior high. Classes in literature consisted mostly of *dictée*, where the teacher read aloud long passages and had us write them down to test our vocabulary, spelling, punctuation, and penmanship. Papers and exams were graded on a scale from one to twenty. At first, the *profs* took pity on me and didn't assign marks at all. After the first month or so, I started getting scores like *huit sur vingt* or *dix sur vingt*—eight or ten out of twenty. I was mortified.

I was assigned to an English class, which only added to my sense of grievance. Why did I have to take a language I already knew? I thought. Still, the class did give me one opportunity to be a star pupil rather than the hapless foreigner. The teacher was named Madame Pirolat (pronounced *Pee-roll-aah*), and she would often ask me to repeat phrases so that the other students could imitate my pronunciation. She had a very thick French accent, and she taught British rather than American English, so sometimes I had trouble understanding what she was saying.

One day, we were studying *Rebecca* by Daphne du Maurier when Madame Pirolat turned to me and said: "There is an expression for this, isn't there, Mark? You have to *shiit* for yourself. . . ."

Huh? I thought. *Did she just say what I think she said?*

"You know," she repeated, "you have to *shiit* for yourself!"

I racked my brain for several long seconds before the lightbulb went on.

"Oh yes," I said. "You have to *shift* for yourself!"

Madame Pirolat was what the French call a *"pied noir"*—literally, a "black foot." It was the label given to colonists who had lived in Algeria until they left during the bloody war for independence. Although most had been born in France or had French ancestors, once they returned they might as well have been the darkest of Africans as far as their bigoted countrymen were concerned. The Village Olympique was full of *pieds noirs,* and I saw the way they were treated. If that's what the French thought of them, I wondered, what did they make of me? In school I was *"l'Americain,'* but did my curly hair and light brown skin make the kids think of me as an American black foot?

My battles with the language made me painfully aware of how dependent on verbal expression I was. My brother was much more comfortable communicating with his face and his body, and he could shrug it off when words didn't come out the way he planned. The difference between us became clear one night at Boffres when Grandmaman, as usual, was urging everyone at the dinner table to take seconds. Exasperated, Paul tried to shoo her away with a bit of French slang.

"Grandmaman, tu casses mes pieds!" he blurted out.

Everyone at the table exploded in laughter.

"Non, Paul, c'est tu me casses les pieds!" Grandpapa corrected him, pointing out a small but crucial grammatical distinction between saying "You're getting on my nerves!" and, literally, "You're breaking my feet!"

Unembarrassed, Paul roared out loud with everyone else. At that moment, I felt deeply jealous of him.

To escape my struggles with French homework, I read novels in English at night, the longer the better. I lost myself in *Of Human Bondage,* by Somerset Maugham, gloomily comparing Philip Carey's clubbed foot and trail of misfortunes to my own predicament. I found a translation of *Don Quixote* and savored the funny stories of adventure and self-deception as well as my ability to enjoy Cervantes's irony in my native tongue. By Christmas, I was so miserable and homesick that I told my mother that I wanted to go back to the United States for the rest of the year.

"And where would you stay?" she asked. "With your dad?"

I had put my father out of my mind for most of the time since we arrived in France, but suddenly I flashed back to how angry and disappointed I felt after the aborted spring vacation visit to Princeton.

"No, I guess *that's* not such a good idea," I said.

"Be patient," she told me. "Your French is getting better. The rest of the year won't be so difficult."

Shortly after the New Year, she told my brother and me some dreadful news. Grandmother had written to inform her that my aunt Gertrude's husband, Robert Smedley, the affable truck driver we knew from our yearly trips to Pittsburgh, had perished in an accident right after the holiday. It had been a horrifying death. Transporting a load of steel to Buffalo in the middle of the night, he had veered off the road, probably after suffering a heart attack or falling asleep at the wheel. The truck ran up a mountainside and jack-knifed, and the gas tank stowed on the rig struck a culvert and exploded. Trapped inside, Robert was instantly incinerated, leaving no remains to lie in state at the Edith M. Whitaker Funeral Home.

What my mother didn't tell us was that my father had been visiting Pittsburgh at the time and that Robert's death had abruptly ended his latest attempt at sobriety. "Syl is not doing well at all," Grandmother reported in her letter. "He was getting along fine but began drinking again when Robert died. I talked with him this evening. He needs to be hospitalized again, but the Carrier Clinic won't take him for less than 3 weeks, and he can't get the time off. I don't know what is going to become of him. I am worried sick. He keeps saying he wants to die."

In late February, French schools have a holiday called "*les vacances d'hiver*," and for Louise's family, that meant one thing: a chance to go skiing. With their American cousins living in Grenoble, they decided it would be fun to invite other relatives to join us for a week on the slopes of the French Alps. Louise's oldest, Olivier, arrived from his commune in Paris and brought his sister Catherine. Francoise's four children came up from Montpellier in the south, as did Marianne's three sons from Strasbourg in the north, accompanied by a Danish teenager who was living with them as an *au pair* for the year. Her name was Tove and she was the daughter of Janet Nyholm, my mother's college friend who had married the Danish artist and lived on his fish farm outside of Copenhagen.

I had just learned to ski that winter, traveling with a youth group from the Village Olympique on weekends to ride a T-bar at a small mountain outside the city. But I had never seen anything like Chamrousse, the majestic ski resort above Grenoble where Killy won the Olympic Triple Crown, with its enormous elevations and big ski lifts stretching up toward the sky.

"Alors, tu viens avec moi?" Olivier asked me the morning we all arrived at Chamrousse, inviting me to mount the gondola.

"Je ne suis pas assez doué," I protested, replying that I wasn't good enough.

"C'est rien!" he assured me. *"Viens!"*

I couldn't say no to my tall, charismatic, redheaded cousin. Besides, I knew that he was an expert skier, a former safety patrol, and I assumed that he would help me get down the mountain. We filed into the gondola line and climbed into a moving cabin. My heart began thumping as we ascended up the highest peak I had ever seen. At last, we got to the top, and . . . there was a deep valley and an even higher mountain in front of us! How was I ever going to get down from there? I asked myself anxiously.

"Ca va?" Olivier asked me as we climbed down from the gondola at the Cross of Chamrousse, more then seven thousand feet above sea level.

"Oui, ca va," I responded.

"Bonne chance, alors!" he said. Then he swooshed off, leaving me standing all alone at the top of the mountain.

It took me more than two hours to get down, slipping and falling over the entire way. I cursed and I cried, but I kept picking myself up and getting on my skis until I fell again. By the time I reached the foot of the mountain, every inch of my rented yellow ski pants and jacket was soaked. I couldn't feel my frozen fingers and toes. My entire body shook uncontrollably during the slow car ride down the icy roads back to Grenoble. When we finally arrived at our apartment in the Village Olympique, it took half an hour in a hot bath before my teeth stopped chattering.

Staggering down the mountain, I had told myself that this was one of the most miserable days of my life. Yet once I warmed up and put on a fresh set of clothes, I had a very different sensation. Although the descent from seven thousand feet had been hell, I felt proud that I had managed to get all the way to the bottom by myself. That night, everyone gathered for dinner at Louise's apartment, and she served an enormous pot of pasta. The cousins crowded around her kitchen table, wolfing down second and third helpings. It was just simple spaghetti with tomato sauce, but I ate it willingly and I relished every bite. Olivier regaled everyone with the story of how he had introduced his American cousin to the Alps. In my now fluent French, I described my crazy adventure at Chamrousse, and the cousins all laughed and understood every word.

Over the Easter vacation six weeks later, we went to Boffres. The big stone house was overflowing with family, including four of my mother's sisters and twelve of my French cousins. Over Scrabble one night, Grandmaman reminded everyone that five of the grandchildren present were products of the famous Theis baby boom of 1957 and 1958. Within a twelve-month period, six of the eight sisters had all had children, each in the exact order of their birth. My mother was the eldest, and I was the first of those babies. Jackie's daughter Elizabeth, whom we called Leeza, was the second. Louise's daughter Myriam was the third. Marguerite's son Manouche was the fourth. The fifth was Anna, the daughter of Francoise, who was the younger of the twins, having come out of the womb second, and the sixth was Cecile's son Laurent, who was born weeks before my first birthday, just barely making it into the club.

At the time, I didn't realize that Anna had been among my first crushes, when we met in Le Chambon as one-year-olds and I stalked her with my hands behind my back. Now she was a tall fourteen-year-old with long brown hair and the same huge brown eyes she had as a child. My mother had told me how smart she was and how many books she had read, including *War and Peace* when she was only twelve. But because she was shy, and I had been so self-conscious about speaking French, we hadn't said much to each other during earlier visits that year. Suddenly over Easter, we became constant companions. We took long walks through the hills around Boffres, talking about our favorite books and sharing our teenage musings on the meaning of life. I felt grateful to find someone to confide in and at last to have enough mastery of the language to communicate my thoughts and feelings. When I returned to America, I told Anna, I was going away to boarding school, to a Quaker academy in Pennsylvania called George School. If I liked it there, I suggested, maybe she could come as an exchange student for a year.

When the spring break was over we returned to Grenoble, where I found my last two months of *troisième* as gratifying as the first few months had been maddening. At last I could understand everything my teachers said and raise my hand to speak and write papers and exams with confidence. In literature class, the *prof* assigned us an essay on a typically cosmic French question: "What is the meaning of sports in modern society?" *Now that's a subject that is right up my alley!* I thought. When I got the essay back, I couldn't believe my eyes: the grade was *dix-huit sur vingt*—eighteen out of twenty! "You see, *l'Americain* got the best mark!" the teacher announced to the class, making me want to crawl under my desk with embarrassment.

My brother hadn't had as much success with his classes. By the time we arrived in France, he was already almost six feet tall, and he kept growing all year long. He looked so adult that the school put him in the *quatrième* grade, just a year behind me. While he learned to speak French with an almost undetectable accent, going from sixth grade in Norton High to that level in France was too much of a leap.

Eventually my mother pulled him out of school in Grenoble and sent him to stay with Grandpapa and Grandmaman, who took him to visit Marianne and Jean-Paul in Holland. But at the end of the year Paul returned, and I asked him to join me in a performance for my theater class. Together we enacted a scene entirely in French from the farce *The Bald Soprano,* by Eugene Ionesco, one of my mother's favorite plays, and the class applauded enthusiastically for *"les frères Vit-a-kair."*

Over the summer, my mother rented a car and we drove from the Mediterranean all the way to Scandinavia. We stayed at a campsite on La Grande Motte, a seaside development near Montpellier, where I fell asleep on the beach and got sunburned so badly that all the skin peeled off my back. On the Côte d'Azur, we rented a room at a motel with a cherry tree outside, and Paul and I ate so many cherries that we thought our stomachs would explode. We picked up Gretchen in Paris and headed to Britain, where my mother's college roommate Isabel Kenrick lived. She was a Yankee from outside Boston who had married an English minister and raised her children in London. Driving on the left side of the road flummoxed my mother and she kept taking wrong turns. "Go left!" I would yell, reading the map in my lap, but she would go right or just freeze and keep heading straight. One night she entered a roundabout without looking the right way, and only the strong brakes on the oncoming car saved us from a disastrous crash.

Our last stop was the fish farm in Denmark where my mother's friend Janet Nyholm lived with her artist husband, Erik. They had five children, including Tove, the student who had come to visit us during the *vacances d'hiver.* For a week, we ate smorgasbord and spun pots in their outdoor kilns and trolled for trout in the canals running across their property. Finally eating like a normal human being, I savored a stewed fruit dessert called *rodgrod med flode,* and I amused myself for days trying to perfect the guttural pronunciation.

During our long walks around Boffres, I had told my cousin

Anna that I thought the secret to life was to forget about trying to find happiness and to settle for contentment. In retrospect, it was a pretentious, adolescent thing to say, and no doubt reflected all the unhappiness I had experienced in my life up to that point. But as we were getting ready to leave France, I was conscious of feeling more content than I had in a very long time, as well as a good deal more grown up than when we arrived in Luxembourg a year earlier. I was also amazed that my shy, cautious mother had been so brave as to take us to France and to drive us all the way across Europe. Seeing how relaxed and at home she appeared with her family and friends, I realized that for her returning to her roots may have been the best therapy of all.

At the end of August, we drove to Luxembourg and boarded another Icelandic flight back to New York. When we arrived at JFK Airport, Aunt Cleo and Uncle Gene were there to greet us with hugs and kisses and take us to their apartment in Queens for the night. Paul and I talked excitedly about everything we had done in France and all the familiar foods and pleasures we were looking forward to rediscovering in America. But I was exhausted from the flight, and before long I fell fast asleep on the cot that my aunt had set up in the little study behind her galley kitchen.

My body was still on European time, so I woke up several hours later. My mother and Cleo were talking quietly at the dining table on the other side of the kitchen. I couldn't make out exactly what they were saying, but I heard the word "Syl" and the sounds of Cleo whispering and my mother sighing. I could tell they were discussing my father and that the news wasn't good.

10

He was coming to Norton for Thanksgiving, and I had no idea what
to expect. It had been a decade since were together as a family, just
the four of us. I was arriving from George School, the Quaker academy in Bucks County, Pennsylvania, that I started attending after we
got back from France. I planned to take the train at Trenton, and he
was supposed to get on in New Haven. He was at an addiction clinic
called Silver Hill in Connecticut, and I didn't give much thought to
why he was there in the middle of the school year. All I knew was that
my mother said he needed permission to visit us.

Since returning from France, I had experienced more ups and
downs with him. When I first arrived at George School, he had called
to invite me to Princeton. By the end of September, I was feeling
homesick for family, and I left him a message saying I wanted to take
him up on his offer. The next day, he returned the call while I was in
class, but when I reached him that night he was completely smashed
and had forgotten about his invitation. I wanted to hang up, but he
kept asking me questions about my state of mind and telling me what

I should and shouldn't think of him. Finally I told him that I wasn't the one he should be talking to about his problems.

By Halloween, I missed him again, and I told my mother in a letter that I planned to write him and hoped that he would write back. "The poor guy, he's going to need a lot of support from friends and family to really stop drinking," I said sympathetically. "I think that it's very important for him to feel that people care for him, and it's most important that he knows that he really cares for himself. Well, let's hope that he can really do it."

Later in the fall, he came to visit George School with his girlfriend Barbara Callaway. I didn't recognize her as the second woman whom had he had kissed on Cape Cod all those summers ago, partly because her long brown hair had been cut short and had turned prematurely gray. I also didn't know that she had reentered his life after he had broken up with his fiancée, Sally, most likely over his drinking. They came to see a one-act play that I was directing, and he seemed alert and upbeat, and the visit went better than I expected. I showed him the Quaker Meeting house at the foot of the campus, with the pictures on the wall of graduating classes going all the way back to the school's founding in 1893. He remarked at the Victorian dress of the first students and told me that they were Hicksite Quakers, the same sect that founded Swarthmore.

He was excited to see the tennis courts and to hear that I had made the junior varsity team. We sat for a while on the white swings on the back porch of Main, the big brown building that dominated the center of campus, and looked down the sloping hill where students sunned themselves in the warm weather. I didn't tell him that at night you could stand on the porch and see little specks of light in the distance, the evidence of the potheads who snuck down to the bottom of the hill to smoke dope.

I introduced him to my roommates, and as usual he was quick to inquire about their families and backgrounds. Joel Roos was a redheaded skier from the Northeast and Alberto Gutierrez was a curly-haired soccer whiz from Bogota, Colombia. He met my friend

Greg Silverman, a funny New Yorker with a big Jew-fro whose father owned a store in the Diamond District. I informed him that another classmate was Donzaleigh Abernathy, the daughter of Ralph Abernathy, one of Martin Luther King's top lieutenants. Did he know that the civil rights leader Julian Bond had also graduated from George School? I asked. He said that, yes indeed, he did.

One reason I was glad to see my father was that at George School, for the first time in my life, I was reflecting on my racial identity. Until then, I had spent most of my life in small college towns where there were hardly any black people of my age, or any age. During our visits to Pittsburgh, I connected with that part of my heritage, but apart from that I knew only the virtually all-white environments of Norton, and Swarthmore, and Grenoble. Now at George School, I was reading *Native Son,* by Richard Wright, and James Baldwin's *Go Tell It on the Mountain,* with their bracing portraits of what it was like to be black in places like the South Side of Chicago and Harlem. Although written in a previous generation, they raised powerful questions about whether any black American, of any shade or upbringing, could be untouched by racism, conscious or unconscious.

When I asked my father what he thought, he responded with his familiar murmur. For the first time, I noticed that it wasn't so much a "hmmm" as a "hmmph," with a soft snort of judgment at the end, as if to indicate that he was thinking about your question but that he couldn't possibly do justice to the complexity of the matter in just a few words.

"I've been wondering how long it would take for you to ask me that," he said finally. "You won't believe this, but some of your ancestors looked even less black than you do. My mother's father was so light that he could pass for white. But that doesn't matter as far as American society is concerned. Mixed race, light skin, we're all black. But I want you to know that it will be up to you to decide *how* you want to be black. That will always be your choice."

Boarding school was the first place that had ever given me that option—of how I wanted to identify myself and who I wanted to be my friends. I realized that I was already starting to answer the question, and that I was doing it with his example in mind. I knew how at home he was in the black worlds of Pittsburgh and Africa, but I had also seen how open he was to other cultures, and friendships, and romances. Although in 1973 the pressure to "self-define" as black was in the air even at a place like George School, I saw no reason why I should be reduced to one thing or the other, why pride in my black heritage should rule other relationships and experiences. I didn't want to limit my horizons any more than he had.

On the day before Thanksgiving, as planned, I boarded the Amtrak at Trenton, and my father joined me at New Haven, and we chatted for the rest of the way to Providence. He asked about the George School friends whom he had met, and I told him how my courses were going. I also delivered my big news: that I was thinking of going straight to college after my junior year was over, and that I wanted to follow in his footsteps and apply to Swarthmore. I thought he would be flattered, but his response betrayed a surprising ambivalence about his alma mater.

"I hear they call Swarthmore the jewel of the little Ivies," I said, thinking that description would please him.

"Swarthmore is a jewel all right," he replied, "but sometimes it can be a jeweled prison."

When we arrived at the Providence station, my mother was there to pick us up. She must have been worried about how we would all get along in the small apartment in Norton, because she immediately suggested that we go see a movie. She said she already had a head start on cooking for the big meal the next day, so we could eat an early supper and head out.

It was a cold night, and an icy wind blew through the screened porch behind our apartment as we left to drive to the mall in Brockton, a nearby town. I had on a sweater and a scarf around my neck, but nothing else covering my upper body.

"You should put on a coat," my father said.

At the time, I didn't like wearing coats. At George School, I went outside with only a sweater and scarf well into the depth of winter.

"That's okay, I don't need one," I said.

"I'm telling you to put on a coat!" he snapped.

"No!" I responded curtly. "I'm fine like this."

My father glared at me for several seconds, then he shook his head in disapproval. During the ride to the mall, he sat in the front passenger seat of the car, next to my mother, and didn't say a word. When we got inside the movie theater, I could see that he was still sulking.

What is he being such a baby about? I thought to myself. *Does he just expect me to obey his every command?* During the movie, I kept looking over at his brooding face in the dim light of the theater, and bit by bit I felt myself filling with a silent rage. *What gives him the right to tell me what to do?* said the voice inside my head. *Does he think he can just waltz back into my life and start ordering me around?*

As we drove back to Norton, he continued to say nothing and to stare straight ahead out the front car window. Once we were inside the apartment, Paul went off to his room, and my mother and father took off their coats and sat down in the kitchen, looking as though they didn't quite know what to do next.

Summoning the courage to say the words that had been forming in my mind all evening, I stood up and faced my father.

"What makes you think you can tell me what to wear?" I said. "As far as I'm concerned, you forfeited that right when you divorced Mom!"

My mother sighed anxiously.

"You have no right to say that!" he shot back. "I'm still your father! I'll always be your father!"

My hands were gripping the kitchen counter behind me, and I could feel the knuckles tighten and hear my voice getting louder and louder.

"Oh yeah?" I shouted. "If you cared so much about being my father, why were you never there for us? Why didn't you ever call us? Why didn't you visit us? Why didn't . . ."

"Mark, maybe this isn't—" my mother said, trying to calm me down.

I cut her off. "Why didn't you pay child support when you were supposed to?" I said, tears rolling down my cheeks.

He glowered at me. "You little shit," he said, under his breath. "That's a low blow!"

"Syl, Mark!" my mother exclaimed. "Both of you, stop it! Stop it right now!"

Stop it? I thought. Why should I stop? He deserves to hear every-thing I'm saying! And "little shit"? "Little shit," huh? Well, fuck you, Dad!

My chest was heaving, and I was sucking in loud gasps of air. But I wasn't about to stop until I made him feel just as worthless as he had tried to make me feel.

"You weren't a father!" I cried. "You weren't a man! Paul and I needed a man in our lives, and you weren't there!"

My eyes were so full of tears that I could barely see my mother and father sitting at the table in front of me. They were just a blur. I ran out of the kitchen and down the hallway to my bedroom, and without taking off my clothes I threw myself on the bed covers. My body was in spasms, and as I cried myself to sleep, I felt not only the fury that had boiled up inside of me at the movies and come spilling out in the kitchen, but a sense of righteousness that I had stood up to my father and spoken for my mother and for brother too, because I was the only one strong enough to do it!

The next thing I remember, my mother was tapping me on the shoulder. The sun was streaming through the bedroom window, and I realized that it was morning.

"Come say goodbye to your father," she said. "He's leaving. We've been up all night. He's been drinking."

He was sitting at the kitchen table, in the same place I had left him the night before, but now he no longer looked defiant, just foggy-eyed and inert. In the seven hours or so since I had run out of the room, he had consumed every ounce of Scotch, bourbon, gin, and vodka that my mother kept in a cabinet underneath the silverware drawer in the corner of the kitchen.

"Mark, the trouble with you is . . ." he started, and then his voice trailed off as he lost his train of thought.

"The trouble with me is what?" I said. "What? Come on, Dad, I'm waiting."

But I didn't feel like starting up again. Now all I felt was contempt for him, because he looked so pitiful. He couldn't even fight back like a man; he just made himself so helpless that I wouldn't have the heart to attack him. As I looked at my mother's worried expression, I was full of scorn for her too, for sitting there passively while he guzzled her liquor and drank himself into oblivion.

She could have just told him to call a taxi or a car service, but instead she said she was going to drive him all the way back to Silver Hill. I didn't give him the satisfaction of hugging him goodbye; I just watched as he stumbled out the back door and climbed into her Pinto. But as the car pulled away, I was aware of another sensation, a sudden stab of guilt. What if he had actually been on the road to sobriety, and I had ruined it? What if he had missed his best chance at drying out because of me?

What I didn't know yet was just how many times he had already tried to give up booze, only to fall off the wagon. Nor did I realize that when he finished his treatment at Silver Hill, he wouldn't be going back to his job at Princeton.

The story of how my father returned to Princeton in the first place, I discovered, had begun four and a half years earlier, with the takeover of New South Hall. It was the end of the 1960s, and students across America were occupying administration buildings in protest over Vietnam, black studies, and university investments. In April 1968, New York City police had stormed the campus quad at Columbia to end a weeklong siege of Hamilton Hall and Low Library. At Harvard, state and local cops with billy clubs and mace were called in to eject students from University Hall. At Swarthmore, black students protesting the dearth of minority undergraduates and faculty occupied the admissions office, taping black paper over the windows and bolting the doors. As the sit-in dragged into its second week, Courtney Smith, the man who had made life so difficult for my parents, showed up for work at Parish Hall, sat down at his desk, and dropped dead of a massive heart attack.

By comparison, the occupation of New South was a tame affair. Several dozen black students sat in for less than a day to dramatize their demands that Princeton pull its investments from South Africa. Unlike the showdown at UCLA, no one was packing heat, and before they left the students cleaned up the building so as not to create more work for the black janitors and cleaning ladies.

In the following days, Princeton's president, Bob Goheen, and provost, Bill Bowen, deliberated about how to defuse the crisis. They quickly ruled out expulsions or suspensions, since more than two-thirds of all the black undergrads and grad students at Princeton had participated in the sit-in. On the other hand, they had no intention of heeding the divestment calls. "That's when we learned that Princeton will give up its God before it gives up its money!" one protester told me.

In the end, Nassau Hall, as the university leadership was known, gave in to two other demands: enrollment of more black students, and the creation of an African-American studies department. The protesters and their supporters on the faculty were excited by the idea of a black studies program but also worried about what traditionalists would think. They knew that most white faculty and students at Princeton didn't view the study of black history and culture as a legitimate academic discipline, on a par with economics or political science. If the new department was going to gain any respect, they decided, it was imperative that they recruit an impressive chairman.

A search committee was formed, and one name quickly rose to the top of the list: C.S. Whitaker Jr. of UCLA. No one could dispute his academic credentials. His published work on political development in Nigeria was considered first-rate. His forthcoming book,

The Politics of Tradition, was already being touted as a major work of scholarship. What was even better, he was a Princeton man, the first black to ever earn a doctorate in politics. The professors who had taught him as a graduate student all spoke very highly of him. Both Goheen and Bowen remembered him well, and when they were briefed on the idea, they signed on enthusiastically. Princeton should do whatever it took to get Syl Whitaker back!

The job of closing the deal was given to a black grad student named Badi Foster. It was a fitting choice. A tall, light-skinned alumnus of the University of Denver, Foster was Princeton's second black doctoral candidate in politics, having enrolled in 1964, two years after my father left. From Hube Wilson, he had heard story after story about his first black protégé. Hube roared about the tiny attic that Syl Whitaker had lived in when he was commuting from his home in Swarthmore: It had no bathroom or toilet, so the landlord gave him a milk bottle to do his business! Wilson also confirmed Foster's suspicion that the Politics Department had an unspoken policy of admitting only one black student at a time, and that knowledge only increased Foster's sense of kinship with the first "only."

Officially, Badi was still a grad student, but because there were so few blacks at Princeton he was frequently enlisted by Nassau Hall as a Minority Mr. Fixit. Sometimes his job was to greet visiting black dignitaries and carry their luggage. At other times, he was given weightier assignments that the powers-that-be thought would benefit from his "sensitivities." When a black administrator was caught in a scandal, for instance, it was Foster's job to make the problem go away by finding a cushy sinecure at a faraway university. Now the mission was recruitment, and he was dispatched to California with the academic equivalent of a blank check.

When he arrived in Los Angeles, my father was staying at a fancy estate in Brentwood, house-sitting for a traveling colleague. His student Jerry Bender, now an Angola scholar on the UCLA faculty, was spending a lot of time there too. Foster was immediately struck by their laid-back lifestyle; unlike the uptight professors at Princeton, they lingered over meals and hung out by the pool, and every night they hosted cocktails and dinner or took him to a party at someone else's house. He didn't see them doing much work, but he figured maybe that was just the way it was in L.A.

"So what will it take to get you back to Princeton?" Foster asked.

From his high-school days playing poker in Pittsburgh, my father knew a strong hand when he saw it, and he played this one for all it was worth.

What would Princeton think of granting him, up front, a paid year-long sabbatical so he could travel around the world? he asked.

"I think that could be arranged," Foster told him.

He also didn't want to get bogged down in administrative details. Would Princeton hire his administrative aide too?

"Done!" Foster said.

Relieved to have an excuse to leave UCLA after the traumatic shootout between the Panthers and the United Slaves, my father accepted the offer. There was just one formality: a visit to Princeton. It went swimmingly, with the community welcoming him back like a long-lost son. There was just one awkward moment. The official "interview" for the department chair was scheduled for ten o'clock in the morning, and as it began his hands were shaking. "Can I have a glass of wine?" he asked.

What? Badi Foster thought. Where was he going to find wine at that hour of the morning? Conveniently, Hube Wilson's secretary was nearby, and she had a big jug that Wilson kept on hand for wine-and-cheese parties. She filled a large paper cup, and once my father took a few sips his hands stopped trembling.

For the next year, he traveled the globe while Badi Foster babysat his possessions. The green Mercury Cougar was shipped from L.A., and Foster found a garage and started the motor every week. My father sent back artwork and furniture and suits from his stops in Africa and India and Hong Kong, and Foster arranged to get them through customs. He even sat at the sleek wooden desk that my father had ordered for his office at the new African-American studies headquarters at 70 Washington Street. As part of his deal, he had demanded that the department have its own building and negotiated for a budget to decorate it. The Danish Modern furbishings were a welcome contrast to the usual dark wood and leather of the Ivy League, without coming across as a Kinte-cloth caricature. Syl Whitaker had class, Foster had to admit.

When my father finally showed up for work at Princeton in the fall semester of 1970, everyone was impressed with his gravitas. On his best days, chairing meetings in the mornings, he was masterful at guiding discussions toward Quaker-like consensus. He never lost his cool and let everyone have a say. He had a sixth sense for how to give "face" to all the big egos in the room. For anyone who might doubt his credentials, he invoked his bona fides without ever appearing boastful, casually throwing out literary references that belied any preconceptions about the limits of black intelligence. Watching him in action, Badi Foster thought, was like observing an academic high priest: He knew how to swing the chalice and dispense the Host and had a flawless command of the scholarly liturgy.

He also had a sense of vision that was both practical and inspiring. People relate to heroes, he told his colleagues, black people more than anyone. Think of Joe Louis, he said, or Jackie Robinson. What African-American Studies should look for were role models of scholarship and public service. Whenever he had the chance, he held up the example of Ralph Bunche, the political scientist who helped found the United Nations and won a Nobel Prize for his role in ending the war in Palestine. The world needed more Ralph Bunches, he argued: strong advocates for racial and international justice who weren't militant "race men."

"But what is the noble purpose?" he would ask when a discussion was bogging down in trivial issues or petty disputes.

Yet soon after my father's return to Princeton, Badi Foster and other admirers also began to see another side to him. Publicly, it was most apparent when the "firemen" came to town. "Firemen" was Hube Wilson's nickname for the dignitaries whom the Politics

Department invited to the university: renowned scholars from other universities, retired government officials, famous authors and activists. My father was first introduced to this tradition in his graduate student days, and it had been one of his favorite things about going to school at Princeton.

When Wilson was hosting, the visits involved drinks and meals at the Annex, his favorite haunt. It was a small, below-ground Italian restaurant on Nassau Street, directly across the front gate of the university. Wilson had a special table reserved at the end of a long hallway, right next to a cigarette machine, so fresh smokes were always within reach.

Once he returned to Princeton, my father rejoined Wilson's fraternity, and he began hosting firemen himself. He saw bringing prominent blacks to the university as a way of legitimizing the fledgling African-American studies program, and also helping his guests by sprinkling them with Princeton's holy water. Firemen visits were a way to make connections with rising political and cultural stars and to collect IOUs that could be cashed in later. One example was a promising black writer and a single mother who was looking to make a name for herself in the New York publishing world. My father invited her to give several talks at Princeton, and before long Toni Morrison had a book contract with Knopf.

Naturally, being a good host meant keeping everyone well plied with food and liquor. A typical fireman visit started around noon with burgers and martinis at the Annex. Then the group would proceed to 70 Washington Street or to the Woodrow Wilson School for "visiting hours," from two to four o'clock in the afternoon, when students from across the university could come by to meet the honored guest. Afterward my father hosted a cocktail hour and a dinner with steak and salad and wine and beer at his apartment, or Hube Wilson did the honors at the Farm, his country property just over the state line in the Bucks County town of Solebury.

Most of the invitees usually went home by midnight, but my father and Wilson would keep talking and drinking into the wee small hours. By then they were riding the hard stuff: bourbon for Hube; Scotch or gin for Syl. On some days, my father paced himself so well that no one would have known how much alcohol he had consumed. His buzz was like a coal furnace that was banked and fed so that the fire never went out and never flared out of control. But the next day was another story. More and more, instead of appearing steady and in command at his morning meetings, he looked exhausted and bloated, and his hands trembled uncontrollably. "It was like the shadow of death was upon him," recalled one student.

When he wasn't working, he went on daylong benders. One weekend, his old friends Michael and Barbara DeLaszlo came down from Manhattan to visit, and he was three sheets to the wind by the time they arrived in the early afternoon. For some reason, he told them that he wanted to fetch a tennis racket from his office. Could they drive him there? he asked. But when they climbed into Michael's car, he couldn't remember where his office was. They drove around Princeton for an hour as he tried to point them in the right direction. Finally he got out of the car, staggered around, then fell to the ground weeping. "I'm so sorry!" he cried.

On another summer weekend, the DeLaszlos invited him to the beach house they rented in Peconic, a town on the northern side of Long Island Sound. My father started knocking back Bloody Marys over breakfast and kept drinking for the rest of the morning and straight through lunch. In a catatonic haze, he took a plastic boat attached to a little rope that belonged to the DeLaszlo children out to the beach. For several hours he dragged the children's toy back and forth across the sand, his torso turning from nut brown to a blistered red in the blazing Hamptons sun.

Exactly when the president and the provost became aware of his condition is unclear. From my ill-fated spring vacation visit in 1971, I know that he had begun checking himself into a local clinic to sober up as early as his second semester on campus. Word might have filtered back to Nassau Hall from that facility. Or the powers-that-be might have heard something from other faculty members or students who were concerned about his health or worried that his behavior might hurt African-American studies.

One student was particularly appalled. Bob Curvin was the third black student admitted into Princeton's doctoral program in politics. He was a military veteran who lived off campus with his wife and children and had already cut his teeth as a campaign aide for Ken Gibson, the first black mayor of Newark. He arrived in the early 1970s just as Badi Foster was leaving for Rutgers, and Foster gave him a gift from one "only" to the next: his notes for "American Politics," one of five general exams Curvin would be required to take. But Curvin had no sympathy for the first "only." As far as he was concerned, Syl Whitaker's drinking was an embarrassment to Princeton. What was more, Curvin didn't mind telling people that my father was hurting the cause of all black scholars who wanted to be taken seriously.

If the only charge against him had been his drinking, Nassau Hall might still have turned a blind eye; after all, Princeton had tolerated sots on its faculty for centuries. What landed him in serious hot water, his allies were convinced, was when the university leaders started to hear about the women. It came to their attention that Dr. Whitaker had propositioned the wife of a faculty member at a dinner party. Then they received another such report, and another. Now they had a more serious problem on their hands, the kind of thing that could end up in the newspapers and do damage to the entire institution. Race and sex were not words that they wanted to see together in headlines about Princeton!

Did my father even know what he said to the women in question? Or was it all lost in blackouts, as so many of his evenings were by then? Certainly flirting with white faculty and wives and students, and expecting them to be receptive to his advances, had been his modus operandi going back to his college days. It had worked with my mother, and with his mistress Gina and with Adele Leopold and with Barbara Callaway and with one-time fiancée Sally. But what he might not have understood, particularly once he had more than a few too many, was how much times had changed. By the early 1970s, it wasn't just racial taboos but the women's movement that had placed a certain kind of behavior beyond the pale.

What he did know was that Nassau Hall was pressuring him to seek help. They sent him to a psychiatrist, then paid for more stints at the Carrier Clinic, and then two months at Silver Hill in Connecticut. Barbara again started urging him to go to Alcoholics Anonymous, and finally he agreed. But when he got to the church where the meeting was being held, he wandered into choir practice instead. "That wasn't so bad!" he said when he got back.

He managed to quit numerous times, but each time he went back to the bottle almost immediately. To Bill Bowen, the Syl Whitaker issue was starting to look less like a personal tragedy and more like an administrative headache that he wanted off his desk. Things might have played out differently if Bob Goheen were still president; he was known as a listener, a leader who liked to take his time getting the "holistic" sense of a problem before he moved to action. But the bow-tied Classics scholar who was in charge of Princeton when my father returned had retired in 1971, and the new president, Bowen, an economist by training, was more of a yellow-legal-pad type of decision-maker. His academic work focused on racial issues, and he would later co-author a widely acclaimed book in defense of affirmative action. As a fellow social scientist, he viewed Syl Whitaker's unraveling as a great waste, but he was the type of executive who would cut Princeton's losses and move on if his list of cons outweighed the pros.

Bowen was also relying on advice from an unlikely black consigliere: Conrad Snowden. Snowden had been one of the first new friends that my father made when he returned to Princeton—the guy who played touch football with my brother and me during our summer visit in 1970. But since then, a distance had grown between them. Now he was Bowen's associate provost and chief surrogate on "minority issues." Behind his back, at least one member of the small fraternity of black administrators at elite institutions viewed Snowden as a "House Negro"—their term for blacks who not only did what was required of them but deliberately manipulated "the Master," feeding him gossip and playing on his insecurities and anxieties. I don't know if my father would have used the term, but he would have seen Snowden's role in handling the "Whitaker problem" as a personal betrayal. And he didn't forgive betrayal.

By the spring of 1973, less than three years after my father's triumphant return to his alma mater, Bowen met with him to offer a deal. The university would send him back to Silver Hill, one of the most expensive substance abuse facilities in the country, the place where celebrities like Truman Capote and Edie Sedgwick went to get clean. Princeton would foot the entire bill—$1,500 a week—for four months. But when he was released, he would look for a job elsewhere.

My father was furious and humiliated, but he was also desperate for help and saw that he wasn't being given a choice. The whole matter was dressed up with all the civility and generosity that Princeton could muster, but there was no question that he had been fired.

11

After the disastrous Thanksgiving in Norton, the next time I saw him was at the end of the Christmas holiday. Having finished his treatment at Silver Hill, he was teaching at the State University of New York at Purchase and living in a rented second-floor apartment in a drab little building in White Plains. My mother took my brother and me to visit him there on our way back from celebrating New Year's with Aunt Jackie and Uncle Jack in Philadelphia. He was wearing a light blue stretch leisure suit that had grown tight around his belly and thick thighs, and for the first time in my life I had an impression of my father as overweight.

I had worried that I might get angry and that we would have another fight, but once I saw him I felt something closer to shame. I had never heard of Purchase, but I knew he would never have taken a leave to teach there and be living in such a pitiful place of his own volition. Nobody said anything, but I figured out that he must have lost his job. I wondered if that was why he seemed so jittery: He chain-smoked through the entire visit and talked faster and laughed louder

and more afraid of [...] ... [...] ... [...] ... [...] ...

[...] ... [...] ... [...] ... [...] ... [...]

[...] ... [...] ... [...] ... [...] ...

than usual. We didn't stay long, and I was glad to get out of there, but as we left I found myself hoping that his weight gain was at least a sign that he was gorging instead of drinking.

Returning to George School, I made good on my plan to leave for college a year early. In the fall, I had borrowed a bike on a cold Saturday morning and cycled into the nearby town of Newtown to take the SATs before any of my classmates. When the envelope came in the mail in January, I was relieved to see that my scores were high enough to give me a shot at getting admitted to Swarthmore as a junior.

In retrospect, I'm not sure why I was in such a hurry to leave George School. I had made some good friends and I would be missing out on the fun and perks of senior year. My French cousin Anna had come to spend the year as an exchange student after all, and I had enjoyed having her around. But I was driven by an inner restlessness born of . . . what? A desire to relive my parents' lives, as if searching for a better ending? A yearning to revisit the town where they fell in love, where we had been together as a family, where everyone had once been happy?

Over the summer, my father phoned us in Norton with his latest news: He was back in New Jersey, living with Barbara Callaway, and he had been named the Martin Luther King University Professor at a place called CUNY.

"What's CUNY?" I asked. "I thought you were at SUNY." To myself, I thought: So was he fired from that job too?

He explained that CUNY stood for the City University of New York and that he would be teaching at Brooklyn College.

"Can you come to see us before you go to Swarthmore?" he asked. "Is a birthday celebration a possibility?"

I was momentarily startled that he remembered when my birthday was, since it had been so long since he acknowledged it in any way. But I took the invitation as a peace offering and thought it might be a chance to make a fresh start with him, so I accepted. As the date approached, I received a letter about all the plans he was making. He wanted to take me to a faculty reception at Brooklyn College and had bought tickets for *Good Evening,* a comedy revue starring the British actors Peter Cook and Dudley Moore. He was eager to introduce me to his latest find, a big outdoor clothes and food market near his new home in New Brunswick called Englishtown.

"It would be worth it for you to wait and buy clothes at Englishtown," he wrote. "More and/or better for the money will be yours . . . the only hitch is getting up early Saturday morning which is *de rigor,* and having lots of stamina for tramping around vast fields. I find it a lot of fun, but I am temporarily worn out."

When I arrived in New Brunswick and we made the trek to Englishtown, it turned out to be more of a flea market than the wondrous bazaar he had described. I let him buy me a synthetic suede coat for my birthday, but I was leery of spending my own money, having always lived by my mother's counsel that when you're poor it's better to buy things of quality that will last than cheaper goods that won't. But I had to admit that it was entertaining to watch him browse and bargain and boast about his purchases. Even the smoked salmon and bagels and Greek olives that he bought for brunch were "just as good as New York!" he proclaimed, improbably.

He and Barbara took me out that evening to celebrate my seventeenth birthday, and we ate the lox for breakfast the next morning, but I never made it to the Brooklyn reception or to the Dudley Moore play. On Monday morning, I woke up in their little white house on South First Avenue in New Brunswick and saw evidence that he had been drinking through the night. There was the smell of Scotch, the ashtray full of cigarette butts, the glass tumbler in the kitchen dish drain. It brought back the awful visit to Norton and the trip to Princeton when I was thirteen. Only this time, I was determined that I would leave him, rather than the other way around.

In the year since the Thanksgiving fiasco, when I had worried that I had driven my father back to the bottle, I had done a lot of reading about alcoholism. I had talked to our old friend Barbara DeLaszlo, who had quit drinking herself and become a substance abuse counselor in Manhattan. She told me how important it was for family members and friends not to blame themselves for relapses, and she talked about the phenomenon of "enabling" and said that sometimes the best thing you can do for alcoholics is refuse to stick around when they are drunk.

When my father came downstairs in his bathrobe, I got to the point.

"I can't stay here if you're going to be drinking," I said.

He frowned. "Mark, please don't judge me," he said.

"I'm not judging you," I said. "I just don't want to fight again."

He sighed, the worry lines in his forehead deepening. "I wish you didn't feel that way. It has nothing to do with you."

"I know that, but I still think I should call a cab."

As I spoke, I felt as though I was outside of myself, observing and listening, and I was amazed at how calm and in control I sounded compared with my hysterics in Norton a year earlier.

He gazed sadly at me for what seemed like a long time, but I sensed that he saw that my mind was made up.

"At least let me drive you to the station," he said.

"Are you okay to drive?" I said.

"I'm fine. Let me take you."

I could see the hurt in his eyes, and I didn't want to add insult to injury. He had had time to sleep it off, I figured, and the station wasn't far.

"Okay, " I said, "but I want to leave now."

I packed my things and we went outside to the green Mercury Cougar, which stood out more than ever among all the boxy suburban sedans on the block. He was still unshaven and in his bathrobe, and the car swerved over the center line on the road several times as he drove. He had turned the radio on, and it began to play "Alone Again, Naturally," a Gilbert O'Sullivan ballad that had been a big hit a few years earlier about a jilted lover who thinks of throwing himself off a "nearby tower."

"For a long time, that was my song," he said as the radio played.

"And you know, Mark, there have been times when I've thought about climbing up to a tower myself."

Finally O'Sullivan sang the refrain: *"Alone again, naturally . . ."*

"Hmmph!" my father snorted.

The tune was catchy enough that I couldn't help feel a twinge of sadness, but the teenage cynic in me scoffed at the idea that my father would see his sad life summed up in a corny Top of the Pops ballad, let alone that it would lead him to thoughts of ending it all.

By the time the song was over, we were at the train station. I said goodbye and gave my father a weak hug.

"Wish me luck at Swarthmore," I said.

"I beg you not to think that any of this is your fault," he repeated.

"I don't, Dad," I said. "Take care. Maybe I'll see you later in the term."

I hopped on the local to 30th Street Station in Philadelphia and then changed trains for Swarthmore. Once school started, I quickly saw what my father had meant by "a jeweled prison." The classes were stimulating and the teachers were impressive, but the social life was insular and angst-inducing. I made some nice friends, but I felt trapped. The entire student body ate every meal at the Sharples Center dining hall in the center of campus. How would I ever make new friends without offending the friends I already had? I worried. I had brief flirtations with a few girls, but I was haunted by thoughts of having to see them every day if we ever broke up.

One afternoon, I returned to my dorm room on the outskirts of campus and my hippy roommate John with the truckin' gait and hair down to his shoulders was having sex on his bed with a big-breasted blond girl. They were both stark naked and going at it so hard that the metal bed was jumping up and down on the floor. I immediately shut the door and made myself scarce, filled with mortification and more claustrophobia than ever.

The fact that so many people at Swarthmore remembered me as a small child only made matters worse. I never knew when some professor I didn't recognize would come up to me out of the blue and say:

"Are you Jeanne and Syl Whitaker's son? I heard you were here!" On Sundays, I went to the open house that the Enders hosted every week for students. They would have a warm fire blazing in their living room, and Aunt Abbie would serve sugar cookies and mugs of Earl Grey tea. It was a nice break from the limited life on campus, but then Uncle Bob would start telling stories about what my mother was like as a teenager and what I was like as a baby. He meant no harm, but it was hardly what a college freshman doing his best to impersonate an adult wanted to hear.

With each week, I became more convinced that I had chosen the wrong school. I desperately wanted to be in a larger environment with more people to meet, more things to do, and more places to hide out if I felt like it. One of the friends I had made was a witty sophomore named Ben Brantley who was planning to take a leave of absence for a semester and had lined up a job as the assistant to the editor of the *Village Voice*. When I asked the freshman dean and the financial aid office if I could do the same thing, they didn't discourage me. If I got into a bigger school, I told myself, I could start college over again with classmates my own age; if I didn't, I could always come back to Swarthmore.

I became obsessed with the crazy scheme and started spending hours in McCabe Library poring over course catalogs from Ivy universities. I called my mother to gauge her reaction. "Whatever you think is best," she said, showing an astonishing faith in my teenage judgment. Having persuaded her that it all made sense, I burrowed myself in the stacks with the aim of getting straight As in my first term. It was "study, study, study for me," I reported in a letter home to Norton, with only a short break to see a campus screening of *A Streetcar Named Desire*. I knew that the only way a place like Harvard or Yale would take me after only one term at Swarthmore was if I left with a flawless transcript.

Even then, I knew that it was an incredibly rash decision. Having left George School after my junior year, I didn't even have a high-school diploma. Now I would be a college dropout after only one semester. I needed a great deal of financial aid to afford college, and I was gambling that another school would be as generous as Swarthmore. But just as I had been at George School, I was driven by a desire to find something—I didn't know exactly what—that I thought I was missing.

One thing I knew that I wanted to do during my "semester off" was to make another attempt at reconciling with my father. So once I had left Swarthmore, I phoned him to negotiate the terms of a visit.

"I promised myself I would work during this semester," I said pridefully, "so I'd like to do something to earn my room and board. Is there work I can do for you around the house?"

I heard his familiar chuckle. "Well, we've just moved, and my books and papers are a fair mess," he said. "You could help with organizing them."

"And you know the other condition," I said.

"Yes, I know," he replied. "We'd love to have you stay with us, but can you give us a few weeks to get everything ready?"

"Sure," I said, not thinking what "getting ready" might mean.

It was coming up on February 15, 1975, my father's fortieth birthday, and Barbara was planning a party for him at a restaurant in Manhattan. We decided that I would join them there and return with them to New Brunswick. The celebration was a warm occasion: The DeLaszlos came, and my father was in good form and was particularly glad to see his old friend Julian Franklin, a professor of political philosophy at Columbia University who had been one of his teaching assistants when he was a student at Princeton. I don't remember exactly where the restaurant was, but it must have been near the Bowery, because I saw that famous street sign for the first time. *That's where the drunks live on the street*, I thought, and I briefly had a vision that my father could end up there one day.

When I arrived at my father's new house, on Graham Street in New Brunswick, there were no cocktail tumblers in sight, just cans of Tab. He had made up the guest bedroom and set aside towels and washcloths. He ushered me into his new study and showed me dozens of boxes of books and papers that had yet to be unpacked. He was right about the "fair mess"; there would be real work for me to do. We ate a nice supper topped off with a dessert of Breyer's ice cream, which I discovered had become a nightly treat in the Whitaker-Callaway household. Afterward my father turned on a little Mr. Coffee coffeemaker and brewed a small pot. I had grown up drinking drip coffee made with beans that my mother ground in a wooden box, but I had never seen an automatic coffeemaker before.

He took me back to Englishtown, and this time I was more receptive to his offer to buy me clothes. I picked out a pair of Earth shoes and bought a thick winter coat with a fake fur-lined hood, in an unspoken apology for my Thanksgiving outburst the year before. "I'm finally staying warm," I wrote my mother afterward. "No more of my (womb-denial?) foolishness." When he saw that I liked to jog in the morning, he located some old sweat clothes and accompanied me to Donaldson Park down the road. He was still out of shape and he huffed and puffed when he ran, but I enjoyed the company. On the days he had classes at Brooklyn, I stayed in the house organizing his bookshelves, or I drove with Barbara to Rutgers to sit in on classes given by two fascinating political theorists whose lectures she had recommended, Carey McWilliams and Benjamin Barber.

Ten days into my stay in New Brunswick, I reported to my mother that I had no regrets about leaving Swarthmore. Then I added: "And, perhaps most important, I've had time to be with Dad in the last week and a half. . . . And I think this encounter, at this point, has been good for both of us. . . . I'm acutely aware of all the many parts of me and my outlook on life that are influenced (inherited?) by him. We've talked about all this, for what is really the first time. . . . His approach to confronting these things with me is more Socratic (not belligerent, but almost belligerent), than yours. But I feel that I'm benefiting from it, now. And I hope that it's helped him. But I can't really tell. I must say that I prefer to react to (that is, appreciate) Dad for what he is at this moment (moment by moment), rather than over-sensitizing myself to 'signs' of his problems, which may be terribly complex, or may be simpler than one would think, but which, in all, I really can't begin to fully understand. So be it."

I wrote those words on a Sunday. Several days later, my father announced over dinner that he was going away the next weekend. An academic journal had invited him to write an introduction to a collection of papers about Africa. He had put it off due to my visit, but the deadline was approaching and he wanted to get it out of the way. A friend of a friend owned a house in upstate New York, in the Catskills near Hunter Mountain, and had offered to let my father use it for a couple of days.

While he was away, Barbara and I had several long conversations. She was quite reserved, and it was the first time I had ever talked to her alone. I had overheard my father teasing her for being a "feminist," and I asked if he had a problem with that.

She sighed. "He thinks he does. When he hears the word *feminism*, he rolls his eyes. It's strange, since he grew up with such a strong mother. And he's always been a big supporter of his female students."

Since we returned from France, I had noticed my mother reading feminist books, and she had told me that they were helping her to understand why she hadn't stood up for herself more in her marriage and in the early days of her career as a teacher. Having seen how domineering my father could be at times, I was glad to see that Barbara was defending her right to be her own person.

On Saturday evening after dinner, we were watching an old movie on TV when the telephone rang.

"No, I haven't heard from him," she said to the person on the other end of the line.

She hung up. "That was a policeman from New York," she told me. "They just found Syl's car sitting in the middle of a road, but they don't know where he is."

Fifteen minutes later, the phone rang again. "Yes, this is she," Barbara answered. "I see. I see. Is he there with you?"

When my mother (top left) arrived in America at the age of fourteen in December, 1940, a *New York Times* photographer took a picture of her and her sisters (left to right) Francoise, Marguerite, Cecile, Jacqueline, and Louise as they sailed into New York Harbor. Fifty years later, the *Times* took another picture of the six Theis sisters when they gathered for a reunion of the child refugees who fled Nazi-occupied France aboard the USS *Cambion*.

My father and his sister Cleo on
their way to Easter services in Rankin,
outside Pittsburgh, where Granddad
opened his first funeral home.

"Junior" with Cleo
aboard his first tricycle.

As a teenager, Dad would get dressed up with his friend Bobby Ayers and his brother for church, then ride the streetcars of Pittsburgh's Hill District after services.

A formal portrait in high school, after he went on strike against the nickname "Junior" and his first name Cleophaus and insisted on being called Syl.

My father's mother, Edith McColes, was born into the black middle class of Pittsburgh Hill District and could afford the flapper look in her twenties.

Left: My grandfather, Cleophaus Sylvester Whitaker Sr., was born on a tenant farm in Texas and worked in the steel mills when he first came to Pittsburgh, but he went by the initials "C.S." once he became an undertaker. *Right:* Edie in the Homewood Brushton years, before she and Granddad divorced.

When Granddad bought the Whitaker Funeral Home on an all-white block, neighbors tracked down the former owner and gave him a beating.

My mother's parents, Edouard Theis and Mildred Dager, met as Protestant missionaries in Cameroon and married in the French colony in 1925.

Grandpapa in his clerical robes outside the Protestant temple in the village of Le Chambon-sur-Lignon, with the local schoolmaster Roger Darsissac.

In 1943, Grandpapa was arrested along with Darsissac and Pastor André Trocmé under suspicion of hiding Jews from the Vichy authorities, and the three were detained for several months at the internment camp at Saint-Paul d'Eyjeaux.

Grandpapa and Grandmaman doted on me as an infant when we visited Le Chambon during the year and a half we spent in England, Nigeria, and France.

My mother met my father when she was the faculty adviser to the French club at Swarthmore College and had to teach him his lines when he played a tribal chief in *Supplement au Voyage de Captain Cook* (here with his roommate Paul Berry).

Dad and Mom on their rainy wedding day in August 1956 in Le Chambon-sur-Lignon.

On their honeymoon in Copenhagen,
where they saw a flea circus.

After Dad returned from a year and a half of field research in Africa, Granddad and Grandmother Edith visited them in Swarthmore (along with my mother's sister Jackie and my cousin Leeza).

When my parents first visited the emirate of Kazaure in northern Nigeria in 1959, my mother took me to visit the women and children in purdah, the separate quarters where they lived according to Islamic law.

The post-Ramadan *sallah* pageant in Kazaure, which I watched transfixed as a one-year-old.

After the divorce, Mom brought us back from L.A. to live in Swarthmore and Grandpapa (here with Paul and me and our cousin Leeza) took a temporary teaching post at a nearby school so he and Grandmaman could help look after us.

Right: Once we moved to Massachusetts and stopped hearing from my father, I went from husky to fat to obese, eventually ballooning to more than two hundred pounds by the time I entered junior high school.

The day I graduated *summa cum laude* from Harvard in 1979, Dad looked at me with pride—or was it bemusement at my enormous afro?

Alexis and me with Mom and Dad on our wedding day in May, 1985.

Dad with our kids on one of his few visits to New York after he moved back to Los Angeles in the late '80s.

On another of the rare family events that brought my parents back together, Mom helped Rachel light the candles on her cake after she became a bat mitzvah in 1999.

At their fiftieth high school reunion in Swarthmore, Mom visited the home where she stayed during World War II with Trudy Enders, the childhood friend who convinced her parents to take "Jeannius" in as a teenage refugee.

At his third wedding, to Shirley Kao, in Palm Springs in 2003, Dad finally asked Paul and me to be his best men.

On his last trip to Nigeria, Dad visited the current emir of Kazaure, Najib Hussaini Adamu, the son of his long-time friend Hussaini Adamu, the former emir.

Rowing in Canaan, Maine, where he spent the last years of his life in a lakeside cabin he christened *She Ke Nan,* which means "Go in Peace" in the Hausa dialect of northern Nigeria.

With Shirley and Jane Goodall, the British primatologist, at the 2007 reunion of directors of her charitable foundation in New York.

Dad's gravesite in the Quaker graveyard in Fairfield, Maine, emblazoned with his graduation photo as the first black Ph.D. in politics from Princeton.

Mom and I visiting my brother Paul in San Diego to celebrate his fifty-first birthday, July 2010.

She shut the door to the kitchen and lowered her voice. Then there was the sound of more dialing and more hushed conversation.

Finally she reemerged into the living room. "Well, we've located your father," she said. "He went to a bar in Hunter and started drinking. He couldn't remember where he left his car. He found a man in the bar and asked him to call me."

"He couldn't call himself?" I asked.

She shook her head glumly. "I guess he had trouble operating the pay phone."

"So where is he now?" I asked. "How will he get back?

"I reached the man who owns the house where he was staying," she said. "He said he would fetch the car and drive Syl back here."

I was too antsy to sleep, so I stayed up with her and watched more movies. At about four in the morning, the doorbell rang. Barbara thanked the man from Hunter, and my father stumbled into the house and sat down on the couch without taking off his coat. His body was trembling, and he clasped his elbows to his chest for warmth.

"You're freezing," Barbara said. "You need a hot bath."

He turned toward me with tears in his eyes. "Mark, don't look at me that way," he said.

"I'm not looking at you any way," I said.

"I never wanted you to see me like this."

"It's okay, Dad," I said.

It wasn't okay, not in the least, but I didn't want to tell him how appalled I was. Before then, I knew my father had a drinking problem, but it never occurred to me that he could get so drunk that he couldn't remember where he parked his car. How long was he in that bar? All day? He was so drunk that he couldn't even operate a telephone! I didn't know *anyone* could get that drunk. And now he had gone and ruined another visit!

"You know I'm going to have to leave again," I said.

"I know, I know. This time I hoped . . ." He didn't finish the sentence.

"Syl, let's go upstairs and get you a bath," Barbara said.

She led him up the stairs, and as soon as it was daylight I called a cab and left for the train station.

Still determined to work during my term off, I spent the next month trying to find jobs in New York City. I stayed with the DeLaszlos for a week in the tiny maid's room behind the kitchen in their apartment, then moved to the International Student Center youth hostel on West 88th Street, where I slept on the floor in a camping bag for five dollars a night. For several weeks I worked in the back room at the New Yorker Book Store on the Upper West Side before taking a job putting boxes on a conveyor belt at a shipping company in Brooklyn. I answered classified ads for other jobs, but the phone call usually ended as soon as the interviewer found out that I was only seventeen and didn't have a high-school diploma.

When I was hungry for a full meal, I ate at Tad's Steak, where 99 cents bought a chewy, overcooked strip of beef, a baked potato, and garlic bread. On other nights dinner consisted of a Cadbury's chocolate bar, consumed in the darkness of the New Yorker Theater. At the time I had a fantasy of becoming a film critic, and I saved as much as I could from my meager paycheck to go to the movies after work. On weekends I spent all day at the Thalia Theater off 96th Street watching European films or at the one movie house in Times Square that wasn't a porno parlor and showed Gene Hackman double features for a couple of dollars.

I took the train to visit Yale and Harvard and found that I liked Yale better. I described it to my mother as "so wonderfully vast in its exclusiveness: Movies every night, plays constantly, chamber music, orchestras, the newspaper." I decided that I would go there if I could, but I was consumed with a dark premonition: that neither place would give me enough financial aid even if I was accepted. The applications asked me to list my parents and their salaries, and I had told the truth and reported my father's new position at CUNY, but with his history of lost jobs and delinquent child support I had no confidence that he could be counted on to help support me.

My mother had written a letter to both universities spelling out the problem and asking them to take only her salary into account. But I wasn't sure that would be enough; independent evidence might be required. I knew that my father was seeing a psychiatrist, so I called Barbara Callaway and asked for his name and address. I wrote a letter to Dr. Weber, and asked if he could communicate with the universities confidentially to explain why my father might be unreliable.

A week later, I got a letter back tersely refusing my request. "You seem to have issues you need to resolve with your father," Dr. Weber said. "It would be inappropriate for me to get involved."

The last week in March, just as I was about to go home to Norton to await the college news, my father called the youth hostel.

"Can you come down here?" he said. "It's an emergency."

"What kind of emergency?" I asked skeptically.

"I'll explain when you get here," he said.

I didn't know what was wrong, but I couldn't ignore the word "emergency," so I made my way back to Graham Street. My father was up and about when I arrived, although his bloated face and the bags under his eyes told me he wasn't exactly sober.

"I want to go on Antabuse, but first I have to go cold turkey," he said. "I need someone here in case I get the DTs. Barbara is away at a conference. Can you stay for a couple of days until I'm out of the woods?"

I knew from my reading that "DTs" stood for *delirium tremens,* the fever and hallucinations that addicts go through during withdrawal. I also knew that in extreme cases, alcoholics who stopped drinking all of a sudden could suffer seizures and die. I was vaguely aware that Antabuse was a drug that made you sick when you drank, and that you had to get all the booze out of your system before starting to take it. I was hardly a medical expert, and I don't know why I accepted the responsibility of looking after my father in that condition, but he had caught me off guard and I felt that I couldn't leave him alone under the circumstances.

"Okay, I'll stay," I said.

For the next two days, he lay in his bed under the covers, moaning and twitching and catching fitful moments of sleep. When he called out for me, I brought him glasses of water and ice cubes to suck on and mopped the sweat off his brow with a washcloth. He smiled feebly but was otherwise too weak to talk. I sat at the foot of the bed long enough to make sure he wasn't going to vomit or seize up, then went back to the living room, where I read books and watched TV on low volume to pass the time.

Finally, after two days, my father got out of bed and came downstairs in his terrycloth bathrobe.

"I think I'll be all right now," he said.

"Then I have to split," I said. "I'm going back to Norton. The letters from colleges should be coming any day."

"So which way are you leaning?" he asked.

"Yale, probably, if I get in," I said. "We'll see."

We said goodbye and I headed home. I had grown hard-hearted enough not to have any expectation that the cold turkey would last. He would be back on the sauce soon enough. So why had he put me through all that? I wondered. Why all the melodrama?

It was only as I reconstructed these events that it occurred to me that it might have been my father's way of getting me to come back. Maybe he just wanted to see me again, even if it meant lying in bed with the DTs as I wiped cold sweat from his face. Or maybe it was his way of showing me the agony he had gone through to prepare himself for all of my other visits. Maybe he wanted me to see just what it took for him to dry out before the Hunter Mountain disaster, or the Thanksgiving in Norton calamity, or the spring break in Princeton debacle. Maybe he was saying: I couldn't stay sober for you, but see how sick I made myself trying. . . .

The following week, I got thick envelopes from Yale and Harvard. My first sensation was relief that I hadn't wasted my time by leaving Swarthmore. The second was an instant transfer of allegiance when I saw which school had offered me only token aid on the assumption that both my parents would support me, and which gave me close to a full scholarship based on my mother's salary. On the spot, I decided to go to Harvard and became a grateful lifelong booster of the university on the Charles River.

When I called my father to tell him the news, I could hear the mixed emotions in his voice.

"A Harvard man, huh?" he said. "Well, too bad for Swarthmore. When you get there, please look up Martin Kilson in the Government Department. He's an old friend."

"Okay," I said.

"What happened to Yale?" he asked.

"Nothing," I lied. "I just decided Cambridge would be more fun than New Haven."

It was the last time I would speak to my father for three years. Once I went to Harvard, he stopped trying to contact me. And deep down, underneath my "enjoy Dad for what he is" pose of detachment, I was furious and sick of being disappointed, and I didn't make any effort to see him or to call him or to write to him either.

12

The December of my first year in Cambridge, on the day I went to try out for the college newspaper, I wrote my mother an anxious note. "Somehow, the prospect frightens me," I said. "I imagine cold, lonely people spewing words like spittle in an absurdist play. But it's surely not so lugubrious as all that."

What I found was the opposite of gloomy. Walking into the newspaper's building near Harvard Yard, I encountered a bracing hive of activity. In the lobby, a gray bulletin board was littered with tacked-up notes, each scrawled with three letters. Student editors traded loud greetings, using each other's initials instead of their names.

"RSW!" called out an attractive, petite girl with long brown hair.

"What's happening, NKS!" replied a bushy-haired boy in a bomber jacket.

I would quickly learn that the *Harvard Crimson* was more than just a hundred-year-old college newspaper; it was a proud society of current and former "Crimeds" with a history and language all their own. They included FDR, Harvard Class of 1904, JFK, 1940, and scores of other famous politicians and journalists. In the hearts and minds of its alumni, it was also a physical space, a small two-story brick building at 14 Plympton Street. Many editors spent more time there than they ever did in their classrooms or dorms. They met life-long friends and made mortal enemies, hooked up with girlfriends and boyfriends and even future spouses, and honed the personalities that they would carry forth into the adult world.

Entering 14 Plympton Street that cold Thursday night, I felt a high that came from more than the plastic jugs of printing fluid that sat in the lobby. The newsroom at the end of a short hallway was full of shaggy-haired undergrads hunting and pecking on manual typewriters. As they wrote, they puffed on cigarettes and teased each other with affectionate insults. In the corner of the room was the night desk, a curved table where an editor was busy scribbling changes on the day's stories. Above it was a huge poster of Che Guevara, an artifact of the trendy left-wing politics that most *Crimson* editors had affected since the Vietnam era. Downstairs other students had started assembling the day's layout with X-acto knives, a ritual that would carry on into the early morning hours.

To join this bustling club, I would have to survive an apprenticeship called a "comp." Along with several dozen other freshmen and sophomores, I was directed to a large room on the second floor called the Sanctum and introduced to our comp directors. One was a skinny junior with blond hair, glasses, and crisply pressed clothes named David Hilder. The other, Mark Penn, was tall and burly, with a messy mop of black hair and shirttails hanging out of his pants. They reminded me of Felix and Oscar from *The Odd Couple*, except that Penn, who on the side was launching a business as a political pollster, was tidy and blunt in his instructions. "Ten weeks, sign up for as many stories as you can, then you're in or you're cut," he said.

I didn't know it yet, but two of the other freshmen in the room would become my roommates. Joe Contreras ("JLC") was an irreverent Chicano from Los Angeles who wore his hair down to the middle of his back and kept a pack of Marlboros rolled up in the sleeve of his

T-shirt. He was the only child of a laundry-truck driver and a secretary who had emigrated from Mexico, and in high school he had worked as a gas station attendant. Joe Dalton ("JWD") came from Clendenin, West Virginia, where his parents owned a department store. In high school he had sported a mullet, driven a Corvette, and gone by his middle name, Warren, but in college he was trying on a new persona as a Southern raconteur in the vein of Willie Morris. Another comper was a curly-haired Midwesterner named Jon Alter ("JHA"). His mother was a well-known Chicago politician, and he walked into the *Crimson* offices with all the confidence of a sociable preppy who had edited his high-school paper at Philips Academy Andover.

I also didn't know yet that we had arrived at the Crimson in the aftermath of a particularly nasty power struggle. Every fall, the seniors who ran the newspaper picked the next leadership "guard" in a vote called "the turkey shoot" because it took place before Thanksgiving. In the shoot that had just occurred, two compelling but very different juniors had squared off for the top job of President.

Eric Breindel ("EMB") had grown up in Gramercy Park, the son of a prominent Jewish obstetrician and his elegant French wife, a Holocaust survivor. He had attended the Horace Mann School and Philips Exeter Academy, where he was not only a star student but a champion wrestler and tennis player. At Harvard, he was rooming with one of Bobby Kennedy's sons. He was known for his quick wit, incisive writing, and strong political views, particularly when it came to defending Israel. But his greatest talent was in cultivating friends and allies, a skill he had used to convince many of the most talented editors in his class to line up behind him on a Breindel "slate."

His opponent, Jim Cramer, represented a slate of one. The son of a gift-wrap salesman, Cramer had attended public schools in the Philadelphia suburb of Wyndmoor and didn't have Breindel's easy confidence and charm. He didn't even have a middle initial. To play the *Crimson* naming game, he had doubled his first initial to make "JJC." But Cramer was a fanatical worker who had all but lived at the *Crimson* since his freshman year. He did every job at the paper, writing a story a day and signing up to edit on the night desk every week. Many nights, he stayed well past midnight pasting up layouts and was still there at four o'clock in the morning to help bundle papers as they came off the printing press in the basement and to deliver fresh copies around campus as the sun came up.

Once I asked Cramer how he got by on such little sleep.

"Coltrane, MTW!" he said, with all the ebullience he would later become famous for as a business television star. "Every morning, as soon as I get up I listen to 'My Favorite Things'! All I need to get me going!"

As the turkey shoot progressed, the departing guard was split in support of the two candidates. Everyone looked to the incumbent president, Nick Lemann, to break the tie. Although competition for the top job was usually intense, Lemann had been a rare consensus pick. The son of a lawyer from New Orleans, he was shy and spoke in a soft voice. He had to stand on an overturned wastebasket to address the newsroom, and he nervously tore matchbooks into shreds as he spoke. But he was universally respected as a thorough reporter, a thoughtful writer, and a patient diplomat who could make peace among warring factions and big egos.

In the end, Lemann cast his vote for Cramer. Although he admired Breindel's intellect, he thought his opponent had done more to earn the post. Breindel was named editorial chairman, overseeing the opinion page, but he was livid. He and some of his supporters stormed into 14 Plympton Street on the night the results were announced and physically threatened some of the seniors, and for months after they refused to step into the building except to discuss the week's editorials on Sunday night.

Eventually the wounds would heal, but at the time it made for a very tense atmosphere. It also meant that Cramer had to rely on compers to get the paper out. During my ten-week tryout, more than a dozen of my stories ran on the front page, including everything from a whimsical piece on the early onset of spring to stories on a federal review of Harvard's affirmative action program. My first long feature was on the controversy over the university's hiring of Fred Malek, a former Watergate-era aide to Richard Nixon, to teach a seminar at the Institute of Politics. Nick Lemann edited the story himself, and he taught me an invaluable lesson.

"Read the story out loud," he said as we sat upstairs in the Sanctum.

"The whole thing?" I asked.

"Yes, then you'll see if it really makes sense," he said.

As tempers cooled, Breindel and his friends started to drift back into the building, and they struck me as the coolest people I had ever met. There were three juniors named Kaplan—Jim Kaplan from Chicago, and Peter Kaplan and Seth Kaplan from New Jersey—who roomed together, and all had blazingly fast minds and wits. Breindel and Seth Kaplan, who had gone to Exeter together, let me tag along to highly entertaining lunches in the dining hall at Adams House, next door to the *Crimson*, where I would later live as an upperclassman.

At the start of the comp, I had burned with a competitive desire to outshine my fellow initiates—to get the most stories published in the newspaper and to win the most praise from the upperclassmen. But once we were all elected editors, I had a far more gratifying sensation: of having found a home. I had never had that feeling about George School or Swarthmore, but now I had found it at Harvard, thanks to the *Crimson*.

That summer, I took a job with the American Friends Service Committee, working for an inmate-support program in Walpole prison. I needed the money to put toward the work-study requirement of my financial aid package, and I figured that it would give me a chance to reconnect with my mother. Since I had started going away to school, she had become increasingly involved with the AFSC, helping to set up an office in Providence and serving on a committee that oversaw its activities across New England. Once the regional director heard that I was working for the AFSC as an intern, she invited me to join that group too.

Yet as the summer wore on, I grew increasingly disenchanted with the Quakers and their worldview. Under the influence of Eric

Breindel, I had become engrossed by the politics of the Middle East, and I chafed at the AFSC's knee-jerk criticism of Israel and romanticization of the Palestinian cause. I also saw the unintended consequences of their patronizing liberalism, specifically their decision to hire two excons to run the prison program. One was a jovial Irishman who was supposed to have given up drinking but would go on benders and disappear for days at a time. The other was a slick black con man who charmed the AFSC officials while pilfering the program's funds. It all left me quite cynical and more convinced that my mother and her friends, while well meaning, were hopelessly naive and had no clue how the real world worked.

One college friend remembered me during this period as being in open rebellion against both of my parents. Yet as I revisited those years, I couldn't escape all the signs that I was unconsciously still very much under their spell. Returning to school for my sophomore year, I didn't throw myself back into journalism and the *Crimson* like my roommates but retreated into the lonely world of academic study that I associated with the two of them. Having grown up around her books on psychology and his books on politics, I applied to major in the Social Studies Department, an interdisciplinary program that taught students to study the world by the light of Freud and Erickson as well as Plato, Locke, and Rousseau. And in the spring, I signed up for a course on international relations with a professor who would become one of my two mentors on the Harvard faculty, Stanley Hoffmann, a political scientist like my father who—was it any coincidence?—also happened to be French like my mother.

The second mentor was also someone I met thanks to my father: his friend Marty Kilson. He was the first black ever to have received tenure at Harvard and was still one of the few professors of color on the faculty, and shortly after arriving on campus I went to introduce myself. His official office was in Litthauer, the headquarters of the Government Department, but he had an unofficial lair in Apley Court, a building two blocks west of Plympton Street. When I knocked on the door, he was sitting in the corner of the book-filled room behind a huge desk, a rumpled tweed hat on his head and a pipe curling smoke around his brown, leathery face.

"Ahhhh, Syl Whitaker's boy," he said in a professorial mumble. "How is your father?"

"Fine," I mumbled back, embarrassed to admit that I wasn't in touch with him.

Raised in a textile-mill town north of Philadelphia, Kilson was the son of an African Methodist minister and had attended Lincoln University, the black college where my mother taught briefly before she got her job at Wheaton. He did graduate work at Harvard and made his reputation as an expert on the West African country of Sierra Leone, which is how he met my father, although by the time I got to know him he was spending most of his time writing and thinking about black politics in America. He dressed and talked like a cross between a preacher and an Oxford don, and he loved to engage in intellectual combat, a penchant that, in addition to the aggressive way he flirted with co-eds, repeatedly landed him in hot water. But in the absence of my father, he offered another black role model, and he gave me grist for some of my own evolving ideas about racial issues.

Like my father, Kilson was utterly dismissive of calls for "black nationalism." He thought that the best hope for blacks was to work within the system and to integrate into the American mainstream. He admired the Irish and Italian immigrant groups that had won power and acceptance through the ballot box, and he celebrated black politicians like Richard Hatcher and Carl Stokes and Ken Gibson who ran for mayor in, respectively, Gary, Cleveland, and Newark. He also believed that class was becoming as big a divider as race for the black community. He introduced me to the scholarship of William Julius Wilson, a professor at the University of Chicago who was about to publish a groundbreaking book called *The Declining Significance of Race*. Wilson argued that, thanks to civil rights laws and affirmative action, blacks like me and my Harvard classmates could look forward to comfortable middle-class lives, while the black underclass still mired in physical and cultural ghettos was falling further behind than ever.

Every few months, Kilson would drive me and his other protégés to his house in the Boston suburbs, where he would mix Manhattans and hold forth over dinner. One of his favorites was a lively graduate student named Cornel West, who had a huge Afro, wore three-piece suits, and spoke in his own unique idiom mixing the language of radical politics and the black church. Another was a classmate who would become one of my best friends at Harvard: Eugene Rivers of North Philadelphia.

Rivers was already twenty-six, a full eight years older than I was, when we both arrived as freshmen. He had grown up in the Philly slums, joined a street gang as a boy, and was carrying a gun by the time he was in high school. He dreamed of following in the footsteps of his father, an artist who after his parents split up became the cartoonist for *Muhammad Speaks,* the black Muslim newspaper in Chicago. But he was expelled from art school for mouthing off too many times to his instructors, and for almost a decade he bummed around college towns up and down the East Coast, sneaking into lecture courses and educating himself with books he found in libraries.

One day, Kilson was visiting Yale and browsing through the stacks at Sterling Library when he heard an unmistakably black voice discussing the work of the German sociologists Horkheimer and Adorno. Who *is* that brother? he wondered.

It turned out to be Rivers, who was working as a shelf-stocker. Kilson introduced himself and was immediately impressed with Gene's intellect and energy. "You should have a college degree, son!" he said. "I'm going to get you into Harvard!"

Rivers and I were very different in background and in temperament. He was an unmistakably black man who had grown up in the ghetto; I was a light-skinned mulatto who had been raised in college towns. He loved to talk a blue streak of street jive, while I had become quite reserved, particularly with people I didn't know well. But we bonded over several things we had in common. We both fancied ourselves intellectuals and loved to talk about politics. We had grown up without our fathers around and with very little money in the house. And we shared similar views on many aspects of life at Harvard, including the self-segregation of middle-class black students.

One of my *Crimson* "beats" was the Harvard admissions office, so I knew where most of the black students on campus came from: the same place as the white students. Although the college did some recruiting in poor areas, most of my black classmates had attended prep schools and elite public schools just like the white kids. Yet once they arrived at Harvard, they chose to isolate themselves. They sat at "the black table" in the dining halls and applied to live in the Quad, the former home of Radcliffe College, where Currier House was known as "the black house." Such was their prerogative, I thought. Some of them were my friends, and I knew that they were enjoying the opportunity to have a "black experience" after being forced to fit in with white kids in high school. I just thought it was a waste, and Rivers agreed. "A *damn silly* waste!" he said. "I mean, we're at *Harvard*! Don't treat it like some damn black fraternity!"

In truth, Rivers himself didn't spend much time with white students either. He lived off campus, squatting in a run-down house in Dorchester and working with troubled street kids, a calling that would eventually become his life's work as a Pentacostal minister. But for me, our closeness was proof that I could make black friends on my own terms, without opting for the "black experience" myself. I could hang out with Rivers and still have a Chicano and a Southern good ol' boy as roommates and have yet another life debating global issues and speaking French with Professor Hoffmann and his acolytes at the Center for European Studies. I still had that in common with my father, even though we weren't speaking.

Or at least that's what I told myself. The more complicated reality was that as my sophomore year wore on, I wasn't only withdrawing into my books but also into the solitary shell that I had formed after my parents got divorced. I wasn't just steering clear of the black table; I wasn't making an effort to meet anyone I didn't already know.

Harvard students who didn't know me dismissed me as aloof, and some even thought I was downright rude. "You could say hello!" one girl snapped at me as I passed by her in Adams House without looking her in the eye. But I couldn't help myself. It was as if the longer I was separated from my father, the more I lost touch with the outgoing child who had modeled himself after him.

I might have drifted away from thoughts of journalism altogether if I hadn't gotten a call out of the blue one night that year in Claverly Hall, the Adams House annex where I was living. It was from a black graduate student named Chris Foreman who said that he had read some of my stories in the *Crimson*. "Would you be interested in a summer internship at *Newsweek* magazine?" he asked.

I hadn't looked at *Newsweek* in years, but I had fond boyhood memories of seeing my father reading a copy on Cape Cod and getting a subscription for my tenth birthday in Norton. I also knew that I would need another work-study job that summer, so when Foreman told me that the internship paid, I didn't think twice. "Sure," I said.

I discovered that Foreman was acting as a talent scout for the magazine's news editor, John Dotson, who ran the internship program and was looking for black students who would have a knack for *Newsweek*'s blend of in-depth reporting and colorful writing. A former L.A. bureau chief, Dotson had light skin, a bureaucratic manner, and a private passion for helping minorities break into the business. Several weeks later, he showed up in Boston and engaged me in a friendly interview, and soon afterward he called back to say that I had made the cut and would be sent to the *Newsweek* bureau in San Francisco.

I had no idea where to stay while there, so I got in touch with the only person I knew of who lived in the city, the father of a Harvard classmate. He turned out to be a kindly out-of-work gentleman who rented a room in a seedy hotel at the corner of Jones and Taylor Streets. I inquired and found out that the hotel had another room available: a tiny cubbyhole in the back of the lobby, with no windows and a "closet" that consisted of a steel rod behind a shower curtain.

But it cost only $90 a month, so I took it. The place was so depressing that I spent my nights roaming the hilly streets of the city, which, after Paris, I found the most beautiful place I had ever seen. Still experiencing sensory overload several days after my arrival, I wrote my mother that "the first three days have been confused, bewildering, fascinating, encouraging, friendly, traumatic, crazy, spooky, thought-provoking, fatiguing, hectic, eye-opening, culture-warping and very investigative. But never dull."

By then I had already reported my first big "file," the dispatches that reporters in the field sent to New York writers who crafted the stories that appeared in the magazine. The hard-charging editor, Ed Kosner, had ordered up a cover on the craze over Laetrile, a supposed miracle cure for cancer that was made from apricot pits. The San Francisco bureau chief was a laid-back veteran named Jerry Lubenow who had taken me out to lunch on my first day on the job. When we got back to the office, he told me to go interview a woman in the suburbs who claimed that Laetrile had saved her life.

"Why don't you take the car I've been using?" he said, handing me the keys to his rental. I went to a nearby parking lot and located the yellow sports car. But there was a problem: It had a stick shift, and I only knew how to drive an automatic. I was too embarrassed to go back to the office, so I decided to try my luck. I turned on the engine and put my foot on the gas. There was a grinding sound and the car bolted underneath me, then it jumped forward and pounded into a concrete wall. I jumped out and saw a big dent in the fender, and I was sure that my internship would end right there. But when I called Lubenow, he calmly assured me that he had taken out insurance and told me to rent an automatic. I drove to the interview, and ten days later it appeared as a sidebar to the cover story.

It was a busy news summer in San Francisco, and thanks to Lubenow's faith in me, I got to cover a lot of it. I did leg work for his files on the lively local political scene. The liberal mayor, George Moscone, was facing a recall over his push for district voting, and a local gay activist, Harvey Milk, was talking about running for city supervisor. *Newsweek*'s star pop culture writer, Maureen Orth, cabled me to do an interview for the Newsmaker page. The rock group Led Zeppelin was on tour and had been trashing hotel rooms across America, and she wanted to know if the rock promoter Bill Graham might cancel their San Francisco concerts.

"A Newsmaker item!" Graham screamed at me when I reached him on the phone. "A Newmaker item! You tell Maureen Orth that a Newsmaker item is when the president's dog pisses on the White House lawn!"

In late June, I cabled New York to suggest a story on a curious local religious sect called the People's Temple. It had strong political connections in the city, but lately defectors had been coming forward with alarming reports of child abuse. The editors bought the pitch, and on a sunny Sunday I took a bus to attend services at the large church in the Western Addition. The Temple's leader, Jim Jones, appeared behind a massive pulpit, looking more like a car salesman than a minister in his leisure suit and tinted glasses. He launched into a fiery sermon that was greeted with repeated standing ovations. But when an usher saw that I wasn't getting up with the rest of the crowd, he came over to the end of my pew and motioned to me to stand up and then instructed me to leave. Flustered, I beat a hasty retreat and quickly typed up my file, and a week later *Newsweek* published one of the first articles to appear in a national publication on the sect that would later flee to Guyana and perish in the biggest mass suicide in American history.

At the end of July, I wrote my mother to tell her that I was sitting in Lubenow's office while he was on vacation because "the new third man in the bureau, a nice but very New York-y black guy has arrived and taken over my territory." The new correspondent in question was Steve Gayle, an intense, uninhibited former *New York Post* reporter and City College graduate from Queens who over the next month would become like an older brother to me.

After work, he took me under his wing and freed me from my street-wandering solitude. We went to the Keystone Korner jazz club to listen to the drummer Roy Haynes and his band, and during a lackluster warmup set he stood up and shouted, "I remember Dolphy!" Lubenow assigned me to do a story on a hot new restaurant called Chez Panisse, and I took Gayle along. He ordered one of the most expensive bottles of champagne on the menu, and later Lubenow called me into his office to quiz me about the expense report. Steve encouraged me to read his favorite books, *Under the Volcano* by Malcolm Lowery and *Last Exit to Brooklyn* by Hubert Selby. On the weekends, he invited me to stay with him and his girlfriend, a white single mother named Ann, in her plant-filled house in Berkeley.

"Can you come and get me, man?" he said when he called me on the last Saturday in August, the day before I was scheduled to leave San Francisco. "The bitch is throwing me out!"

I crossed the Bay Bridge over to Berkeley in my rented Buick Opel. When I arrived at Ann's house, Steve was sitting in the living room next to an empty gallon jug of white wine. They must have had a doozy of a fight, because she didn't even come downstairs to say goodbye.

As we drove away, he stuck his head out the window. "Hey, Berserkeley!" he shouted. "Hey, Bersekeley! You think you're so cool, but you ain't shit!"

I took him to a hotel, and as he was checking in, he turned to me and said: "Do you know today is my thirtieth birthday?"

After that, I couldn't leave him alone, so I took him to a nearby restaurant for dinner and encouraged him to drink coffee while he gave me a rambling lecture.

"There are two kinds of people in the world, man," he said. "There are people who have the worst day of their life when they turn thirty. And there are people who have the worst day of their life when they turn forty. I'm the first kind. I'm thirty and I haven't done shit with my life. You're the second kind. You're going to go back to Harvard and go work for *Newsweek* or some other fancy job and get married and have kids and have the perfect life. And it won't be until you turn forty that you'll realize that it's all shit and that you fucking missed out on your youth!"

As I listened to his rant, I thought to myself that Gayle was a lot like my father after all: a drunk who considered himself more of an expert on my life than I was. But I still hugged him goodbye and told him that I wanted to keep in touch. I wrote him a few letters when I got back to Cambridge, but I didn't see him again for another four years. I had moved to New York after graduate school and he was working for *Black Enterprise* magazine and he had just been promoted to managing editor. We met for a nice lunch and he told me that he had stopped drinking, and I was looking forward to having my black big brother back in my life. Then he went out to the Hamptons for the weekend and was playing volleyball with friends when he dropped dead of a heart attack, still six years away from being able to test his theory about fortieth birthdays.

While I was in San Francisco, my mother phoned me one day, very upset after visiting Grandmother Edith in the hospital. At the time, all I knew was that she had suffered a stroke some months before, and my mother reported that she was not recuperating well. She couldn't walk or get up by herself, and her words were difficult to understand. After hanging up, I became quite emotional and I decided to write her. Then I sent the following letter to my mother:

Dear Mom,

> *I just wrote a letter to Grandmother, right after I spoke with you on the phone. Writing her is very difficult. It is such a delicate task to let her know how much we care and think about her and to say how hard we know her illness must be for her, while still trying to offer support and cheer her up. Mostly I feel badly because I am at the age when I would have liked to go beyond just knowing and caring for her as my grandmother, but as a fascinating, entertaining, powerful lady. At this state in*

my life I need very strongly to find out and think about where I've come from and what the lives of people I grew up attached to only in that vague, child's way were like. It's sad to think that because of her stroke and sad times and faltering memory, I may never really benefit from knowing Grandmother as she once was.

It's very sad. There are a lot of things in our family that have been very sad. I don't know. But I wish I knew more.

Pensively and kind of broken up,
Mark

When I returned to Harvard for my junior year, I didn't shoot for one of the top jobs at the *Crimson* and instead asked for a lowly position on the new guard with no specific responsibilities. I crawled back into my books, and one night over the winter, as I was returning from the library, I found a note posted on the door of my room in Adams House. "Call your father," it said.

My pulse started racing. I hadn't talked to him in almost three years. What did he want from me?

I went to the dorm pay phone and dialed the number on the note.

"Hello," he answered.

"Dad, it's me. You called?"

"It's good to hear your voice, Mark," he said. "I'm sorry it's been so long. A lot has happened since I last saw you. I've stopped drinking. I know you've heard that story before, but I've been sober for more than a year now, and this time I think it's for good. I've been thinking about you a lot and I'd like to see you. Do you think Barbara and I could impose on you for a visit to Cambridge sometime soon?"

"O . . . kay . . ." I answered slowly, trying to process my emotions. For three years I had put my father out of my mind. Was I ready to start up again with the disappointments and the fights or whatever it was going to be this time around?

"I'm so glad," he said. "You really have been on my mind. I have much I want to say to you. Shall I write you, and we can figure out a propitious date?"

"Maybe . . ."

But before I could respond, he hung up.

"Bye!" he said.

It seemed like a strange and abrupt way to end a call that he had initiated, so unlike the phone marathons we used to have when he was drunk and would talk my ear off and not let me get off the line. Maybe it was a sign, I thought, that something had finally changed.

13

This story too, came to a head over Thanksgiving.

It was the fall of 1976, a year and a half after I nursed my father through the DTs. Grandmother Edith was coming to New Jersey for the holiday, and he dreaded having to witness her deterioration. Since her fifties, she had suffered from terrible arthritis in her knees, exacerbated by all the excess weight she carried. Now, in her sixties, she had had both kneecaps removed, and accidents and medical mistakes had repeatedly set back her progress. After the first procedure on her left knee, she was putting on her underwear after a whirlpool bath in the hospital when the metal chair gave way and she fell on the slippery floor and busted up her entire leg. After the right knee was taken out, she was in so much agony that she went for a second opinion and was told that her first doctor had botched the operation.

He also wasn't looking forward to her lectures, the ones that made him feel guilty for squandering the gifts that God had given him. He could still remember the letter she had written him when he was a graduate student at Princeton and didn't get a grant he coveted. "My

dear Son, please always remember that *Life itself* is one disappoint-
ment," she had said, "if for no other reason than that the world we
live in has turned out to not be the world we thought it would be. Do
not let this go too deep, as there will be other disappointments ahead,
even deeper ones, so this one will make you stronger for the ones
to come. You are so blessed that you have had so many wonderful
things happen to you so soon in your lifetime. You are also wonderfully blessed in having such a wonderful devoted wife who must be
such a comfort, then your adorable boy! Always 'Keep on Keeping On'
regardless of what comes or goes."

Now he would have to see her in a wheelchair and hear her
reproaches, spoken and unspoken, about what had become of that
"wonderful" marriage and his life in general since those glory days of
his early twenties. She planned to stay with his sister Cleo and her
husband, Gene, who had moved with their two boys to a house in
Princeton several years earlier, after visiting him there and discovering that the town had good public schools and a small but welcoming
black population. That would make the visit a bit easier, but it also
meant that his mother and his sister would be free to talk behind his
back. And he had to figure out what he was going to tell Grandmother
about the latest deep water he was treading, this time at Brooklyn
College, the job that was supposed to be his professional life raft.

Like the African-American studies program at Princeton, the Martin
Luther King Distinguished Professorship had been created in response to pressure from black students. In 1967 the City University
of New York had announced plans to woo outstanding scholars with a
handful of special honorary chairs. In the wake of Dr. King's murder,
black students had demanded that one of the positions be awarded to
a black scholar. The funds had been set aside, but the university was
still looking for a candidate it deemed distinguished enough in 1974,
the year that my father left Silver Hill for his dispiriting job and apartment in Purchase.

A Princeton colleague alerted my father to the opening, and as luck would have it, he had a connection. An exprofessor of Barbara Callaway's named Sam Gyandoh knew the head of CUNY's search committee. Barbara told Gyandoh that her friend Syl Whitaker might be interested. "If you'll write a nominating letter, I'll sign it," Gyandoh said.

The search committee was excited to get an applicant of my father's caliber and didn't look into why he had left Princeton. In the fall of 1974, he was named to the Martin Luther King chair and was told that he would be assigned to Brooklyn College's Department of Africana Studies.

As soon as he showed up for work, however, he discovered a problem: the Africana studies program was a joke. Formed just a few years earlier, it was staffed with adjunct professors, many of whom had sparse scholarly credentials. The chairman, Willie Page, was a slender, carefully dressed man who was still working to earn his doctorate. My father considered his departmental meetings disorganized, even farcical, with no agenda and no rules of protocol. Students were allowed to attend and to monopolize the discussions with arbitrary and irrelevant demands, and even the receptionist who answered the phones was given a vote.

Trained at Swarthmore, Princeton, and UCLA, my father felt he knew proper academic governance when he saw it, and to him Page's operation didn't come close. He wasted no time in making his disapproval known to CUNY's leadership. He argued that Africana studies needed a proper set of bylaws and that only professors who were on a tenure track should have a say in its affairs. Privately, he told Barbara Callaway that it was a form of patronizing white racism for the university to tolerate the situation. "It's like they built a balcony and put all the colored people on it!" he said. "And I've been hired to add some class to that balcony!"

In CUNY's Political Science Department, he found a few kindred spirits. He became particularly close to Herbert Weiss, an expert on the Congo, and Philippa Strum, a specialist in civil rights and the politics of the Middle East. As his battle with Willie Page escalated,

Herb and "Flip" decided to attempt an experiment in mediation. They invited my father and Barbara to dinner at Flip's apartment in Manhattan, and, without telling them, they asked Page to come as well.

When his nemesis walked through the door, my father was furious, and the tension was etched on his face.

"Syl, would you like a drink?" Herb asked, hoping to lighten the mood.

Barbara lowered her head and whispered under her breath: "Please, God, no . . ."

Her silent prayer went unanswered. My father asked for a Scotch. The first drink relaxed him and he started chatting amiably with Page. Then he accepted a refill, and another, and another. His speech started to slow and then to slur. As he kept asking for more and more Scotch, he was becoming less and less coherent, until by the end of the evening the evidence of his addiction was obvious for everyone in the room to see.

When he awoke the next day, he had forgotten most of what happened, but he realized that he was in trouble. He had gone gunning for Page and now he had given his enemy ammunition to fire back.

In the following weeks, Page began investigating my father's past, calling administrators and former colleagues at Princeton and UCLA to dig up dirt. He invited students and adjunct faculty of the Africana studies program to report on Professor Whitaker's coming and goings. Did he show up for class? How did he look? Did he get his papers graded on time? Page assigned him an extra course to see whether he could handle the workload. Around campus, he disparaged my father as a drunk unworthy of his distinguished chair or any association with the hero it was named after.

At the same time, my father was dealing with another humiliation: His psychiatrist had dropped him. Dr. Weber was a medical school professor with a busy private practice, and my father had started seeing him when he moved to New Brunswick. Early in his treatment, Barbara tried to warn Weber that his new patient was an alcoholic and that she thought he needed to stop drinking before he could deal with other issues. But Weber was just as dismissive with her as he would be with me when I asked him to write a letter to colleges about my financial aid predicament. "You're not part of the therapy," he told her. "Butt out."

At first, my father charmed the doctor. Weber found him intelligent and observant and wondered how bad his drinking problem could really be. But then he missed a session, and then another. Weber reminded him that he had an ironclad policy: No cancellations. The next time it happened, he informed my father that his treatment was over. "Weber fired me!" he told Barbara when she returned home that night.

In letters to friends, Barbara described the summer and fall of 1975 as "a disaster." Either my father was in a drunken stupor or a dry fury after going cold turkey. "Syl's periods of not drinking were almost (that's an exaggeration, of course) as unbearable as the drinking because his infamous temper was raging unceasingly," she wrote. "I felt like I was living in the midst of a tornado. Things were not helped at all when Brooklyn notified us that they would not be interested in rehiring Syl, ever."

At wit's end about what was happening at home and irate at Dr. Weber for not listening to her warnings about my father's addiction, she turned to the head of the Rutgers employee-counseling program, Ann Baxter. Baxter was not about to take sides against Weber, but she was sympathetic to Barbara's argument that something needed to be done about my father's drinking before therapy could do him any good. She recommended a rehabilitation facility in northwest New Jersey called Alina Lodge. "It's like the Reverend Moon camp of AA," Baxter said, "but it has one of the highest success rates with chronic alcoholics in the country."

A former apple farm near the Delaware Water Gap, Alina Lodge was a long-term residential treatment center for alcoholics and drug addicts that adhered strictly to the philosophy and methods of Alcoholics Anonymous. In my father's book, that meant by definition that it wasn't for him. He had gone to AA meetings in L.A. and Princeton and found them cultish and superficial. He still had no intention of saying out loud, or admitting to himself, that he was powerless over alcohol. But Barbara put her foot down. "In desperation I finally decided I had had it and Syl was on his own," she wrote, "UNLESS he committed himself to a hospital and an AA rehabilitation program."

He agreed reluctantly, checking himself into a hospital to dry out and then heading to northwestern New Jersey to start rehab at Alina Lodge. For a time, it seemed to go better than Barbara had dreamed to hope. "It's been three weeks now and he's still there," she reported. "It's a minimum commitment of six weeks. The place is super-tough AA. No telephone, no visitors for the first three weeks, no exercise (you can imagine how that goes over with Syl), no television, lights out at 10:30, non-stop AA lectures, film strips, tapes, discussions, etc. all day long with written evaluations every morning!! It does sound dreadful. . . . But, it just seems as though any kind of less fanatical approach is manipulable—soooooo. There it is. I have now had two letters from Syl and much to my surprise and relief he seems to think this is not a bad program. . . . I'm not sure I want to believe in miracles, so I'm trying to temper my reaction with caution."

Before the six weeks were up, Barbara got a letter from my father saying he wanted to leave. She called the lodge, but the woman who ran the place refused to let him go. When the mandatory stint was finally over, she drove to pick him up, and on the ride back he was full of scorn for Alina and its lady director. She was an Irishwoman in her early seventies with a beehive hairdo and an autocratic manner. A reformed drinker, she was full of AA jargon and all sorts of my-way-or-the-highway rules.

What was more, he fumed, she had a completely inflated sense of her own worth. "Her name is Geraldine O. Delaney and she signs papers with her initials, G.O.D.!" he said. "Can you imagine the gall?"

Within two weeks he started drinking again, and the next year passed much as the previous ones had: with bouts of incapacitating inebriation, followed by dry-outs that never lasted long and left him boiling with rage. He managed to get another one-year contract at Brooklyn College, but Page was still on the warpath, monitoring his every classroom appearance and nonappearance. Finally, as Thanksgiving drew near, Grandmother's impending visit spurred him to go cold turkey again. When she arrived, he met her at the airport and helped get her settled in his sister's spare bedroom.

The next day, she called him in an emotional state. She said she had had a fight with Cleo, who had accused her of favoring my father when they were children in Pittsburgh. His sister said that it was because he was the boy and her only biological child, and she blamed the way Grandmother spoiled my father for the fact that she hadn't been able to go to college. As he listened to his mother's account, my father was beside himself. How could Cleo suggest such a thing? No one had made special sacrifices for him! He had earned scholarships the entire way, from the Quaker work camps to Swarthmore to Princeton! And how could she upset their mother that way? Didn't she care about her fragile health?

When Grandmother, Cleo, and Gene arrived at his house on Graham Street for Thanksgiving dinner, he didn't know how he was going to get through it. He was dying to give his sister a piece of his mind, but he didn't want to make a scene. He needed something to calm his nerves, so he fixed himself a cocktail. The rest went as it always did: He kept drinking and drinking all the way through dinner until he could no longer put words together or stand up without stumbling and falling. He could see the worry and hurt in his mother's eyes, but he couldn't stop himself.

When she left New Brunswick that night, Grandmother was more heartsick than ever about what had become of her beloved son. For years she had observed the consequences of his addiction: his lost jobs, the relapse after Robert Smedley's death, the time she flew to Princeton to take care of Paul and me while he went back to the Carrier Clinic. But she had never seen him bomb himself into such a state of utter oblivion.

Two days later, Cleo called him in a panic. "Mom suffered a

stroke!" she said. "They took her to Merwick Hospital! It's bad: She can't walk and she's having trouble talking!"

He rushed to his mother's side and was devastated by what he saw. Her body was immobilized, her beautiful face badly contorted. Her speech was so impaired that he could hardly understand what she was saying. Her corpulent frame was barely covered by a green medical gown and industrial sheets, and nurses had to be summoned to turn her from side to side. All the elegance that he associated with his mother was gone.

He came home to Graham Street that night as upset as Barbara had ever seen him. She was sure that he would use his mother's illness as yet another excuse to get drunk. Would he simply draw the shades and go on a bender, as he had done so many times before? Would she eventually have to call an ambulance to take him to the hospital too?

But that's not what happened.

"I want to go back to Alina Lodge," he said.

Barbara was shocked, given how vehemently he had denounced the rehab center after his first visit. She also wondered whether it was the right time to return there. It was almost Christmas, and the rules of the lodge would forbid him from having any visitors or phone calls for at least a month. Did he really want to be separated from his mother so soon after her stroke? Could he handle being alone for the holidays after everything that he had just been through?

But he was adamant. "I want to go now," he said.

There is no record of his thinking, but my guess is that my father wanted to return to Alina Lodge because he could no longer stand to be anywhere else. He didn't want to go back to Merwick and see his mother in her horrific condition. He didn't want to spend another holiday with Barbara or Cleo or anyone else he knew, for that matter. He had had it. He had had it with disappointing his loved ones. He had had it with losing jobs. He had had it with feeling so much guilt about his divorce and his two boys and everything else in his past. He was sick and tired of feeling sick and tired, as one of his civil rights heroes, Fannie Lou Hamer, once said. He must have felt it in his weary bones. For at last he was ready to do whatever it took to free himself, even if it meant putting himself in the hands of "G.O.D."

At Alina Lodge, Geraldine Owen Delaney wasn't only known by her initials. She had a cushion on the chair in her office and a coffee mug on her desk emblazoned with her other nickname: "The Boss." In the lodge's nursing station, there was a sign on the wall that read:

Rule 1: The boss is always right.
Rule 2: If the boss is wrong, refer to Rule 1.

She had first come across Alcoholic Anonymous in a frantic effort to help her brother. His name was Oskar and he drank so much that she worried that he was going to die. Desperate for a cure, she reached out to Bill Wilson, who had just founded AA in the 1930s, and his wife, Lois, who had started a program for family members of alcoholics called Al-Anon. In 1941 "Bill W." sponsored Oskar, as they say in the program, and Delaney's brother became one of AA's early success stories.

It took her several years after that for "Gerry" to admit that she was a drunk too. She worked as a marketer for a lucrative traveling medical practice and enjoyed the nightlife on the road. During Prohibition, she would smuggle Canadian whiskey over the border between her legs to bring to parties. One night she was at a club in Chicago with a group of doctors and had a few too many and started to take her clothes off in an impromptu striptease. Worried about getting written up in the local papers, the doctors had her temporarily locked up in a psychiatric ward. When she woke up the next morning, she was lying on an iron bed in a tiny cell with bars over the windows and a door with a peephole and no knobs.

"My name is Gerry and I'm an alcoholic," she admitted as she stood up at her first AA meeting. "I'm awful nervous so I think I'll sit down."

Thanks to AA, she got sober. Then she met Ina Trevis, a German actress and recovering addict who dreamed of opening a rural treatment center. Trevis teamed up with a lawyer named Al Silverman and found an eighty-acre property on the Paulinskill River in New Jersey called Little Hill. They didn't have enough money to buy the farm, so Trevis borrowed $50,000 from Gerry Delaney and her husband, Tim. She named the retreat Alina Lodge, after Al and Ina. Four months later, Ina didn't show up for an appointment to sign a new will, and later that day she was found dead of a heart attack on the second floor of the farm's Stone House.

Gerry was left with a mortgage on Little Hill and no one to pay her back, so she quit her job and took over the operation. Over the next thirty-five years, she developed a highly structured, no-nonsense treatment program that became famous in AA circles for its success in treating the hardest of hard-core cases, or the "reluctant to recover," as she called them. Her methods were so notorious that she often received letters from addicts whom she had never met thanking her for helping them get sober. Just the threat of being sent to Alina Lodge had been enough to scare them straight!

Her secret was an extremely tough form of tough love. She had a simple definition of addiction: "pain plus learned relief." To unlearn that relief, she believed that addicts had to be "brainwashed" into learning how to function without booze or drugs. She called her patients "students" because they had to be instructed in a new way of life. She also believed that the only way to achieve that was with "the tincture of time." She insisted that addicts stay at Alina Lodge for six weeks at an absolute minimum and often for six months or longer. She refused to take medical insurance because she didn't want bureaucrats trying to cut short stays or question her methods. "I think I will bring you in for the long, long-term program—five to twenty-five years," she joked to particularly recalcitrant addicts.

My father certainly fit that description when he arrived for the second time at Alina Lodge in early December 1976. Over the previous decade, he had made two trips to Silver Hill, had multiple stays at the Carrier Clinic, and repeatedly tried to quit cold turkey, all without success. The rehab equivalent of a country club prison hadn't worked; he needed maximum-security lockup. It began with Mrs. D.'s first rule: no contact with the outside world for an entire month. So he kissed Barbara Callaway goodbye, knowing that he wouldn't see her for Christmas or New Year's Eve, and instead would spend the holiday with strangers, all of them white.

They were also all men; Mrs. Delaney had a strict policy against mixing the sexes. And like everything else at the Lodge, there was a G.O.D. story associated with the no-fraternization rule. If students wanted personal items like razors or deodorant, they were told to submit a request in writing. One day a man asked for binoculars, claiming that it was to observe the wildlife on the farm. Mrs. D. was convinced that he just wanted to scope out the women in the female section of the lodge. "Look in the mirror," she wrote back. "You will see all the wildlife you need."

At the orientation session the first week, my father listened to the counselors lay down the law. G.O.D also stood for "Good Orderly Direction," they explained. "Students" were required to get up and go to bed at the same hour every day, and allowed only short naps in the afternoon. There would be daily lectures and films about the effects of alcohol and the teachings of Bill W. During group sessions, they would share their stories, but only after admitting out loud: ". . . and I am an alcoholic."

Dining rules were nonnegotiable. Everyone was required to attend breakfast, lunch, and dinner and to wear jackets and ties as a sign of respect for each other and for themselves. They weren't allowed to reserve seats and they had to stay for at least an hour so they would get to know each other. On the podium in the dining hall was a sign that read: "I never said it would be easy. I said it would be worthwhile."

As for reading, only material approved by Mrs. D. was allowed. She put out the AA "big book" and other works about alcoholism, and there were copies of *Guidepost* magazine and prayers everywhere you turned: the Lord's Prayer, the Serenity Prayer, the Prayer of St. Francis. At first, my father dismissed all the religiosity as impossibly trite, but as the weeks went by he came to see the spiritual dimension of Alina Lodge as the most important part of the treatment.

Mrs. D. liked to say that of all the ways alcoholics fooled themselves, the greatest delusion was control. They believed that they could control their drinking, and drinking made them feel in control of their lives. But in fact, alcohol made them *lose* control—of their health, their jobs, their money, their friends, and their families. That was the point of all the prayers and teachings: to help students accept that *they* weren't in control; a Higher Power was. "Religion is about how you set the table," she liked to say about organized faith. "Spirituality is a belief in a power greater than myself. Ultimately, it boiled down to: Know myself. I'm the problem."

Her other favorite line about religion was: "I don't know about you, but I wouldn't want to meet my Maker half-bombed."

A month after my father entered Alina Lodge, Barbara was finally allowed to visit him for the first time. She found him quiet and pensive, as though he was still figuring things out and letting the "instruction" sink in. There was none of his usual self-assurance and eagerness to charm. For the next five months, Barbara drove the sixty miles from New Brunswick to Blairstown every Sunday. When she got there, they were required to attend classes together and not spend much time alone. The lodge called it "Education Day" rather than "Visiting Day." Week by week, he appeared stronger, more alert. He was able to call himself an alcoholic and describe it as a disease, and he told her that once an alcoholic starts drinking he can't stop, something that in the past he was never able to admit.

One Sunday in the third month, he greeted her with a big smile. "G.O.D. talked to me the other day!" he said. "She said she thinks I'm going to make it!"

When he had first arrived at Little Hill, he had viewed Mrs. D. as a preposterous disciplinarian. He scoffed at her intimidation tactics, like the billy club that she kept in her office. She called it "the Tire Whomper" and would wave it around while she talked. But he had come to understand why, after threatening them with the club, she gave her students a big hug. She loved alcoholics not for who they were when they drank but what they became once they faced themselves in the mirror and took responsibility for their lives. As she liked to say: "Our students are the worst of the worst, and they turn out to be the best of the best—if they stay sober!"

In June 1977, six months after he had arrived, Geraldine O. Delaney told my father that he was ready to leave Alina Lodge. Barbara drove up to collect him and his things, and he said goodbye to the bossy Irishwoman who had saved his life. He got in the car and drove away, and he never touched another drop of alcohol again. He had freed his body and his mind and learned the humility embodied in Reinhold Niebuhr's "Serenity Prayer," which he framed and put on the wall of his bathroom in New Brunswick when he got home:

> *God grant me the serenity*
> *to accept the things I cannot change;*
> *courage to change the things I can;*
> *and wisdom to know the difference.*
> *Living one day at a time;*
> *Enjoying one moment at a time;*
> *Accepting hardships as the pathway to peace;*
> *Taking, as He did, this sinful world*
> *as it is, not as I would have it;*
> *Trusting that He will make all things right*
> *if I surrender to His Will;*
> *That I may be reasonably happy in this life*
> *and supremely happy with Him*
> *Forever in the next.*
> *Amen.*

But if my father had embraced a new life of serenity, he had a funny way of showing it. After leaving Alina Lodge, he didn't visit his stricken mother in the hospital or call his estranged sons at college. The first thing he did was go to war. Brooklyn College was still trying to get rid of him, and he wasn't going to let them get away with it.

14

In May 1977, just as my father was leaving Alina Lodge, Hube Wilson retired from teaching. His Princeton mentor, who had championed his career and fed his addictions, retreated to the Farm, his rustic home in Bucks County. Three months later, he was mowing the lawn when a swarm of bees attacked him. Highly allergic, he rushed toward his pool, but he was stung before he jumped in. When his body was pulled out of the water, doctors determined that he had died from anaphylactic shock before he drowned. The hundreds of admirers whom "Hubey" had accumulated at Princeton and around the world were stunned but not entirely surprised. After all the heartache that two dead wives and his own demons had visited on their friend, it seemed like one last cruel twist of fate. "What a shock it was to hear of Hube's dreadful death," Mary Tyfield wrote my mother from London, "like a Greek tragedy and really a fitting end to such a tragic life."

In the past, my father might have responded by going on a binge, just as he did after Uncle Robert was killed in the truck accident or when Hube's second wife, Cora, died of cancer. But this time, he simply closed the book on Harper Hubert Wilson. When Barbara Callaway urged him to go to the funeral, he declined. "That part of my life is over," he said.

Barbara knew that living with him wouldn't necessarily get easier when he stopped drinking, but the reality was more nerve-racking than she had even imagined. In his best moments, he was sweeter than ever, and more intellectually captivating. But when he got angry, it was volcanic, and now that he was sober there was nothing to quiet the eruptions. They would fight, and he would storm out of the house. She would sit by the phone waiting for a call from a bar. Instead, he went to AA meetings.

The mess he confronted when he returned to Brooklyn College didn't make matters easier. While he was on leave at Alina Lodge, his adversary Willie Page had mounted an all-out campaign to push him out. He instructed aides to search my father's office for bottles. He went to the heads of the college and the university with reports of what happened to Syl Whitaker at Princeton. When my father arrived back on campus, he confronted a scene out of Franz Kafka: His office had been taken away, and he was treated as though he no longer existed.

He tried to go above Page's head to Nate Schmuckler, Brooklyn's dean of social sciences. Schmuckler first refused to take the meeting, then informed him curtly that his contract would not be renewed. When he appealed the decision to the president of Brooklyn College, he was instructed by an administrative assistant to stop using the title of Martin Luther King Professor.

"The aptly named Schmuckler has left me no choice," he told Barbara. "I'm going to have to sue to keep my job."

Michael and Barbara DeLaszlo urged him not to do it. Barbara, who had become a counselor at Smithers, an addiction clinic on Manhattan's East Side, reminded him that the process of recovery involved not taking on additional stress or making major life changes in the early stages of sobriety.

"I'm worried that if you go ahead with this lawsuit, you might start drinking again," she said.

"I'm worried that I'll drink if I don't sue!" he shot back.

His friends thought they had his best interests at heart, but he didn't see it that way. He interpreted their lack of support as an act of treachery, so he stopped talking to them. Now even the DeLaszlos were banned!

While my father may have viewed Page as a clown, he didn't underestimate what he was in for. In a court battle, he would be up against not only Africana studies and Brooklyn College but the entire CUNY power structure. If he was going to have a fighting chance, he needed to get the best lawyer he could find. He inquired around New Jersey legal circles and one name came up over and over again: Emil Oxfeld.

A veteran civil rights attorney in his early sixties, Oxfeld was part passionate crusader, part gentle eccentric. For almost forty years since graduating from Harvard Law in 1939, he had used his Ivy League training to defend unions, victims of discrimination, and opponents of forced prayer in school. He had founded the New Jersey chapter of the American Civil Liberties Union and fought McCarthyism before most people ever heard of Joe McCarthy. In 1951, he had gone all the way to the Supreme Court to challenge the constitutionality of a New Jersey state law that required public school teachers to take an anti-Communist oath.

An opera buff, he whistled arias in the courtroom whenever there was a lull in the action. In his spare time he collected photographs of steelworkers. While most lawyers hid behind careful legal jargon, he relished skewering his adversaries with colorful metaphors and righteous language. Wiretapping is "a general dragnet embracing all the fish in the water without distinction as to size, nature, or color, season of the year or status," he wrote in a 1955 ACLU brief opposing efforts to water down New Jersey laws against electronic eavesdropping. "Wiretapping is a dirty business, and it is impossible for anyone to involve himself in it without contributing to the lowering of standards of justice."

My father retained Oxfeld because of his long experience representing university professors in hiring and pay battles. But as the lawyer listened to his story, he realized that it wasn't just another run-of-the-mill grievance case. Syl Whitaker wasn't denying that he was an alcoholic, even though he had been sober for more than six months. Quite the contrary, his "education" at Alina Lodge had made him view alcoholism as a lifelong condition. He believed that Brooklyn was firing him due to that illness, not because he was unfit for his job. Viewed that way, the matter was not an administrative dispute; it was a discrimination case. And it landed smack in the sweet spot of the hottest new area in civil rights law in the 1970s: protecting the rights of the handicapped.

With Oxfeld's help, my father filed *Whitaker v. Board of Higher Education of New York*. It charged that Brooklyn College's attempts to push him out violated the Rehabiliation Act of 1973, which prohibits recipients of federal funding from discriminating against "otherwise qualified handicapped individuals." The Board of Ed countersued to dismiss the case, arguing that it was nothing more than an administrative matter. The American Council on Education filed a friend of the court brief supporting CUNY's position. But my father got a break from the Feds: Jimmy Carter's Justice Department found that he had enough cause to merit a hearing "without prior resort to administrative proceedings."

That was enough to catch the attention of the *New York Times*. On May 16, 1978, the following blast appeared on the Gray Lady's venerable editorial page:

> At the end of this term, if Brooklyn College has its way, Dr. Cleophaus Whitaker, a professor of Africana Studies, will be out of a job. He has been denied reappointment "for academic reasons." According to Dr. Whitaker, who is suing the City University, the reasons are not all that academic. He says they relate to alcoholism; he has been an alcoholic, he concedes,

but is being treated and is on his way to recovery. . . .
We do not dispute the description of addiction to
drugs or alcohol as a handicap, but we question
whether it makes sense to classify addicts as handicapped for the purposes of job protection. . . . As long
as a person remains an addict, his performance will
always be chancy. The only thing that can turn an
alcoholic into a dependable worker is an end to his
drinking—the aim of all cures.

When he opened his *Times* that Tuesday morning, my father hit
the roof. He knew that Bob Curvin, the former black graduate student in politics who had turned against him at Princeton, had joined
the newspaper's editorial board, and he saw Curvin's fingerprints all
over the editorial. As my father imagined it, his old nemesis would
have known how much it would irk him to be called by his first name,
"Cleophaus." He would also have understood the insult in describing him as "a professor of Africana Studies" rather than the "Martin
Luther King Distinguished Professor." In any event, in talking about
"former alcoholics," the *Times* had shown its ignorance about the
disease: No alcoholic was ever "former"! What was more, he fumed,
the editorial never addressed the fundamental flaw in the Board of
Ed's case! The *Times* suggested that Brooklyn College had grounds to
dismiss him because of his drinking, but that wasn't what the Board
of Ed and its lawyers were arguing. They were contending that he
had no claim to the job in the first place. They didn't have the guts to
admit why they really wanted to get rid of him!

In the proceedings that followed, the Board of Ed counsel proved
no match for my father's *La Boheme*–humming advocate. Oxfeld carefully reconstructed the details of his hiring. When Thomas Birkhead,
then the dean of Brooklyn College, had first offered him the Martin
Luther King chair in March 1974, he said it was a one-year appointment but that it could be converted into a tenured position if my
father was interested. In November of that year, Willie Page himself

had written a memo to Birkhead to "formally request consideration for appointment of C.S. Whitaker Jr. permanently to the Department of Africana Studies as Martin Luther King Professor." So much for CUNY's assertion that the chair was never more than temporary!

Oxfeld also attacked Page's attempts at vilification. The complaint outlined my father's allegations: he had only missed three classes, yet Page had claimed that he routinely skipped lectures and arranged for colleagues to cover up for his absences. The department chairman had written a letter to the president of the college describing Dr. Whitaker as "morally derelict." He had pressured department members to vote against reappointment. He had even addressed my father in obscene terms in front of other faculty. Dramatic testimony came from Barbara Johnson, a secretary for Africana studies. Under Oxfeld's gentle but persistent questioning, she described how boxes of files were removed from my father's office. When they were returned, precious documents had disappeared, including the only existing copies of several typed articles that he had written for prominent scholarly journals.

My father's side did have one bad moment when his friends Flip Strum and Herb Weiss testified. The university's attorney grilled them about the disastrous dinner with Willie Page at Flip's house. They tried to describe his drinking that night in as sympathetic a light as they could, but the picture they painted was still hurtful. Angry and embarrassed, he consigned Strum and Weiss to his list of banned betrayers, and from that day on he never spoke to either one of them again.

Before there was any ruling, my father threw a curve ball, informing the court that he no longer desired to be reinstated as Martin Luther King Distinguished Professor. In the months since he filed the lawsuit, Rutgers had offered him a position as director of its international studies program. As it turned out, the university had kept its eye on him ever since Ann Baxter recommended that he go to Alina Lodge. A university vice president had quietly indicated to Barbara Callaway that if my father completed the program and stayed sober for a year, Rutgers might find a place for him. Now *Whitaker v. Board of Higher Education* was no longer a demand for redress; it was simply a quest for vindication.

On October 17, 1978, the court's top magistrate handed down a ruling refusing to dismiss my father's complaint. Judge Jacob Mishler began by noting dryly that the complaint was "hardly a model of draftsmanship." Still, the judge found it sufficient to suggest that he did have some claim to the Martin Luther King chair and that the dismissal could damage his reputation. In the language of civil rights law, he was entitled to defend his "property" and his "liberty."

In the most legally significant portion of the ruling, Mishler rejected Brooklyn's argument that my father should simply file a complaint with the Department of Health, Education and Welfare. Because HEW had the power only to withhold federal funds, the judge ruled, that route did not allow him to fight back against a violation of individual rights. For years afterward, that part of the decision in *Whitaker v. Board of Higher Education* would be cited in other cases where institutions tried to dismiss disability discrimination cases as purely administrative matters.

In the end, Mishler slapped both parties on the wrist. Because my father was no longer asking for his job back, he rejected the original request for an injunction preventing the university from stripping him of the Martin Luther King professorship. But he also denied CUNY's motion to dismiss the case and declared that the university should have allowed my father to defend himself under the "due process clause" of the Civil Rights Act.

In my father's book, that amounted to victory. He was free to move on to Rutgers with his head held high, having punched back at Page's perfidy. In the following months, CUNY quietly offered him a $25,000 settlement to drop the case, and he accepted. The least Brooklyn could do was help him to pay Emil Oxfeld's fee!

While *Whitaker v. Board of Higher Education* is now a matter of legal record, there is no evidence of whether my father saw the larger ironies in his lawsuit. But they seem unmistakable to me. He may not have marched in Selma or Montgomery, but he had turned himself into a crusader for civil rights. He had universalized his recovery by taking on a battle on behalf of all alcoholics, just as he based an entire theory of political change on his legwork in the bush of northern Nigeria. And he had identified himself with his mother even as he was refusing to visit her. Throughout the months he spent litigating, Grandmother lay in the Princeton hospital and then at home in Pittsburgh immobilized by her stroke. She sent word that she wanted to see her only son, but my father refused to go to her side until the very end, when she was near death. He told Barbara that he couldn't stand to see her again in that compromised state and that it might cause him to drink. But he was still with her in spirit, publicly declaring himself a "disabled" American and fighting for her rights too.

My father and Barbara finally showed up at Harvard in the spring of my junior year. He looked grayer than when I had last seen him and was sporting a bushy mustache. I introduced them to my roommates, the two Joes, and showed them our room in Adams House, a sty of strewn books and soda cans and cigarette butts. I took them to the *Crimson* newsroom and to a late-night hangout on Mount Auburn Street called Tommy's Lunch. "You know when I was in high school in Pittsburgh, I was a pretty mean pinball player," he said, pointing to an old Bally machine in the corner. We paid a visit to Marty Kilson in his bunker in Apley Court and took the obligatory tour of the Yard. But I could tell that my father wasn't quite comfortable being around me yet, and I was uneasy too. I was proud to show off Harvard but jealous of preserving it as my sphere of influence, the place where I had made a home for myself without any help from him.

I had even more mixed feelings after I told him about a strange experience I had recently had with two of my professors. Orlando Patterson was a pipe-smoking black sociologist from Jamaica who had just published a book called *Ethnicity: The Reactionary Impulse.* Ostensibly, it was a history of ethnicity as a social phenomenon, but it was also a not-so-veiled attack on "neo-conservatives," the mostly white and Jewish former liberals who had become more hawkish as a result of their support for Israel and antipathy to 1960s radicalism. Michael Walzer was a shy, mop-haired political philosopher and expert on just-war theory who was also the chairman of the social studies department in which I was majoring.

Walzer had agreed to debate Patterson about the book, and on a cold winter night roughly fifty students and interested Cambridge residents came to watch them face off in a lecture hall in the Yard. Patterson started the exchange by summarizing his thesis: that "ethnicity," while it might sound harmless enough to modern Americans, had been at the root of some of history's most pernicious political movements, from the Spartans to the Nazis. When his turn came, Walzer admitted that he wasn't an expert on the subject but said that he wanted to defend ethnicity as a positive force in his own life. As he had grown older, he had felt a need to proclaim his identity and sense of place as an American Jew, and to pass it along to his children.

When the floor was opened to questions, I raised my hand and stood up. "So Professor Walzer," I said, "what would you tell someone who didn't *have* a clear ethnic identity? For example, what would you tell someone who had one parent who was black and another who was white? Who had one parent who was American and another who was European? Who had moved dozens of times as a child and didn't have a specific place to call home? And not to be coy about it, I'm talking about myself."

Walzer pondered my question for a while. "I guess I would say that that's too bad," he answered finally, "and that in the future I hope we don't have too many more people like you."

Several people in the audience gasped. The rest sat in awkward silence.

"That is, what I mean to say is . . ." Walzer resumed haltingly, realizing how hurtful his words sounded.

"Look, I think I understand what you're saying," I said, sensing his discomfort. "But I guess I would say that it's not a matter of choice: The world *is* going to have a lot more people like me."

When the debate was over, a number of people in the audience came up to me to offer their sympathies and to share their own stories of mixed upbringings and marriages.

"Some nerve!" my father said when I told him what Walzer had said. "As I always say, scratch a white liberal and you'll find a bigot."

"I actually don't think Walzer is a bigot," I said.

"Hmmph," he snorted, as if to say: Son, that's noble of you to defend your professor, but you're being naive.

As we talked, I started to regret having told him the story. I realized that I had done it to show off, to elicit sympathy and to invite a moment of racial bonding. But now I found myself annoyed that he was appropriating the incident to support his own resentments. The truth was that I honestly didn't see Walzer's comment as evidence of prejudice against me or black people or mixed-race people. I saw it as a kind of Freudian slip, exposing a wish to hold on to a sense of certainty about his roots in the face of a gathering demographic storm that threatened to wash them away. I could understand that, even though I knew in my bones that those forces would only grow stronger. For the first time, my father's reaction also made me aware of a generational gulf between us: He carried a chip on his shoulder about the racist past that didn't burden me, but perhaps I was more alert to dangers as well as possibilities over the horizon.

At the end of that summer, he invited me to visit him at a little red cabin that he was renting on a lake in Maine. It was deep in the heart of the state, an hour and a half northwest of Portland, in a tiny town with the biblical name of Canaan. A former colleague from Brooklyn College, a sprightly, bow-tied North Africa scholar named Stuart Schaar, owned the cabin and a similar one down the road. My father was wearing blue jeans and work boots when he picked me up at the Portland airport, and he seemed more relaxed than I had seen him in a long time. He took me fishing on the lake, in a little rowboat he kept moored to a dock just a few steps from the cabin. We drove to his latest find, a diner called the Red Barn along a highway north of Augusta. The place served the biggest helpings of fried clams and wedges of blueberry pie I had ever seen, and he seemed to know every waitress and regular in the place.

Schaar came over for dinner several times and brought a house-guest named Eqbal Ahmad. He was a Pakistani who had also done graduate work at Princeton and had gone on to become a left-wing journalist and antiwar activist. In the early seventies, he had been indicted for hatching a wacky plot to kidnap Henry Kissinger. We had long debates about Jimmy Carter's Middle East peace policy, which Ahmad dismissed as a naive example of liberal imperialism. Echoing my friend Eric Breindel, I defended Israel's need to cut a deal that would secure its borders and allow it to remain a Jewish state. Although they were arguing with me, I was flattered that my father and his friends took my opinions so seriously.

I was even more flattered several days later when he asked me to read an academic paper he was writing.

"What do you think?" he asked as soon as I finished.

"I think it's smart," I said. "What's you're basically saying is . . ." and I summarized his argument.

"That's it exactly," he said.

"So why don't you just come out and say it, rather than using all this jargon?"

His eyes widened, as though I had said something scandalous.

"Because without the jargon, it wouldn't be political science!"

We both laughed.

I filled him in on how I had spent the rest of the summer, working for *Newsweek* in its Washington bureau. My first internship in San Francisco had gone well enough that the news editor, John Dotson, had invited me back after my junior year. I had rented a house in Glover Park with Joe Dalton, Jon Alter, and several other college friends who also had internships in DC. *Newsweek's* offices were at 1750 Pennsylvania Avenue, just a half-block from the White House, which I thought was a pretty glamorous address except for the fact that the city was in the middle of a transit strike and I had to walk three miles to get there. Every day I would dodge the neighbor's affectionate dog, Mel, as I set off through the clammy summer heat, and by the time I got to the bureau I was drenched in sweat.

Unlike San Francisco, where everyone in the bureau showed up around nine in the morning and knocked off before sunset, the Washington bureau was a round-the-clock hive of nervous activity. The chief was also named Mel—Mel Elfin—and he looked like a cross between a drill sergeant and a 1950s insurance salesman, with thick black glasses and a crew cut and pants hitched up around his stomach. As the magazine's end-of-the-week deadlines approached, he would roam the hallways demanding copy. "Peris! Peris!" he shouted, asking for small political gossip items for the Periscope page. The twenty or so correspondents who occupied a rabbit warren of small offices ranged from rising stars like Eleanor Clift, Gloria Borger, David Martin, and John Walcott, who would go on to become among Washington's best-known reporters, to crusty newsmagazine veterans who delighted in bending my ear or testing my mettle. "You know, I have a friend about your age who has your generation summed up," John Lindsay, a salty Capitol Hill correspondent with a thick Boston accent said when I introduced myself. "He tells me you're just a generation of aaaaasholes!" I smiled gamely, and his blue eyes twinkled.

Yet as heady as it was, I found reporting from the nation's capital frustrating. "New York so obviously takes Washington more seriously than any other branch of the magazine," I wrote my mother, but I was low man on a very big totem poll, so I was mostly given go-fer assignments. I helped a reporter named Lars Erik Nelson stake out the home of Martha Peterson, a former counsel in the U.S. Embassy in Moscow whom the Russians had accused of being a spy. Elfin assigned me to "Goober Watch," putting me on the press plane that followed Jimmy Carter to New York, but not a word of the president's speech made it into *Newsweek*. Asked to report for a back-of-the-book story on the *Rocky Horror Picture Show* craze, I sent in more than three thousand words, enough for an entire cover story, only to see two sentences from my file used in the final story.

The experience left me more confused than ever about whether

I wanted to be a journalist, or what kind of journalist I wanted to be. There was always something new to cover in Washington, but the life of reporters there struck me as quite ephemeral. As I put it in one letter, "every breaking story assumes immense proportions, is debated and exhausted, and by evening is so old hat that you get hooted at for even mentioning it." I was also getting a better sense of the unsatisfying lot of newsweekly correspondents in the field. Under the "filing" system, they got to cover the world firsthand, but the words that appeared in the magazine were controlled by writers in New York who only left their cubicles to go to bars. By the end of the internship, I was all too happy to head back to Harvard and another year of study before I figured out what I wanted to do with my life.

While I was in Maine, I asked my father for details of Grandmother Edith's funeral. She had passed away at the beginning of the summer, after two miserable last years as a stroke victim. He had finally gone to her bedside shortly before she died, and he was stunned to see how much she had wasted away. He came home and told Barbara Callaway that she looked "like a Holocaust victim." I had just started the job in Washington when my mother called to tell me the news. I asked if I should go with her to the service in Pittsburgh, and she said that it wasn't necessary, but I deeply regretted it later and wrote her that I hoped that it "was not too terribly solemn; she was a magnificent woman, who led a full life, and I'm sure everyone there remembered her that way."

"She was very proud of you boys," was all that my father said about the funeral, before changing the subject. I was upset that he didn't have more to say about Grandmother, and it didn't occur to me that he might not want to dwell on upsetting subjects that could endanger his hard-won sobriety.

He spent most of the next academic year traveling to scholarly conferences around the world, so I didn't see him again until my college graduation in June 1979, which he attended along with Barbara Callaway and my mother and brother. He and Paul showed up in identical three-piece gray suits and I wondered if they had shopped for them together at Englishtown. I had spent most of my senior year buried in the library stacks producing a hundred-page senior thesis on Henry Kissinger, comparing his scholarly writings with his actions as Secretary of State. My two readers, Stanley Hoffmann and Marty Peretz, a part-time social studies tutor who owned the *New Republic*, both gave it a summa grade. That allowed me to graduate with the words "summa cum laude" on my diploma, and I was happy to give my family something to celebrate together after all the many difficult things we had been through.

Before I put on my black gown and mortar hat with the red summa tassle on it, Barbara snapped a picture of my father and me standing on Mount Auburn Street outside of Adams House. Studying it later, I couldn't tell if he was looking at me with pride or bemusement at my enormous Afro. I had neglected to get it cut for the big day, and my hair was stacked so high that my friends had taken to calling me "Eraserhead."

Earlier in the year I had received a Marshall Scholarship, a grant from the British government that sent several dozen Americans to English universities every year. I told my father that I had decided to go to Oxford's Balliol College to study international relations.

"So what are you planning to do after Oxford?" he quizzed me.

"I don't know," I said. "I don't want to think about it now. I have a couple of years to figure it out."

"With your summa, the world could be your oyster," he said. "I hear that Harvard has a program that allows you to get a law degree and a business degree at the same time. That would really set you up for anything."

"Yes, I know about that program," I said impatiently. "But I'm not sure if I'm cut out to be a lawyer. I looked at one of those prep books for the law school admissions test and it put me to sleep."

"Don't rule it out," he said, sounding hurt that I was rejecting his counsel.

I tried to change the subject.

"John Dotson invited me to visit *Newsweek*'s headquarters in New

York," I said. "They want me to work as a stringer in the London bureau while I'm in England, and they want to hire me once I'm finished at Oxford. Dotson even said that if I played my cards right, I might be a senior editor some day."

"And what did you say to that?" he said

"I told him, why not the top editor?"

He gave me a stern look. "Do you really think *Newsweek* is ready for that?"

I shrugged. "That's what Dotson said: *Newsweek* isn't ready for a black editor. But who knows, maybe it will be some day."

From the look in his eyes, I got the feeling that he was assessing me, trying to figure out who I really was and what I wanted out of life.

"I just don't want to see you disappointed," he said. Then his dimples appeared and he let out one of his soft chuckles. "But then again, you know what they say: Beware of what you ask for because you might just get it."

I had never heard that expression before, but I liked it. At first, it sounded like another of my father's bon mots, his collection of clever lines. But the more I thought about it, the more I thought that he was trying to tell me something deeper. He wanted me to know that life is full of ironies and uncertainties, and that sometimes success can bring its own disappointments. I didn't know why, but that struck me as a nice graduation gift, certainly more welcome than all his pushy advice about law school.

15

Grandpapa turned eighty in June 1979, just a few weeks after I graduated from college, and all eight of his daughters and most of his twenty-three grandchildren gathered in Boffres to honor him. There was an air of sadness about him that he had carried ever since Grandmaman's death from cancer five years earlier. One afternoon, he drew the eight sisters around him in the little yard outside the parsonage to tell them how much he missed their mother. But otherwise it was a happy occasion, and on the big day we all assembled for a celebratory dinner at the little *auberge* in town. Because Grandpapa was a teetotaler, the inn had been instructed to serve only water and grape juice, but my brother and several of the other cousins convinced the waitress to fill several carafes with red wine, and throughout the rest of the meal they giggled and made frantic hand signals as the forbidden beverage was passed under the table and around the guest of honor's back.

At it turned out, it was fortunate that we could all be there, because his decline began soon afterward. Within a year, he had grown so sickly and forgetful that his daughters decided that he could no longer live on his own. He moved to a nursing home in Grenoble, near Louise, and when I called him there one day from Oxford he didn't recognize my voice.

"*Salut, Grandpapa, c'est Mark,*" I said.

"*Qui?*" he responded.

"*Ton grandfils, Mark!*"

"*Nom de famille, s'il te plait!*" he bellowed, asking me to tell him my last name so that he could distinguish me from his other grandsons.

In the fall of 1981, my mother, her sister Louise and Gretchen Ellis went to visit him at the nursing home on the way to a meeting at the Le College Cévenol, and he asked that they take him with them. One last time, he was able to visit the unique academy that he had willed into existence almost half a century earlier and to walk the streets of the little village that he had helped turn into an international symbol of moral courage. But then my mother had to return to America, and she was only able to see him for brief visits over the next few summers as he succumbed to the ravages of old age that would take him away four years later.

Yet all the while, she comforted herself with the thought that he would have approved of the work she was doing at Wheaton. Grandpapa had always been a fervent believer in equal education for women, both as a father and as founder of Le College Cévenol. So he would have applauded the direction that the women's studies movement had taken at my mother's college since its first stirrings after the Kent State strike a decade earlier. While other colleges and universities around America were adding separate courses or departments in the field, the faculty at Wheaton had embarked on a bold journey toward a "balanced curriculum," where the study of women would be fully integrated into every aspect of their teaching.

"Today's liberal arts curriculum still reflects the bias of male-centered culture," wrote the provost, Ruth Schmidt, in applying for a federal grant to help fund the transition in 1980. "The development of women's studies courses and programs has so far produced only minimal impact on the core of the liberal arts curriculum. Wheaton, as a college committed to the education of women for almost 150 years, proposes to integrate the study of women into the core of our curriculum through a systematic examination and revision of our introductory courses in all disciplines where faculty express a conviction that research on women is relevant."

While I was at Oxford, my mother wrote me dozens of letters full of excitement about the "balanced curriculum" project. She also informed me that she was working on an article for an academic journal with her friend Carlota Smith, a linguist whom she had met at Swarthmore, when Carlota was married to one of my father's political science professors. It was the first thing she had ever tried to get published, and it had her thinking about finally contacting Bryn Mawr to finish her doctoral dissertation on the French poet Charles Baudelaire, the one that she had abandoned twenty years earlier under the stress of motherhood and moving, divorce, and depression.

She also confided her worries about my brother. For college he had chosen Wesleyan over Columbia, like me because it offered him more financial aid, but he found the place clubby and competitive and was starting to have anxiety attacks when he took tests or had papers due. In the middle of his junior year, he announced that he couldn't stand it anymore and intended to drop out. He wanted to move to San Francisco, and to earn money for the trip he applied for a job at a facility in upstate New York for what were still coarsely called "retarded" young people. Feeling for him, I wrote him several letters at the Elmswood Rehabilitation Center, and he wrote back, telling me that he found the work gratifying but was shocked by how ill-informed and provincial many of his fellow attendants were. "I can't bear the hare-brained conversations that some of the staff have— throwing out bits and snatches of unreflective topical commentary," he said. "It's so boring. I prefer talking to my students much more."

When my mother told me how upset she was about the idea of his traveling alone to San Francisco, I took his side. At the time, I had a theory about the roles that she had unconsciously assigned the two of us. I was supposed to be the successful son who went forth into the world and earned her reflected glory, while Paul would be the helpless one who was so dependent on her that he would never venture far from home. The differences in the way she treated us bothered me on both of our accounts, and now I found myself rooting for him to escape her fretful orbit.

"I agree with you about Paul," I wrote. "It is scary, someone in his position setting out across the country, without specific plans, without a degree, and without a great deal of experience of fending for himself to fall back on. But if he has made up his mind himself that this is what he must do, he should do it. . . . Let Paul find his own way. Please. It is the only way that that way will get found. The only thing, and the best thing, that you and I can do for him now is just to pray for him."

In the end, he didn't need our prayers. He made his way to San Francisco safely, spent several months working as a dishwasher and a busboy, then returned east to get a degree from Hampshire College and eventually a doctorate in psychology from the State University of New York at Stony Brook. We stopped corresponding, although not before I added another awkward chapter to our complicated history. Feeling flush with my Marshall Scholarship stipend, I had bought a raincoat when I arrived at Oxford, but I found it too small and offered to give it to Paul. He happily accepted, even though it was going to be even smaller on him. Then I forgot to send him the coat, and he had to remind me repeatedly. When I finally did mail it to San Francisco, I neglected to pay the import tax, so it wasn't a free gift after all. "Thanks so much for the coat," he responded dryly. "My first reaction in fact was to send it back but Mom said, 'no, no, it'll get lost or something,' so I just paid the fee after questioning it at the P.O. Oh well, spilt milk." When I came across that letter, I winced, realizing how thoughtless and self-absorbed his older brother must have seemed to him.

In most of the letters I wrote to my mother from Oxford, I was trying to make her laugh. After I matriculated in tails and white tie · with hundreds of other students on a cold October morning outside the Sheldonian Theater, I described it as looking "a bit like an after-Christmas sale in the Antarctic." I told her that I was determined to be a "Paragon of Friendliness" after my standoffish behavior at Harvard and offered funny descriptions of the friends I had made among the Marshalls and Rhodes Scholars as well as the other Americans, Brits, Scots, Canadians, Indians, and South Africans I had met. She was particularly tickled by my accounts of Bennett Freeman, a Berkeley graduate and history and punk rock aficionado with unruly hair and a passion for all of Oxford's strange quirks and rituals.

In one episode I recounted, Bennett and I had attended Balliol's annual St. Catherine's dinner. Named for the patron saint of philosophers and held in the college's ornate dining hall, it started with sherry and made its way through multiple courses to a dessert of plum pudding and port and cheese. "Gentlemen, you may smoke!" the master cried out, and a red-faced Classics scholar rose to give an after-dinner speech about the dangers of isolationism. The evening ended with a tradition called "the Loving Cup," in which we bowed and took gulps of hot mulled wine from silver bowls and shouted, "Here, here!" and "Well done!" when there were empty. "Hey man, this is Oxford!" Bennett crowed. "This is it! This is what it's all about! And we're here, and we're citizens, and we're not subjects, and it's great!"

At other times, my mother and I debated politics, and I continued to challenge what I saw as the naive perspective she shared with her Quaker friends. "The kind of reaction you sketched for me of the AFSC increasingly galls me," I lectured after she told me how incensed they all were when Jimmy Carter pulled America out of the Olympics after the Soviet invasion of Afghanistan. "The American liberal-Left continues morbidly to subject only the U.S. to criticism, rather than weighing comparative evils. It goes on acting as if the U.S. were operating unilaterally in some idyllic vacuum, instead of in a cutthroat international arena where if you don't look after your interests yourself somebody else will."

Yet as I pored through those old letters, I also found one that startled me, not for its irreverence or its argumentativeness but for its willingness to drop those defensive poses and admit to my mother how much I missed her. Was it any accident that it was written the day after Thanksgiving, the holiday that had always been so full of heartache for our family?

"My Thanksgiving was made something truly special by being able to talk with you yesterday," I wrote after phoning to wish her a happy holiday. "I hope that even at those moments when I give you a difficult time you realize how very much I love you. Your faith in me, your respect for me, and your confidence in me are more than anything else responsible for whatever I am and whatever I have been able to do with my life so far. I want to be a good son to you. More than anything, I want to repay your faith in me."

In college, my roommates and I had come up with a wise-aleck theory about the girls who were attracted to us. We called it "the zoo factor." We joked that we were all such unusual animals—the cynical Chicano from L.A., the yarn-spinning good ol' boy from West Virginia, the studious mulatto from Massachusetts—that dating us was like adopting an exotic pet. But of course that was just a pose too, a way of keeping deeper emotions at bay. For me, it masked a deep-seated fear that romance could lead to premature marriage, which would lead to divorce and unhappiness, which is what the story of my parents taught me happened when you fell in love too young.

In Paris, those fears finally began to melt away.

After another internship in London before I went to Oxford, *Newsweek* had offered to send me to Paris the following summer. I had gotten to know the bureau chief, an irascible former *Baltimore Sun* editor named Scott Sullivan, when I was in Washington and he was covering the State Department. He had barely given me the time of day then, but when I showed up in France he took to mentoring me with city-desk gruffness. The bureau's other reporters were away on assignment: A young dynamo named Elaine Sciolino was covering the American hostage crisis in Iran; a laid-back veteran named Ron Moreau was in Afghanistan monitoring the Russian invasion; and *Newsweek's* debonair chief foreign correspondent, Arnaud de Borch-grave, was always somewhere interviewing foreign heads of state. So I was left to cover what passed for news in France in July and August—a shipping strike in Calais, a tourist-overcrowding crisis on the Côte d'Azur—mostly for the "overseas edition," where my reporting was crafted into stories by a newly hired writer named Alexis Gelber.

The slow pace left plenty of time for other affairs, as it were. A month before I left for France, a girl I will call the French Major wrote to tell me that she would be there for the summer too. She had been my most serious flame in college, a chestnut-colored brunette whom I had dated in the spring of my sophomore year. We were introduced by my roommate Joe Contreras, who had become smitten with her, but she decided she liked me instead. We went to European movies at the Brattle Street Theater and sipped bourbon and gimlets in Cambridge bars and made out in the doorway of her entry in Mather House. I had hoped that we would stay together as juniors, but she moved on to other boyfriends. Now she had written me at Oxford to say that she hoped to see me in Paris, dropping suggestive references to Henry Miller and teasingly declaring that *"la reve est maintenant!"*

When she showed up in town, I was housesitting in Scott Sullivan's palatial apartment in the 7th *Arrondissement* while he was on vacation. I invited her over to cook dinner and we shopped for ingredients at the local markets and bought a bottle of wine and laughed as we tried to figure out which of the elegant sets of china in the kitchen we could possibly use. But she kept talking about her latest boyfriend back in the States, and I realized that she no longer made me weak in the knees. I didn't want to risk our friendship by trying to get intimate again, and I sensed that she felt the same way, so for the rest of the summer we kept our old flame on simmer.

One Saturday in late July, I met the Opposite Number. She was a stringer in the Paris bureau of *Time* magazine, and when she introduced herself at a party, I had a funny feeling that I had seen her somewhere before. It turned out that she had gone to Harvard too, and had been in an introductory Greek class that I took freshman year. I remembered that she sat in the front row and seemed very familiar with the professor, who, unbeknownst to me, was engaged to one of her girlfriends. She had chin-length blond hair and was very witty as well as very attractive, so the next day I sent her flowers with a note asking if I could take her out on a date.

She phoned me immediately and said that a "date date" was out of the question but asked if I wanted to go for a camel ride. I went over to her apartment on the Rue du Bac and, sure enough, she took me to a nearby park where you could climb onto a camel for a few francs. That evening, two visiting *Washington Post* reporters had invited her to dinner at a Mexican restaurant and she suggested that I come along. We laughed at each other's jokes, and then we all went dancing at a Paris disco. Maybe it was the time of night or the margaritas we had consumed, but at three in the morning she decided that she liked me well enough to spend the rest of the night at my place, another apartment I was housesitting on the Rue Mozart.

I wouldn't call what happened next a romance; it was more like a dalliance, in the desultory French sense of the word. We knew it was unlikely to last past the summer, and it had the added *frisson* of sleeping with the enemy, so to speak, since *Newsweek* and *Time* were such fierce competitors. She was older, by two years, and more experienced, so she called the shots. She would summon or dismiss me, according to her whim, but I didn't mind, because I always found her amusing even when she wasn't in the mood.

The French believe that things come in threes, and in the last weeks before I left Paris I had another brief interlude with a girl whom I will call the Art History Major. She had dark hair and intelligent eyes and a French father, and her combination of reserve and quiet humor reminded me of my mother. She had also gone to Harvard, and we had first met when a mutual friend introduced us in the Adams House dining hall. We cooked dinner in her little apartment near the Arc de Triomphe and I took her on a story assignment to check out an experimental glider at the Paris Air Show. But the resemblance to my mother was a little eerie, and she also had a boyfriend at home, so that romance ended once I returned to England as well.

While none of these relationships lasted, they introduced me to the simple pleasures of companionship and gave me a better sense of what kind of girls appealed to me. As it turned out, they were like my mother in some ways—their intelligence, their interest in books and culture—but they were also able to stand up for themselves in a way that she never had with my father. I had seen the way he could behave with women, like a cruel bully or a selfish baby, and I desperately didn't want to end up like that. If you had asked me in the summer of 1980 what I thought about the prospect of getting married one day, I would have recoiled, associating it with pain and hurt. But as it turns out, I was preparing myself to recognize the person I could share a life with when she finally came along.

"Foot fault!" my father cried as we were playing tennis on Oxford's grass courts.

"What?" I said incredulously. "You're calling me for a foot fault? Who made you the referee? And how can you see my feet from all the way over there?"

"I can see perfectly well, and you foot-faulted," he said. "My point!"

He and Barbara Callaway had come to visit me in the early spring, just as the endless gray of English winter was finally beginning to lift. Before their arrival, I had written to my mother that "something tells me that Dad may expect some sort of heart-to-heart, future-charting, law school–deciding talk, and I am not into it." When they arrived, I showed them my room in Holywell Manor, a former asylum for unmarried mothers that was Balliol's graduate student annex, took them to eat "in Hall" and introduced them to my international relations tutor, a burly, irreverent, and aptly named Australian named Hedley Bull. My father and I played tennis, and I beat him in straight sets, which caused him to resort to calling me for foot faults in the final points. He sulked afterward, and I had to make more small talk to diffuse the tension, but he eventually snapped out of it and returned, as I had predicted, to the subject of my future.

"Dad has arrived and, as feared, has wasted little time in launching into an extended pep rally—exhorting me to stay for a third year and get a D.Phil and go on to BIG THINGS," I reported in a sarcastic letter home to Norton. "But it becomes more and more obvious that Dad's major interest in my modest exploits stems from his sentimental need to relive his own somewhat squandered past—and although I suppose there are worse ways of exploiting your offspring (he has already treated me to several of them), it makes it doubly difficult to impress upon him that we are in fact two quite different people."

He wanted me to come see him in Africa, but I never did. He and Barbara were making plans to take a sabbatical in Nigeria for a year and a half, and we went back and forth in letters and postcards about the possibility that I might visit them there. "We look forward to seeing you in Nigeria," Barbara wrote in a Christmas card at the end of the year. "All's hectic now. Nothing compares with your father getting ready for an 18 month trip!" By May, I hadn't made travel plans, and she wrote to say how disappointed he was. "Syl had once hoped you were coming for several months," she wrote. Several months? I wondered. How did he get that idea? Didn't he know I was in school? But the truth was that I didn't want to face more of his counseling, because after my summer in Paris I had decided that I was going to leave Oxford without finishing my doctoral degree and accept *Newsweek*'s offer of a job in New York.

Yet while I was rejecting his career advice, I was taking after him in another way. Just as he had in the year after leaving UCLA, I was planning a trip around the world. In those days, Pan Am had routes across the globe and sold a "Jules Verne ticket" for £1,200, or less than $3,000 at the time, that allowed you to go anywhere the airline flew within eighty days. I had calculated that if I saved enough of my Marshall stipend and my *Newsweek* stringing fees, I could just afford it. So I plotted my itinerary: Tel Aviv, Bombay, Bangkok, Hong Kong, Tokyo, and L.A., where I would visit my roomate Joe Contreras before ending the odyssey in New York.

At the airport in Tel Aviv, I was pulled aside for questioning by guards who thought I looked Arab. (Later, when I took a bus across the Sinai Desert to Cairo, the Egyptian authorities would ask if I was Israeli.) But once that interrogation was over, I found the country utterly captivating. I toured the Golan Heights, swam in the Dead Sea, and took a bus to the Negev Desert. I spent several days in Jerusalem, so stimulated by its energy and sense of history that I forgot to eat. I found Egypt interesting for the majesty of the Pyramids and the Sphinx, but that trip and a tour of the West Bank left me with a depressing sense of how backward the Arab world was compared with the dynamism of Israel. The disparity was captured in a scene that I witnessed on the Mount of Olives. I had ridden on the efficient Israeli buses to visit Gethsemane and the Tomb of Zechariah, but I was curious about what was farther up the road, so I climbed to an Arab neighborhood called al-Tur. When I reached the top of the hill, I heard a loud bleating sound, and I looked down to see an Arab man in a headdress struggling to push a bucking donkey into the back of a battered white station wagon.

In India, I came down with a bad case of dysentery on the train from Bombay to Madras. Luckily, the man sitting next to me was a doctor from the southern city, and he invited me to stay with his family for several days while he treated me with antibiotics and electrolyte powder. I continued my recuperation by taking a boat to Sri Lanka, where I went running on a beach near Colombo and a pack of urchins chased after me shouting "Muhammad Ali! Muhammad Ali!" I was startled at first, but then I laughed at the thought that I was the closest thing they had ever seen to the world's most famous athlete. As I made my way to Calcutta and the Taj Mahal, I took trains at night and slept on wooden planks that folded down from the walls. When I reached New Delhi, I looked up a *Newsweek* stringer named Ramanujam Ramanujam, or "Ram" for short. As he drove me around the villas where the foreign correspondents lived, I felt grateful that I had traveled through India the way I had, third class all the way, because I figured if I ever came back with money I would never get as close a look at the poverty and fatalism that permeated so much of the country.

During the rest of my trip through Asia I visited the usual tourist destinations in Thailand, Malaysia, Singapore, Hong Kong, southern China, and Japan. But I also spent a lot of time hanging out with local *Newsweek* and *Washington Post* reporters. When they heard that I was headed for a writing job in New York, they were only too happy to take me to meals and bars on their expense accounts and ply me with gossip and complaints about their editors. As I listened to their grumbling, I saw more clearly the downside that came with the glamour of being a foreign correspondent, and I formulated a theorem that I would see proven again and again throughout my career: A reporter's paranoia about his editors increases in direct proportion to his distance from headquarters.

I don't remember how I learned that my father would be in Los Angeles when I got there. But I had a phone number for him, and he suggested that we meet for breakfast at Ship's Diner at the corner of Olympic and La Cienega. He looked even heavier than I remembered, although everyone in America looked heavy after three months in Asia.

"I don't think I've ever seen you so dark," he said. "You're blacker than I am!"

"All the sun in India, I guess." I shrugged. "How's Nigeria?"

"Wonderful! We've been spending time with my old friend Hussaini Adamu. You knew him when you were a baby."

"I don't remember," I said.

"Yes, of course. Well, he may be an emir some day. The emir of Kazaure. We took you there too, when you were little."

"Sorry, I don't remember that either."

He must have sensed that I didn't really want to talk that much about Nigeria, so he changed the subject to my plans.

"So, *Newsweek* it is, then?" he said.

"Looks that way," I said. "Sorry about the law school thing."

"You know, there was a time when your old man thought about becoming a journalist. When I was in Nigeria as a graduate student, I filed several dispatches to a journal called *West Africa*."

Oh, brother! I thought to myself. *First he wanted me to be a lawyer; now that I've decided to become a journalist, he can't just let it be my thing.*

"So do you still have your sights set on becoming a senior editor?" he asked.

"I don't know," I said. "I think I might want to become a foreign correspondent. But I'm going to take it one day at a time. You know about that, right?"

He nodded.

"How's Barbara?" I asked.

"She's in New Jersey handling the paperwork on our new house before we go back to Africa. I came here to talk to people at UCLA about the Awolowo project, which is really turning into something very special."

My father talked about "the Awolowo project" as if I should know what it was. But I didn't ask any questions. It had been nice to see him, but I wasn't hungry for my pancakes anymore and I was ready to let him get the check. I had my own life to lead now, and I wanted to get on with it.

What I didn't bother to learn that morning at Ship's Diner was that he had come to L.A. to persuade UCLA to create a permanent home for the papers of Chief Obafemi Awolowo. He was one of the founding fathers of Nigerian independence, and my father was working on a book about him that he hoped would be one of the great political biographies of modern Africa.

A slight, serious man who wore round, wire-rimmed spectacles, Awolowo had led an epic life. He was the son of a poor farmer and woodcutter who died when Obafemi was only seven years old. He worked as a stenographer, newspaper reporter, and union organizer before signing up for correspondence courses to further his education. In the 1940s, he traveled to London to get a law degree, and while there he wrote a book called *The Path to Nigerian Freedom,* one of the country's first anticolonial manifestos. He returned to Nigeria and served as the premier of the western region, where he introduced free primary schools and the first television station in all of Africa. He founded a political movement called the Action Party and ran for president in Nigeria's first independent election in 1960. But he lost to Sir Abubakar Tafawa Balewa and had to settle for becoming the leader of the opposition in parliament.

A few years later, he was charged with trying to topple Balewa and was thrown in prison for three years. When he got out, Colonel Jack Gowon was running the country, and Awolowo became his right-hand man. By the early 1980s, a succession of feckless civilian presidents and military strongmen had come and gone, but he was still at the center of power. Many Nigerians saw the chief as the country's greatest leader despite the fact that he had never occupied the presidential palace.

What my father found most impressive about Awolowo was his unique combination of nationalist vision and regional pride. Twenty years earlier, he had built his academic reputation on his insights into the enduring power of tribal and religious identity among the Hausa people of northern Nigeria and his battles with the political scientists who believed that "modernization" could sweep away "the politics of tradition." In Awolowo, he saw a statesman who grasped the delicate balance between the past and the future. A native Yoruba, Awolowo had devoted himself to bettering the lot of his tribespeople, building them the best roads in Nigeria and instituting health care for all children under eighteen. "I cannot be a good Nigerian if I am not a good Yorubaman," he liked to say. But he had also fought to keep Nigeria united during the Biafra crisis, leading a delegation that tried to persuade the Ibos not to secede. A true man of history, he had traveled to India to meet Jawaharlal Nehru, befriended Ghana's Kwame

Nkrumah, and would have felt right at home discussing federalism with James Madison.

When my father first approached Awolowo's aides, they were suspicious. If anyone was going to write his biography, they protested, it should be a Nigerian. But my father won over the chief, who was taken with his magnetism and sensitive understanding of the country's politics. He gave him the run of his personal files, and my father hired a feisty Russian librarian named Lena Young, who happened to live in Kano, to organize them. She made repeated trips to Lagos to sift through Awolowo's personal library while he went in search of an institution that would pay to pack, ship, and create a permanent archive for the treasure trove.

He thought UCLA would be the answer, but after months of negotiations, the university passed. He approached the Ford Foundation, working through an officer named Haskell Ward, who been one of his favorite UCLA graduate students in the 1960s. Those talks broke down too, and he stopped talking to Ward, as he had done to so many other friends who disappointed him. At the end of his second year in Africa, he was forced to abandon the project, and his opus on Awolowo was never written.

In his personal life, the two years in Africa were also a wrenching time. While he was there, he learned that Granddad had died. The driven Texan who had risen from birth on a tenant farm to wealth and status as one of Pittsburgh's first black funeral home owners, only to endure divorce, financial ruin, a heart attack, and a debilitating stroke, had proven tough enough to hang on for almost two decades and outlive his younger second wife, Edith, by three years. My father never made peace with him and did not return to Pittsburgh to attend his funeral. And yet his life had come to resemble his father's more than he ever wanted to contemplate, with its arc of blazing early success fading into self-destruction and financial hardship.

How much did his unresolved anger toward Granddad and his bitterness over the Awolowo book contribute to my father's breakup with Barbara Callaway? She is not certain, and he may not have been fully aware himself, but that sad event occurred during their time in Africa too.

While she still loved him, Barbara had had enough of his temper tantrums. Even after five years of sobriety, he still flew into rages, accusing her of "emotional betrayal" for not understanding him. And for some reason, he would always cite the same bill of particulars, dredging up two incidents that had happened years before and throwing them in her face for hours and hours until she concluded that he was never going to stop.

The first incident dated back to the early 1970s, when Barbara had just come east to teach at Rutgers University and was living with my father in Princeton. Before she left California, an Africa scholar named Richard L. Harris at the University of California, Santa Barbara, asked her to contribute an essay to a book he was editing called *The Political Economy of Africa.* She sent him a paper that drew on many of the insights that she had gained in my father's graduate seminars on the beach in Venice. When it was accepted, she asked my father to read it. He gave her such useful feedback that she suggested they resubmit the paper under both of their names, and he agreed. But when Harris objected to some of the changes, he exploded. He said that they should withdraw the paper and declared the editor "banned"!

Harris was left in a bind. He still needed a paper to complete his anthology, so he made Barbara a proposition. "Why don't I just publish the draft you sent me before Syl saw it?" he suggested.

Barbara didn't say yes, but she didn't say no, and so Harris went ahead and used her original paper. When the book appeared in 1975, it included an essay called "The Political Economy of Nigeria," by Barbara Callaway.

Some time afterward, my father and Barbara were walking across the Rutgers campus when one of her students came over to them. "I just saw your article in Harris's book!" he said to her.

My father hit the ceiling. He accused her of stealing his ideas and going behind his back to further her own career. For years, he brought the grievance up every time they argued, and he was still fulminating seven years later when they were living on the other side of the world in Nigeria.

The second outrage had occurred all the way back in 1967, shortly after they had first met in Los Angeles. Barbara had yet to meet my brother or me, but my father talked about us so much that she was puzzled why he didn't have more contact with us. "Why don't you call them?" she asked. "Why don't you bring them back to California for another visit?"

She was just expressing concern, but he didn't see it that way. He saw an accusation of irresponsibility. Fifteen years later, after everything that had passed between us, he still couldn't forgive her for having the temerity to suggest that he had left a void in the lives of his young sons.

In the end, she was so desperate to end the relationship that she told him to keep their new house. Before returning to Africa, they had purchased a home in Piscataway, near New Brunswick, a three-story colonial with a huge addition and a swimming pool out back. It was considerably more than two academics with substantial debts could afford, but my father fell in love with the property and told Barbara that it would make them feel that life was good even after their worst day at work, his personal standard for appraising real estate. They had used her money for the down payment, but she told him to take the house anyway and to pay her back later. She even allowed him to keep their secondhand Mercedes, another status symbol that they had bought together after his beloved Mercury Cougar gave out.

He finally returned to America in the summer of 1982, just as I was finding a home in New York City with a job at *Newsweek* and a new girlfriend. When he moved into the place in Piscataway that he called his "millionaire's house," he was professionally defeated, physically drained, and, for the first time in decades, all alone.

16

"Why did you and Mom get divorced?" I asked.

Several weeks before I planned to propose to my girlfriend, I had called my father in Piscataway to ask if we could have lunch. He agreed to meet me at the Oyster Bar, the bustling restaurant in Grand Central Station.

The question took him by surprise. He frowned and paused for a minute before answering.

"Do you *really* want to know?" he asked.

"Yes," I said. "I think I have a sense of Mom's side of the story, but I want to hear yours."

"Hmmph, I can only imagine what her version is!" he said. "As for my side of the story, as you so artfully put it, I think I realized it was a mistake on our wedding day. But I felt trapped. We were in France, and her whole family was there."

"Yet you stayed married for six years. You had me and Paul. What happened to make you want to end it?"

"Hmmph . . ." he snorted again. "Well, I can tell you the precise moment that I decided that I couldn't stay married to your mother. One day I asked if she would let me buy her lingerie. Do you know what she said? She said I had a dirty mind. After that, as far as I was concerned, it was over."

Our conversation took place in the fall of 1984, three years after I had moved to New York. At the time, I didn't realize that my mother had uttered that nervous remark when I was four years old and we were living in Princeton. If I had known the chronology, I would have wondered how my father could have possibly asked her to follow him to Los Angeles. How could he have been so heartless if he had already divorced her in his mind? It would have also struck me as disingenuous, since by that point he was already seeing other women and probably looking for a *casus belli,* a justification for a breakup. Yet sitting at the checker-cloth table at the Oyster Bar, I had mixed emotions. I was startled at how intent he was on blaming my mother, but I was also flattered that he was being so candid with me. And I felt relieved. I had asked him to lunch to find out if he might say anything that would cause me to change my plans, but if my parents had divorced as the inevitable result of his initial ambivalence, I was certain that I didn't feel that way about the woman whom I wanted to marry.

She was Alexis Gelber, the *Newsweek* writer who had turned several of my files from the Paris bureau into published stories. In fact, she had written her first piece for the magazine, after she was hired out of the Columbia School of Journalism, from my reporting. It was on the thousands of European vacationers who were stranded on the highways of southern France because the beaches and campgrounds were so overcrowded. When it appeared, the byline read: "Alexis Gelber with Mark Whitaker in Paris." Her cousin Pamela read the story and phoned her to ask what was going on. "You're on the job one week and you're already running around France with some guy?" she said. Alexis had to explain that in *Newsweek*-speak, "with" simply meant that a writer had used a reporter's files.

I had first laid eyes on her shortly after returning from my trip around the world. I was working on Saturday, as all "front of the book" writers did because of the magazine's weekend deadlines. I was returning from lunch with a friend on the international desk, where I had been assigned, and as we walked into the lobby of the *Newsweek* building on Madison Avenue she strode briskly by us and waved hello to my colleague. She was wearing purple corduroy pants, and her large brown eyes and high cheekbones were framed by shoulder-length brown hair. I was immediately struck by her beauty and the aura of energy she gave off.

"Who's that?" I asked my friend.

"Alexis Gelber," he replied.

"Oh," I said, "so *that's* Alexis Gelber."

Several weeks later we had an intense conversation at the *Newsweek* Christmas party, several days after General Jaruzelski declared martial law in Poland. I suggested that we have lunch sometime. She figured it was just a line, so she was surprised when I called her the very next morning. "Sorry, I can't have lunch today," I said. "My mother's in town."

As we got to know each other over the next few months, I saw ways in which she was both like and unlike my mother. She was very smart, but she didn't take herself too seriously. She could be self-conscious but she was hardly shy. She was an English literature major who read a novel a week and played flawless Bach and Beethoven from sight on the piano, but she could be entertainingly irreverent about music and art. Although I didn't reflect on it at the time, she also had things in common with my father: She was sociable and loved to tell stories and had a talent for making friends. But what I liked best about her were the things that she didn't share with either of my parents. She was more at ease hugging and touching and showing physical affection than either of them had ever been, and she could be good company without getting "heavy," as my father would say. And when we fought, she was able to forgive or be forgiven or at least to let bygones be bygones and move on, which was something that I had never remotely witnessed in my family.

Superficially, we were very different: She was white and Jewish, and I was black and had been raised a Quaker. I had moved across the country and around the world as a child; she had spent most of her life within fifty square miles of New York City. Born in Women's Hospital in upper Manhattan, she had grown up on Long Island and gone to college and graduate school at Barnard and Columbia. Yet there were similarities beneath the surface: Her parents were also intellectuals, a university provost and a classical pianist. Like my parents, they had split up when she was a small child. But they had reunited several years later, and as a result, she managed to be loyal and close to her family while also having the skepticism and sardonic view of the world that I had always associated with children of divorce.

She was living with another man when we met, which made for some complicated logistics once we were no longer just office friends. Because we worked on Saturdays, we had Mondays off, so she would sneak away to my walk-up apartment in a brownstone off Columbus Avenue to spend the afternoons. Eventually she broke up with her boyfriend, and I moved into her four-room apartment in an ivy-covered building on West End Avenue. I quit the *Newsweek* bar scene, which I had joined when I first arrived in New York in an effort to fit in, and I went home with her instead. I also stopped drinking hard liquor of any sort, because I was getting bigger assignments and didn't want to fog my brain but also, I acknowledged privately, because I didn't want to tempt fate given my father's history.

We were both low enough on the *Newsweek* pecking order that no one cared much when the cat was out of the bag, and because we worked in different departments we were able to move ahead without our relationship being held against us. She became an editor in the overseas magazine, and I was writing cover stories for the U.S. edition, on everything from the last days of Leonid Brezhnev in Russia to the Falklands War in Argentia to Ronald Reagan's gunboat diplomacy in Central America. Then more opportunity came along when Katharine Graham, *Newsweek*'s owner, fired the editor, a genial veteran named Lester Bernstein, and replaced him with the founder of *Texas*

Monthly magazine, a tall Houston native with curly hair and eerily blue eyes named Bill Broyles.

My boss at the time, a rotund wordsmith named Tom Mathews, felt so threatened by Broyles's arrival that he started having heart palpitations and went on medical leave. The top writer in our department had to fill in for him, which meant that I got more cover stories to write. When Princess Grace of Monaco died, Broyles decided to put the story on the cover and didn't change it on Saturday when news broke of the massacre at the Sabra and Shatilla refugee camps in Lebanon. He was widely criticized and felt so burned that he began ordering up foreign covers left and right. Eventually he quit and moved to the West Coast to become a Hollywood screenwriter, and Mrs. Graham promoted an insider named Rick Smith, who had been a foreign writer and reporter and was disposed toward even more international coverage.

My dream job in *Newsweek*'s Paris bureau eventually opened up, and I was tempted enough to ask for a month-long try out. Alexis came to visit me and thought I wouldn't come back. But after she left, I realized that I didn't care as much about being a foreign correspondent as I cared about her, so I returned to New York. For two years, we lived together and worked together and vacationed together until one day I decided that I couldn't imagine not being with her. I took her out to dinner on her birthday, the fourth of December, at a restaurant called Cellar in the Sky at the top of the World Trade Center and proposed over dessert. When we got home, we stayed up all night talking about what we were going to name our children.

By this time, Alexis's parents had made me feel like part of their family, and she had met my father and hit it off with him, but the three of them had never met. So once we were engaged, we invited them all to Sunday brunch at a leafy restaurant on Broadway. My father turned on the charm, and it happened that they all knew someone in common. Alexis's father, Sidney Gelber, had helped create the State University of New York at Stony Brook with a man named Alec Pond who later became a top administrator at Rutgers, where my father worked. They all agreed on what a fine man Pond was, and everyone seemed to get along very well.

As we walked back to West End Avenue, my father pulled Alexis's mother, Anita, aside.

"How do *you* feel about your daughter marrying my son?" he asked.

"I'm delighted," she answered. "In fact, when I first met Mark, I predicted that he would be the one!"

"I ask because I know that not all Jewish people would be comfortable with having a black son-in-law—"

Anita cut him off. "Syl, I'm offended that you would even think that!" she said sharply. "What do you take me for?"

I heard about the exchange several weeks later, when Anita told Alexis. The next time I talked with my father, I asked him if he had actually said such a thing to my future mother-in-law.

"Indeed I did," he said with a chuckle, "and she gave me the business. I guess it runs in the family. The Gelber women are feisty!"

I didn't think it was so funny. Why had he doubted Anita's open-mindedness, when I had never given him any reason to? Hadn't he had Jewish friends and supporters and girlfriends going back to high school and college? I was reminded of how he had reacted to my Michael Walzer story in college, and I wondered again if he had more of a racial chip on his shoulder than I realized. Or did it go even deeper than that, to insecurities about what the Gelbers might really think of *him*?

Alexis and I had decided on a Jewish wedding, and when we discussed who might perform it we both came up with the same name: a rabbi named Emily Korzenik. Her son had been a classmate of mine at Harvard and a high school friend of Alexis's former boyfriend. When we called her, she invited us to her home in Scarsdale, and instead of the predictable chitchat, she told us the story of Gluckel of Hameln. A seventeenth-century Jewish businesswoman and twice a widow, Gluckel had devoted her life to making sure that her twelve children got good religious educations and found proper Jewish spouses. Getting to the point, Rabbi Korzenik told us that she would marry us on one condition: that we raise our children as Jews.

That was fine with me, because I had been moving spiritually in that direction in any event. I admired the fact that Judaism, like Quakerism, stressed leading an ethical and socially meaningful existence in the here and now, rather than focusing on the questionable promise of an eternal afterlife. But I had also come to appreciate other dimensions to my wife's religion that I found lacking in my family's faith. In the previous year, several young Jewish friends had died tragically, and attending their sad but cathartic funerals had convinced me that coping with death and celebrating the key passages of life called for more ceremony than the Friends had to offer. And as I listened to Rabbi Korzenik talk about Gluckel of Hameln, I realized that there was something else that was drawing me toward Judaism: that it was a religion that celebrated not just faith but a sense of family, which is what I so badly wanted to create in my adult life after my own unhappy childhood.

The wedding took place at a sunny restaurant called The Terrace on the top of a dorm building on the Columbia campus. There was a tense moment when Alexis's Grandpa Irving, doubting a female rabbi's authority, challenged Mrs. Korzenik on a point of liturgy, but she shrewdly co-opted him with an offer to say the *hamotzi* prayer over the hallah bread. I had asked my brother to be the best man, and over lunch Paul proposed a toast and then held up . . . a piece of toast.

My mother wore a blue dress and seemed in a daze the whole day. At the time, I felt annoyed that she couldn't look happier for me, and I wondered if it was because she was jealous of Alexis or felt upset that she was losing her son to another family. My father came in a dark blue suit and had the time of his life. He chatted with all our friends and Alexis's relatives as if he had known them for years, and afterward everyone told me how charismatic he was. We had invited my aunts Cleo and Gertrude and Della and one of my Smedley cousins from Pittsburgh and her handsome teenage sons. My father put them all up at his house in Piscataway, and I was glad that the wedding had offered a pretext for reunion and perhaps even reconciliation between my father and his sisters.

After the reception my friend Bo Baskin, a Texan whom I had met at Oxford, hosted a get-together at his apartment. My mother begged off, saying she had to drive back to Wheaton to teach a class the next day. That cleared the way for my father to bring his new girlfriend, a high-school teacher from New Jersey named Janice. Alexis and I had met her several times over dinners at the Hunan Balcony on Broadway, and she had invited us to a fiftieth birthday party she threw for my father in Piscataway where she handed out tapes of his favorite jazz vocals in little plastic boxes with the title "Nailing It!" Janice didn't seem as cerebral as other women who had dated my father, and with her blow-dried blond hair and tall, curvy figure, she struck me as almost a caricature of his "type." But she was friendly, in a brassy sort of way, and was good about reminding him to stay in touch with his family.

The day after our wedding, Alexis and I flew to Italy for a three-week honeymoon. We used up all of our vacation time and had to work for the rest of the summer. Before I knew it, it was the first week in September, and my father actually called me on the phone to wish me a happy twenty-eighth birthday.

"And I have exciting news!" he said. "Janice and I are getting married! We're planning a December wedding, and we hope you can come."

"That's nice," I said, trying not to betray my surprise.

When I hung up, I told Alexis the news.

"Exactly how long has your father known Janice?" she asked.

"I don't know," I said. "About a year."

"Isn't it awfully soon to be getting married?" she said.

"I can't figure it out," I said. "He's been with all these women since my parents got divorced and he's never married any of them. He lived with Barbara Callaway for fifteen years and they never got married. And now he's marrying someone he just met?"

Alexis arched an eyebrow. "Maybe he's just being competitive with you!" she said. She was half-joking, but the more I thought about it, the more convinced I was that my wife had nailed it.

When I asked my mother, in the course of my reporting, about her behavior at my wedding, she insisted that she *had* been very happy for me. She had had the blue dress she wore made especially for the occasion, and had even taken dancing lessons, and she arrived determined to "be a respectable mother of the bridegroom." But she confessed to being uneasy when she saw my father.

"Were you still angry at him?" I asked.

"No, not anymore," she said. "I just didn't want to be charmed by him."

It had taken her twenty years, but she had finally come to see how she too, unwittingly, had contributed to the death spiral of their marriage. Returning from our year in France in the mid-1970s, she had found the Wheaton campus abuzz with talk of feminism and the insights of books like *The Feminine Mystique* and *The Female Eunuch* and, a few years later, *The Women's Room*. Reading those works and discussing them with her friends, she came to see how weak she had been, how easily bullied, not because she was a bad wife, in the way she had blamed herself at the time, but because of what the social code of the day made her believe was expected of a woman. She had been the older one, the tenured professor, the world traveler, and yet she had allowed my father to call all the shots, to convince her that his career and his whims and his appetites came first. She hadn't been able to stand up to him then, but now, in her own small way, on my wedding day, she was asserting her right not to be influenced by him.

That summer, she traveled to Kenya on a trip sponsored by Wheaton, which had broadened its push toward a "balanced curriculum" to the next phase of encouraging the cross-cultural study of women. The Third World Conference on Women happened to be taking place in Nairobi, and she proudly attended several sessions. She took a bus ride from the capital all the way to the eastern coast, and the sights and smells and sounds of the African countryside brought back her first childhood memories of Madagascar, as well as her five months in Nigeria when I was a toddler, although this time she was content to be experiencing it all on her own terms and not under my father's headstrong sway.

At the time, I too associated the attribute of charm with my father, and as a result I distrusted it. All too often, I had seen the way he turned it on with people he barely knew, while neglecting his own family and oldest friends. I was determined not to be like him in that way, to the point of seeing my own reserve and aloofness as a moral virtue. But in the years after my wedding, my hard-hearted views on the subject began to soften, at least in part because of two indelible figures whom I met through my work at *Newsweek*.

One—ironically enough, since I had written a college thesis about him—was Henry Kissinger. By the late 1980s, I had become *Newsweek*'s business editor and was busy overseeing the magazine's coverage of Black Monday, the insider-trading scandals, and the savings and loan crisis. But the Communist empire was also collapsing, and when Kissinger was signed up to write several essays a year for the magazine, I became his editor.

In those days, the former Secretary of State was still an incorrigible technophobe. He would only compose his essays in longhand and insisted that his assistant type them up because he didn't trust anyone else to read his handwriting. When we worked together, I had to engage in my own version of shuttle diplomacy: I waited for faxes from his assistant and then traveled to wherever Kissinger was to go over the story line by line. We would meet at his office on Park Avenue, at his home on the East River, at hotels on the road or at his country estate in Connecticut. Once we were driving there from Manhattan and editing a piece in the backseat of his chauffeured Mercedes, when he asked the driver to pull over at a soft ice cream stand. "You musn't tell Nancy!" he said in his Germanic baritone. "My wife thinks I need to lose weight!"

There was always grumbling at the magazine when Kissinger

pieces were scheduled, by staffers who thought he was getting too much space or who still blamed him for Vietnam and Cambodia. But I enjoyed working with him, and I was impressed by his ability to see around historical corners: As soon as the Berlin Wall fell in 1989, he predicted that it would lead to German reunification, and he made a very early forecast of the breakup of the Soviet Union. It was also amusing to watch him disarm his fact-checker, Nancy Stadtman, an unreconstructed 1960s liberal. "Nancy, I know you think that I am a war criminal, but you are a remarkable woman!" he would tell her flirtatiously when she spotted an error in his copy.

Getting a close-up look at how Kissinger exercised his charm with everyone from my colleagues to heads of state he invited to dinner to his beloved dogs, I realized how calculated it was, but also how effective. I could see why it had made him such a masterful diplomat, quite apart from his analytical powers. I also observed its effect from the point of view of the recipients, who were perfectly capable of understanding that they were being manipulated and still taking pleasure in it. After all, I thought, if Kissinger could light up Nancy Stadtman's day, didn't that make his flattery not just an instrument of control but also an act of generosity?

The second charmster was Nelson Mandela. From my early days on the international desk, I had chronicled the violent protests over apartheid in South Africa, so when Mandela was finally released from prison in 1990, Rick Smith asked me to write the cover story. When Mandela emerged, he looked old and gray and frail, nothing like the youthful figure in the last photo the world had seen of him. "Damn!" Rick said. "That's not a great cover!" But as soon as Mandela walked through the prison gate, he raised his fist in a Black Power salute as a delirious crowd shouted "*Amandla! Awethu!*" Rick told the art editor to mock up that photo with the word "Free!" not stopping to think that people around the world would see that cover line and assume that *Newsweek* was being given away for nothing.

Four years later, when Mandela ran for president, I visited South Africa and interviewed several of his top aides, and in 1998 I finally got to meet the great man himself, when he came to New York to address the U.N. General Assembly. He summoned a delegation from *Newsweek* and the *Washington Post* to his suite in the Plaza Hotel. Breakfast was served, even though it was ten-thirty in the morning. Mandela pushed away his plate of eggs, but Katharine Graham kept pushing it back toward him.

"No thank you, madam," he said, looking a bit perturbed.

"I want to make sure you have a chance to eat," she said.

"I already have, thank you," he replied. "But allow me to say, madam, that perhaps it is you who should be eating! You know, in my country we like women to have a little meat on their bones!"

There were nervous glances all around the table, but Mrs. Graham roared with laughter. I thought to myself that only Nelson Mandela could get away with saying something like that to the owner of the Washington Post Company!

During his stay, Richard Holbrooke, the American ambassador to the United Nations, invited Alexis and me to a dinner in Mandela's honor at his official residence in the Waldorf Astoria towers. The guest list included some of the most powerful journalists, politicians, diplomats, and financial leaders in New York, so I was startled and grateful when Holbrooke and his wife, Kati Marton, seated me at Mandela's table, within chatting distance of him. I was never so happy to talk about how I had lived in Nigeria as a child and grown up listening to my parents' Miriam Makeba records, and how my father had taken on the modernization zealots in the 1960s with his theories about the politics of tradition.

"Your father was corrrect!" Mandela said, fluttering his *rs* in the South African fashion. "This is what I confrront to this day in South Afrrica!"

At the end of the meal, I did something I almost never allowed myself to do while on the job as a journalist: I asked for his autograph. I told him that it was for my kids.

"I cannot, not herre," he said. "If they see me, I will have to sign autogrraphs for everryone in the rroom."

I told him that I understood and assumed that would be the end of it. But ten minutes later, as the guests were drinking coffee in the living room, one of the president's aides approached me and said that "Madiba" wanted to see me privately. He escorted me to the library, where Mandela handed me a dinner menu inscribed with his signature.

"You are not to tell anyone, or I shall be into terrrible trrouble!" he said with a wry, dimpled smile that I realized seemed not unfamiliar to me.

My father and Janice were married in the Kirkpatrick Chapel on the Rutgers campus, a nineteenth-century Romanesque church built under the direction of Henry Janeway Hardenbergh, the architect who later designed the Waldorf Astoria hotel and the Dakota building on Central Park West. Seeing the venue on the invitation, Alexis and I assumed there would be hundreds of guests. But when we arrived with my brother, we were surprised to find only about a dozen people sitting in the front pews. As the vows were exchanged, Paul and I eyed the fellow standing next to my father, a squat white gentleman with a comb-over whom we had never seen before. After the ceremony, my father introduced us to Nat Pallone, his "closest friend." I looked him up later and discovered that he was a Rutgers psychologist with an expertise in substance abusers. Paul and I glanced sideways at each other and didn't have to say what we were both thinking: Leave it to Dad to choose someone he's only known for a few years as his best man rather than one of us!

We visited Piscataway about a month later, and he showed off an ornate white wedding album that Janice had already assembled. I leafed through the pages and noticed pictures of a wedding reception at the Rutgers Faculty Club that seemed to have had hundreds of guests. Why hadn't we been invited to that event? I wondered. And what did my father have against all these supposed friends that so few of them had been at the wedding itself? I also didn't see any sign of Barbara Callaway, who was still a Rutgers dean. In our interviews, she told me that she only learned about the wedding on the day of the reception, when a colleague asked why she wasn't going. After all their years together, she couldn't help feeling that my father was trying to get back at her by marrying another woman so soon after their breakup and that his decision to hold a reception at the Faculty Club with all their friends and not invite her was "a pretty big f-you."

"How old do you think Janice is?" Alexis asked my brother and me as we drove home from the church service. We all agreed that it was hard to tell: midforties, maybe older, maybe younger. Alexis kidded us that she might be young enough to have a baby and that we might soon have a step-sibling, a prospect that neither Paul nor I found very amusing. A couple of months later, we learned that Alexis herself was pregnant, and she kept teasing me with the possibility that my father would try to compete with me in that arena too. So when he called to invite us to Easter dinner and announced that he had "big news," Alexis thought her suspicions had been confirmed.

"Janice iiisss . . ." he began theatrically.

I knew it! Alexis thought.

". . . crocheting her head off!" he said.

When we arrived in New Jersey for Easter weekend, Janice presented us with a beautifully crocheted white baby blanket. She served an elaborate holiday feast with ham and mint jelly and led us to a guest bedroom that she had redecorated with flowery furniture. She showed us the wall calendar in the kitchen that she had marked with all the family birthdays. "Syl and I can't wait to circle the birth date of our first grandchild!" she gushed.

The summer passed and September came, and for the first time in decades I was expecting my father to call me on my birthday. But he didn't. I knew that he and Janice had gone to his cabin in Maine for the month of August, and I wondered if they hadn't returned yet. Then two more weeks went by and I figured that he must be back at Rutgers for the fall semester, so I called his house and, sure enough, he was there.

"I've been meaning to get in touch," he said sheepishly. "It's been a difficult few months. Janice and I are getting divorced."

"Divorced?" I said. "So soon? What happened?"

"I won't go into details," he said. "Suffice it to say that Maine made some fundamental incompatibilities apparent."

"I'm sorry to hear it," I said. "Are you okay? Would you like us to visit? We still have a couple of weeks before the baby is due."

"I don't want to trouble you," he said, with more than a hint of self-pity.

"Don't be silly," I said. "We'll come this weekend."

This time, the guest room in Piscataway was empty, except for a bed frame and a mattress. Every trace of Janice and her florid furniture was gone, as though she had never even been a part of my father's life.

"That must have been some month in Maine!" Alexis said.

"Yeah, like *The Shining*," I joked, referring to the Stanley Kubrick thriller where Jack Nicholson goes crazy in a remote hotel and starts terrorizing his wife with an ax.

In my mind's eye, I actually imagined a more emotional form of torture. To begin with, Janice was enough of a suburban queen bee that she must have hated the primitive little cabin on the lake. Once she was alone with my father in the wilderness, she probably got a heavy dose of his mood swings. When he was mad, I pictured him lording his erudition over her and inflaming her intellectual insecurities. But unlike my mother and Barbara Callaway, I imagined her giving it right back to him, which must have made him only more combative. In the end, she just didn't care enough about his good side, his brilliance and his soulfulness, to put up with it. In Barbara's words, "She didn't have Syl in her heart." Or maybe it wasn't that complicated. Maybe she was simply every bit as unforgiving as he was, and they had each said things in anger that the other decided was the last straw. Whatever it was, my father didn't want to discuss the breakup when we visited him, so we passed the weekend talking about our plans for the baby, and I kept my suppositions to myself.

Rachel Eva Whitaker was born at a quarter of three in the afternoon on October 28, 1986. She was "sunny side up" in the womb, so Alexis had to push for two hours to turn her around before she could be pulled out with forceps. When she finally emerged, Alexis told the nurse to give her to me to hold. She was a Whitaker in size—nine pounds, one ounce—and you could already see how pretty she was going to be, with her perfectly proportioned face and wide-set eyes that immediately met my gaze. "Hi, Rachel. Hi, Rachel. Hi, Rachel," I kept saying over and over again. Alexis didn't have an amniocentesis, so we hadn't known the sex of the baby ahead of time, but I told her that I hoped it was a girl. It was partly because I had never had a sister, but I also wanted to be a better father than mine had been to me, and I thought it might be easier with a daughter.

"Make a wish for her!" the nurse said.

I closed my eyes and thought: *Can I have two wishes? Can I wish that she will have a long and happy life? And can I wish that we will all have a long and happy life together?*

Rachel was two weeks overdue, and my mother was so excited about her imminent arrival that she came down to New York from Norton two weekends in a row in hopes of being present for her birth. When I called her with the news, she was overjoyed and said she would be back again as soon as her classes were over. My father sounded pleased too, particularly when he learned that we had given Rachel a middle name beginning with "E" in honor of Grandmother Edith. But he never offered to come to the hospital or to our place once we brought the baby home, and at the time it didn't even occur to me that he might.

Several weeks later we took the baby to Piscataway, and after that I kept hearing from his friends how much he bragged about his granddaughter. After Janice left him, he had reestablished contact with Barbara Callaway, and she sent me a letter saying that "Syl says Rachel is just the most beautiful baby he's ever seen!" Even so, I was always the one who had to take the initiative to involve him in our life. Like a lot of young Manhattan couples, Alexis and I sometimes spent our weekends looking at apartments, fantasizing that we might some day be able to afford something larger than our tiny one-bedroom where Rachel slept in a maid's room behind the bathroom. One Sunday, we saw an ad for a two-bedroom in a building on West 96th Street where one of my father's college friends lived, and, knowing how much he loved house shopping, I invited him to come into Manhattan and look at it with us.

"So what will you do with this room?" he asked Alexis as the real estate agent showed us the second bedroom.

Alexis pointed down at the stroller containing our six-month-old daughter. "We thought it would make a nice room for Rachel," she said.

I thought my father might be embarrassed, but he laughed at his self-absorption. "Oh yes, of course!" he said. "I guess I was thinking it would be a nice guest room for her granddad when he stayed over!"

As it happened, there weren't any of those sleepover visits. A few months later, he phoned to say that he had accepted an offer from the University of Southern California to return to L.A. as a dean of social sciences. I couldn't help but take the news personally, after all the efforts I had made to forgive the past and to try to include him in my life and the life of his granddaughter. Why didn't it surprise me that he would choose another impressive job over staying close to us? Well, so be it, I thought cynically. I had my own family now, no thanks to him, and if he didn't want to remain part of it, that was his problem!

He told me that he was selling his "millionaire's house" and buying a condo in Marina Del Ray. I looked it up on the map and saw that it was a neighborhood just south of his old stomping grounds in Venice. I imagined that he was hoping to lure new young girlfriends there, just as he had done when he was a dashing professor in his twenties. But after a year of reporting, I saw a more complicated picture. In his mind, New Jersey must have come to represent the worst years of his alcoholism and his breakup with Barbara and his disastrous marriage to Janice, and taking the job in California must have seemed like a way to make a fresh start, or perhaps to wind the movie of his life backward and start over again at the part where he moved to the funky bungalow by the Pacific Ocean.

In the winter of 1990, Alexis became pregnant again, and by the summer her belly was swollen and her back was aching and she badly needed a break from the heat of the city. We went on vacation to the coolness of the Catskill Mountains, but we had to rush back when Saddam Hussein's army invaded Kuwait and President George H. W. Bush started laying the groundwork for the Persian Gulf War. Alexis, who was the national affairs editor of Newsweek at the time, would help supervise the coverage up until a week before her due date, while I drove to Connecticut to edit another piece by Henry Kissinger.

Although we wouldn't know it until months later, big changes were also afoot at the magazine. Katharine Graham was preparing to turn over control of the Washington Post Company to her son Donald, and Don was about to promote Rick Smith to run the business side of Newsweek, leaving his deputy, Maynard Parker, in charge of the editorial operation. Two weeks after the end of Operation Desert Storm, the changes would be announced and Maynard would take me out to lunch and ask me to be one of his assistant managing editors. Thirteen years after John Dotson had told me I might become a senior editor if I played my cards right, I would be Newsweek's first black "Wallenda," the nickname that had long been given to the magazine's top editors, supposedly because of the editorial gymnastics required for the job but also, given the history of turmoil at its highest ranks, because of the difficulty of staying aloft on that high wire.

But I didn't know that yet on my birthday, September 7, when our son, Matthew Edward Whitaker, was born. Alexis's doctor had examined her just a few hours before and predicted that he would weigh around eight pounds, but he was another typical Whitaker: nine pounds, twelve ounces. He was long and lean and already had the worry lines in his forehead that I had inherited from my father and passed on to him.

She had had an amnio this time, so we knew that it was going to be a boy. I felt ready to be a father to a son, and I took it as a good omen that we would share the same birthday.

"Happy birthday, sweetheart!" Alexis said to me as the labor nurse handed her the baby.

The nurse thought she was delirious. "It's not *his* birthday, dear!" she said. "It's the baby's birthday!"

When it came to make a wish, I said out loud: "I hope our children will be close." It had always been a source of sadness that it hadn't happened for my brother and me. He had moved to San Diego, where he was building what would become a successful private practice as a psychologist. We saw each other at family holidays and events and got along fine, but then we never stayed in touch. At the time, I thought it might be because we both had such painful memories of our childhood, but it wasn't until twenty years later, as I was conducting my family research, that we finally talked about it. I reminded Paul of how much we fought as kids. He nodded and said, "You know, they say in family systems theory that when siblings fight, it's because they are angry at their parents."

We had given Matthew his middle name in honor of Edouard Theis, his heroic great-grandfather. And three months after he was born, all eight of Grandpapa's daughters arrived in New York to commemorate the fiftieth anniversary of the voyage that brought them to America. The Unitarian Service Committee was holding a celebration to honor the memory of Martha Sharp, the minister's wife who took the refugee children aboard the *Excambion,* and all the surviving voyagers had been invited. We all attended a dinner at a fancy East Side hotel, and Alexis and I took the eight sisters and their husbands to the Statue of Liberty and Ellis Island, to revisit their first moments on American soil.

When we invited everyone to our house for dinner, Marianne brought a pair of blue overalls she had sewn for Matthew and all the sisters passed him around, making the funny faces they had learned from Grandpapa and cooing over the latest member of the Theis clan. Looking back at the time when I first got to know all of my aunts as a skinny, self-conscious teenager in France, I had always dwelled on my struggles with the language and my sense of satisfaction in finally mastering French. But now I see that I was also learning something even more important that year: that not all families are destined to be unhappy.

17

My father retired, abruptly, at the age of sixty.

When he had first moved back to California in the late '80s, Alexis and Rachel and I had visited him each year, and he appeared to be doing well. He had bought a striking if somewhat odd condo in Marina Del Ray with five tiny floors stacked one on top of the other, leading up to a roof deck overlooking the ocean that he called his *"pièce de résistance."* He threw a party on the deck to introduce us to his colleagues at USC, among them a drama professor named Anna Deavere Smith, who engaged our curly-haired one-and-a-half-year-old as though she was a teenager. We played tennis at a club he had joined, and he no longer sulked or called foot faults. "I'm afraid your old man's only a threat in doubles these days," he admitted. As usual, he had new restaurant finds: a bistro with an outdoor patio near the beach and a soul food place in a strip mall that served the best collard greens and chitterlings I had tasted since visiting Grand-mother in Pittsburgh as a child. When I visited in the early 1990s, he talked excitedly about another new friend: Jane Goodall, the British

expert on African primates. "I picked her up at the airport for a talk at the university," he said, "and we instantly became so engrossed in conversation that I got completely lost in traffic."

But when I went back a year after that, something had changed. He was hanging around his condo all day rather than going to campus. He blamed it on the terrible L.A. traffic and said that he had arranged to do most of his work from home. A few months later, he came to New York and invited me for coffee at the Intercontinental hotel with a colleague whom he described as being "on my side." I sensed from their code words and eye rolling that they shared common enemies within the USC administration. In another conversation, he made an acerbic crack about being "the master of what little I survey." Still, I was surprised when I took him out to celebrate his sixtieth birthday in February 1995, and he told me that he planned to accept an early retirement package and leave L.A. at the end of the school year.

"Is everything okay?" I asked. "Is this your decision?"

"Suffice it to say it's by mutual agreement," he replied curtly, clearly not wanting to discuss the details.

USC records show that he was one of five university professors at the time, so if he had become fed up with administrative turf battles he could have retreated into a leisurely life of teaching. But in his own mind he must have been at the end of his rope and impatient to leave Los Angeles, because it was a terrible time to sell his condo. "My place on the water is underwater," he quipped as we took a stroll along the boardwalk in Marina Del Ray. California was mired in a real estate slump, and the property had lost so much value that it was worth less than the balance on his mortgage, so he had decided to walk away from it. He told me that he planned to take his retirement pension and split his time between two small properties he owned: the cabin in Maine, which he had purchased from Stuart Schaar some years back, and a little condo next to the airport runway in Palm Springs that he had bought as a rental property.

"If I can't live in the manner to which I've become accustomed," he said, with one of his mordant play on words, "then I've decided to become accustomed to the manner in which I can live."

I tried to sound sympathetic, but it all struck me as rather pathetic. I felt ashamed that my father would stick the bank with his condo, and I couldn't help seeing early retirement as a disappointing end to his once meteoric career. It didn't occur to me, at least not then, that it might also have been his prideful way of exercising some final control over a life that had been so out of control for so long.

"There's one other thing," he said as we stood in his alleyway, next to a huge black Dumpster. "I haven't told this to anyone else, but lately I find myself fearing that I will die alone."

The confession startled me. Through all my father's ups and downs, I had never thought of him as being without female companionship.

"There's no one in your life right now?" I asked.

"Sadly, no," he said. "And no immediate prospects."

"Well, maybe you'll meet someone in Palm Springs," I said.

"Perhaps . . ." he replied quietly.

Then suddenly the cloud of self-pity passed, and he broke into a dimpled smile.

"Of course, you know the joke about Palm Springs, don't you?"

"No," I said.

"In Palm Springs, it's always the Gay Nineties, because everyone there is either gay or in their nineties."

I had no idea that a year later, while my father was living in his little condo behind the airport in the desert, President Clinton would be urged to name him the next U.S. ambassador to Nigeria.

The suggestion came from John Lewis, the Georgia congressman and brave veteran of the civil rights movement. "Syl Whitaker is one of a very small handful of the country's most eminent authorities on Nigerian affairs," Lewis wrote the recently reelected president in a letter dated December 31, 1996. He went on to tout some accomplishments that I already knew, like the fact that "his book, *The*

Politics of Tradition, is regarded among students of Nigeria everywhere as a masterwork." But he also cited achievements that were news to me: my father's role in raising $4 million for international programs at Rutgers; his tour of five African countries for the World Bank; his co-editorship of a tome on U.S-Soviet cooperation in Africa with Anatoly Gromyko, the son of Andrei Gromyko, the former Soviet foreign minister. In 1992, I learned, he was a member of a delegation that monitored elections in Angola after the bloody civil war. He wrote a final report and presided over a press conference that declared the vote free and fair, despite threats from Jonas Savimbi, the defeated rebel leader, to kill any foreigners who helped ratify the victory of his opponent.

Of course, Congressman Lewis made no mention of some of the less exemplary circumstances involved in my father's career moves as he listed all of the "leading universities" where he had taught. "As U.S. Ambassador," he wrote Clinton, "he may represent perhaps our country's next best chance to forge an improved era in the presently clouded relations between the U.S. and Nigeria, the African country that is perhaps most vital to our interests and to the future of the U.S. role in Africa."

He didn't get the job, which nine months later went to a career diplomat named William Twaddell. He must have known that it would be a long shot, but I suspect that the rejection stung anyway, and it may have explained why he seemed so subdued when I visited him in Palm Springs. Except for attending an occasional academic conference or co-authoring a paper on Africa with his old friend Dick Sklar, he had settled into the passive life of a single retiree: playing senior doubles at a nearby public tennis court in the morning, napping in the afternoon, and spending his evenings watching football and basketball on a huge TV set that he had bought at a salvage store called Mardens in Maine and shipped across the country.

Yet it would be in that solitary, languid period that I would spend more time alone with him than I ever had before. As it happened, *Newsweek* sponsored a pro tennis tournament that was held in the resort town of Indian Wells, half an hour outside Palm Springs, and every year I was invited there to give a news briefing for our advertisers. Each spring I would take the long cross-country flight, and my father would greet me at the airport. I would arrange to get him tickets to the tennis, and he would come to *Newsweek*'s skybox and schmooze amiably with Rick Smith and his salesmen and their corporate clients. He would even nod and laugh at their golf stories, despite the fact that he had always resented the game, having earned pocket money as a teenager by shagging balls at an exclusive country club outside of Pittsburgh where black people weren't allowed to play.

We would go out to dinner at his favorite little restaurants in town, or he would cook dinner in his dinette kitchen, serving up one of his spicy stews with Diet Cokes or nonalcoholic beer. He would ask about Alexis and his grandchildren, but mostly he wanted to know what was going on at *Newsweek,* about the personalities and politics behind the scenes. In the past, I might have deflected his interest, wanting to keep my career to myself, but I found that I welcomed it now that I was helping to run the magazine and had so few other people in whom I could confide.

Ironically, the figure we discussed most was Maynard Parker, who by this time had named me his managing editor. It was ironic because Maynard had become a sort of professional father figure and because he resembled my father in many ways. Although he couldn't have looked more different—he was slender and balding and as WASP-ish as his name sounded—he shared some of the same contradictions. He could be warm and charismatic one minute, cold and judgmental the next. He had a way of getting under your skin, making you love him or hate him or both. And like my father, he was a product of his own creation who had lifted himself from modest circumstances with a sense of ambition and adventure but remained haunted by the insecurities that so often dog self-invented people.

He grew up a pudgy, middle-class kid from the L.A. suburbs who worked on the *Daily* at Stanford and wrote an earnest thesis called

"The Negro in New Rochelle" as a graduate student in journalism at Columbia. It wasn't until he moved to Asia in the early 1960s that he transformed himself into the Maynard Parker of legend. After army duty in Thailand and a stint with *Look* magazine, he went to work for *Newsweek* as Saigon bureau chief. He was known for dressing in suits and shirts tailored in Hong Kong, ordering up helicopters and speedboats and junk yachts at the drop of a hat, and throwing around his own patented military lingo to motivate his troops. He commanded reporters to "scramble the jets" on big stories and accused them of "leaning on shovels" if he didn't think they were working hard enough. But his reporters worshiped him, particularly the scruffy but intrepid war correspondents he hired and, later, the talented women he promoted out of the library and secretarial pool.

Moving to the front office in New York in the early 1970s, he remained a reporter's editor. After the Graham family purchased *Newsweek* in 1961, it had challenged its larger rival *Time* by being less stuffy and conservative and quicker to cover the civil rights, antiwar, and women's movements. But once *Time* started to change with the times, *Newsweek* needed something extra to set it apart, and Maynard provided it: a relentless drive to jump on stories faster, dig up more scoops, offer juicier details. While other "Wallendas" went to bars at night, he took home a weathered briefcase bulging with files to make sure that the best reporting from the field made its way into the magazine. Every week he bounced copy and ripped apart layouts right up until deadline. As much as anyone, he had been responsible for keeping *Newsweek* a "hot book," as they said on Madison Avenue, through the 1980s and 1990s.

But he also had a weakness for secrecy that repeatedly got him into trouble. In 1983 he conducted clandestine negotiations to acquire U.S. rights to secret journals supposedly kept by Adolf Hitler during World War II. When the deal fell through, he pushed for a cover story on "The Hitler Diaries" anyway. The journals turned out to be bogus, and the black eye suffered by the magazine was one of the reasons that the Grahams passed him over when they promoted

Rick Smith. Thirteen years later, he landed in hot water again when our political writer Joe Klein wrote a roman à clef about Bill Clinton called *Primary Colors* and published it under the pen name "Anonymous." Klein denied to me and everyone else that he was the author, but I had my suspicions, since the writing sounded so much like Joe.

"If Klein wrote it, I bet you know," I told Maynard one day. "You're the one person he would have told."

He pursed his lips and stayed mum.

In fact, Klein had confided in him, and Maynard played along with the ruse, even when *Newsweek* published speculation about other potential authors. Eventually a Vassar professor using word-pattern analysis unmasked the real "Anonymous," and Maynard came under withering attack, including a *New York Times* editorial that concluded that the "behavior of [Klein and Parker] violates the fundamental contract between journalists, serious publications and their readers." He didn't lose his job, partly because Don Graham had no intention of taking direction from the *New York Times,* but it cost him his annual bonus and another blow to his reputation.

At his best, Maynard could be unforgettably kind and generous. He would come to the aid of colleagues at times of illness or adversity and urge them to "keep your helmet on." He was devoted to two young sons by a former *Newsweek* editor named Susan Fraker and a daughter by his first wife, and Alexis and I were among the working parents whom he encouraged to make time for school visits and other kids' events. But once I began working alongside him as his deputy, I saw a less attractive side. He "edited by byline," as they said in the hallways, reflexively dismissing the work of any reporter or writer who was in his doghouse. He was incapable of communicating bad news and would reassign stories he was unhappy with rather than confronting the people who had worked on them. His high-handedness had started to create a morale crisis in the ranks, and I was caught in the middle: listening to Maynard complain about the staff, and the staff complain about him.

My father chuckled as I recounted my predicament. "You expect

Parker to be fair and rational, but that's not human nature," he said. "Human nature is to abuse power. You see that in Africa, where there are so few constraints against it. Every soldier at a checkpoint feels free to wave his gun at you. Every customs official feels entitled to shake you down for a bribe."

"So what does that mean for me?" I asked. "What can I learn from Africa?"

"Well, first you can learn that the question is not why people abuse power, but what checks are in place to prevent them from doing so."

"Um hum," I agreed.

"Hmmph," he murmured, and I could tell that he was formulating a deeper thought.

"Look," he said finally, "you also have to realize that most people who abuse power don't think they're doing it. They've justified it based on their own view of the world."

"Um hum . . ."

"An old friend of mine had an expression: Everyone has their own set of jokes. It was a metaphor, but what it meant was that every person, every tribe, has their own traditions and prejudices and ways of defending their actions. You may not think their jokes are funny, but you're not going to convince them of that. And if you want to operate in their world, you have to learn their jokes. So by all means try to be normative, as we political scientists like to say. Do your best to be fair and rational and hope that it will set an example and encourage others to respond in kind. But remember: That's just *your* set of jokes. And don't be surprised if the world doesn't always respond in kind. Because then the joke will be on you."

As I listened to my father's wise advice, so at odds with his own thin-skinned behavior, I couldn't help thinking of all the times that I could have used it when he wasn't around. But I was grateful to get a dose of it now, and I would come to appreciate it even more during the turbulent events that were about to unfold at *Newsweek*.

• • •

It started with the death of Princess Diana. I was filling in for Maynard while he was on vacation in the late summer of 1997, and I had
moved up the magazine's Saturday deadline by a day to give everyone
a long Labor Day weekend. Alexis and I had taken our children to the
country, but when we heard the news of the fatal car crash in Paris,
we rushed back to Manhattan in the middle of the night, bringing
with us a girlfriend of Rachel's who was on a sleepover. The revamped
edition that a skeleton crew put together in the next twelve hours was
a great success, selling more than a million copies on the newsstands,
an all-time record for *Newsweek,* but it also had the effect of making
Maynard even more manic and determined to reestablish his authority once he got back to the office.

In another bid to reassert his command, he convened an offsite
retreat a month later. With his usual flair for the dramatic, he took
the invited group to a resort hotel in Colorado, organized a horseback
ride at sunset, and laid on a Western cookout accompanied by his
favorite pinot noir from Oregon. The next day, after editorial meetings in the morning, he led a hike through the Telluride mountains.
Everyone paired off into twos and threes and got so absorbed in
conversation that they didn't notice when he fell behind. Seeing
people looking back at him, he rushed to catch up. "Got to push
ahead!" he panted.

He didn't know it yet, but his fatigue wasn't a result of the alti-
tude but a symptom of the white blood cells that were multiplying in
his bone marrow and pushing out the healthy red cells that had kept
him so vigorous for fifty-seven years. Once he got back to New York, it
took several weeks of tests to get a clear diagnosis: acute myelogenous
leukemia. His doctors told him that it was a particularly aggressive
form of cancer and that it could kill him in a matter of months if it
wasn't treated immediately.

Finally he called me into his office to tell me what was going on.
He was checking into Sloan-Kettering and opting for the hospital's
most aggressive treatment: a bone-marrow transplant. He was an only
child and would have to use his own stem cells for the operation, but

first he had to undergo three rounds of chemotherapy to cleanse the marrow of cancer.

"You'll have to run the magazine while I'm in the hospital," he said. "But I'll be back between treatments and will stay in touch from Sloan-Kettering."

"Of course," I said. "I'm so sorry, Maynard."

As it turned out, he vastly overestimated how involved he would be able to remain in the magazine over the next eight months. And as he left for the hospital, he took another fateful secret with him.

Six months earlier, Ann McDaniel, *Newsweek*'s Washington bureau chief, had flown on the Delta shuttle to New York to brief Maynard on a highly sensitive matter. Michael Isikoff, our top investigative reporter, had stumbled upon evidence that Bill Clinton may have been having an affair with a White House intern. He didn't know much more, but he was working on corroborating details he had gathered from his sources. Maynard told Ann to keep Mike reporting, but quietly, because he didn't want word to get out that *Newsweek* was digging around for dirt on the president's sex life.

It was a wise precaution, except that he didn't give anyone else a heads-up either. He didn't tell me, his deputy, even after he got sick and knew that I would be running the magazine in his absence. He didn't tell Rick Smith, even though Rick had lectured him about the "no surprises rule" after the Joe Klein debacle. And he didn't tell Don Graham, the owner of the company, the way Ben Bradlee, the legendary former editor of the *Washington Post*, always kept Katharine Graham in the loop when his reporters were unraveling the Watergate scandal or pursuing other stories that might invite retribution.

So when Ann finally called Rick and me on a Thursday morning in mid-January to tell us special prosecutor Ken Starr was questioning a young woman named Monica Lewinsky about her relationship with the president, we had only forty-eight hours to understand the complicated details and decide whether to publish a story that week. During a series of conference calls over the next two days, everyone involved in the deliberations played true to character. Isikoff was the hard-charging reporter, eager to see his scoop in print and privately fuming at the cautious "suits." Rick Smith was the wary publisher, worried that Isikoff had never talked to Lewinsky directly and that his sources had said Clinton told her to lie but had produced only one tape, on which she made no mention of obstruction of justice. McDaniel was the politically artful go-between, trying to follow Rick's lead while not undercutting the reporters in her bureau. Jon Meacham, our young national affairs editor, was the quiet courtroom recorder, remaining silent as he scribbled down details and possible story headlines on a legal pad.

When we finally tracked down Don Graham, he was the booster-ish owner. "Well, congratulations, Mike Isikoff!" he called out heartily over the phone, before telling us that it was our decision but that we shouldn't hesitate to hold off if we weren't certain of all the facts.

I was focused on the sex angle. Based on Clinton's history, I sensed that the story could well be true, but I also thought that it carried a special burden of proof. The reporters in Washington argued that we could run a "Ken Starr story," merely asking why the prosecutor was suddenly investigating Lewinsky. But I thought that no matter how we wrote it, it would be a "sex in the Oval Office" story. That's what people would remember, and they would assume that if we printed the accusation we believed it to be true. Did we have enough to feel confident of that? I kept asking. Without being able to question Lewinsky directly, we were relying on some fairly dubious sources: her gossipy friend Linda Tripp; lawyers for Paula Jones, the Arkansas woman who was suing Clinton for sexual harassment and hoped Lewinsky would bolster her case; and a mysterious book agent named Lucianne Goldberg, who was tied up with right-wing zealots who had been trying to discredit Clinton for years.

"This is the opposite of Woodward and Bernstein," I argued. "They reported pieces of the puzzle, but it took them months to figure out how it all fit together. Mike knows what the whole puzzle looks like, but we're not sure if we can believe all the pieces."

As we were deliberating, I called Maynard at Sloan-Kettering to tell him what was happening. He was weak and groggy from his chemo treatment, so I didn't have the heart to tell him how upset I was that he had kept me in the dark about Isikoff's reporting.

"It's up to you and Rick, but I'll tell you the lesson I've learned," he said. "If the downside outweighs the upside, it's not worth it." He didn't mention the Hitler diaries or Joe Klein, but I sensed the painful memories of those episodes in his answer.

Put that way, it wasn't a terribly difficult choice. The upside, if the story turned out to be true, would be that the magazine would get credit for the biggest story of the year—an unsavory scoop, to be sure, but still a bombshell. The downside would be if we published the story and it turned out to be a "wrongo," as Maynard liked to say. What if Lewinsky was a delusional liar, or Starr dropped his investigation? Then *Newsweek* would be a laughingstock.

We decided to hold off for a week, and the rest, as they say, is history. For two days, Isikoff had been telling his sources that a story might run, and on Saturday night he called them back to say that it wouldn't. The next morning, the Internet tip sheet *Drudge Report* led with an "exclusive" saying that *Newsweek* was sitting on a story about Clinton and Lewinsky. Even though there had never been a written draft, it said that editors had "spiked" the story. By midweek, other news organizations had caught up with the gist of Mike's reporting, and the story broke wide open.

That's when both of my parents phoned me, to see how I was coping with all the harping about *Newsweek's* lost scoop but also to find out what else I could tell them about the scandal.

My mother saw it from a feminist perspective. "Obviously Clinton has no conception of what women are willing to tell each other!" she said.

My father, as usual, was suspicious. He wanted to know if we had reporting on what Hillary Clinton was calling the "vast right-wing conspiracy" that she said had fanned the sex rumors and the legal battles that had kept them alive. "There's such a thing as framing a guilty man," he said.

I kept thinking about my father's question as we scrambled to catch up with a ten-thousand-word version of Isikoff's reporting that appeared in the magazine that week. The following week, we ran another cover story, "The Secret Sex Wars: Inside the Struggle between Clinton and His Enemies," that traced the links between Tripp and Goldberg and Starr and rabid Clinton haters like journalist Ann Coulter and publisher Richard Mellon Scaife. *Newsweek* eventually won an Ellie, the magazine world's equivalent of an Emmy or a Pulitzer Prize, for those two cover stories, but it didn't erase the impression that we had "spiked" the Lewinsky story and that the young managing editor filling in for Maynard Parker lacked *cojones*.

I absorbed the blows and did what I had always done as a boy who had to teach himself to be a man: I reflected on the experience and tried to name my mistakes so that I wouldn't make them again. Publicly, I went on defending the decision not to publish that first week; privately, I concluded that I had been too deferential to my bosses and not confident enough in my own instincts. Although I had traveled many roads in my life, I also realized that I was in new and unfamiliar territory, a place where hard work and good intentions wouldn't always be enough to protect me. I was beginning to see what it was like to be a big media executive in the public eye, and finally understanding what my father meant all those years ago when he warned me, "Beware of what you want, because you might just get it."

Maynard finally returned to *Newsweek* after Labor Day, two months following his bone-marrow transplant, and the troops gathered in the corporate dining room to give him a hero's welcome. Without consulting each other, Rick Smith had bought him a football helmet and I had bought an army helmet, each to evoke the encouragement he always gave others in a time of need: "Keep your helmet on!" He gamely went back to work, but his immune system was shot. He developed an excruciating case of shingles and then came down with pneumonia. At the end of September, he went back into the hospital, and he never came out again.

Shortly before the end, I went one last time to donate blood plate-
lets, and afterward I visited him in the ICU. He was unconscious,
and his swollen body was covered with tubes. "I'm sorry, Maynard," I
said, over and over again, as tears poured down my face. I was sorry
for him, sorry for his wife and children, sorry for the magazine, sorry
for all the critical things I had ever said about him, sorry that I didn't
have a chance to say goodbye. . . .

He died on a Friday, fittingly, as we were closing another issue
of the magazine. The next week, more than a thousand mourners
filled the pews of the Church of the Heavenly Rest on upper Fifth
Avenue for his funeral. In his eulogy, Rick joked that Maynard would
have loved the sight of all the expense account cars parked outside.
His wife, Susan, spoke about his love for his children, his dogs, and
his summer home in Oregon, and by the time she was finished there
wasn't a dry eye in the cathedral.

Several weeks later, Rick asked me to lunch in the company dining room and offered me the job of editor. He asked what I thought
of naming Ann McDaniel and Jon Meacham as co-managing editors.
Both had always been closer to Maynard and to each other than to
me, but I valued Ann's talent for administration and Jon's copyedit-
ing skills, and given everything we had been through together during
Maynard's illness, I agreed that it made sense to form a unity government.

When I called my parents that night, my mother responded with
kind but reserved good wishes. My father sounded proud but pensive,
as though he had been thinking ahead to this day for much longer
than I had.

"Your college graduation prediction came true," he said.

"I suppose," I said, feeling a bit annoyed that he would remind me
of my youthful presumptuousness.

"So you'll be *Newsweek*'s first black editor," he said. "Are you ready
for all the attention and expectations that will come with that?"

Until then, I hadn't really thought about how the outside world
might react if I were promoted. In fact, I didn't even have a publicity

photo on file, and the next day I hurriedly arranged to have one taken. As my father predicted, the words "first African-American" were at the top of the stories that ran in the *New York Times*, the *Wall Street Journal*, and on the Associated Press wire. Over and over again, I found myself telling media reporters that I was proud of that racial first, but that my goal was to the best editor of *Newsweek* I could be, period.

When I flew to Palm Springs for the *Newsweek* tennis tournament, my father threw a party in my honor at his condo. A local caterer laid out a picnic on his lawn, and high-school students played classical music. He invited his tennis buddies and other local friends as well as Rick Smith, Jon Meacham, and some of the *Newsweek* salesmen he had gotten to know at Indian Wells. The sky was overcast but dry, and no planes landed or took off on the airport runway to ruin the atmosphere. I was happy to shake hands and take pictures and give my father *nachas*, as they say in Yiddish, but I couldn't help feel that he was basking in glory for which he didn't deserve much credit.

"Most of your colleagues seem to wish you well," he told me as the party was breaking up.

"Most?" I said.

"Just remember what Shakespeare said: 'Uneasy lies the head that wears the crown.'"

"Meaning what?" I said.

"No leader has only friends."

"All right, Dad . . ." I said, wondering why he was choosing this moment to introduce such a distrustful note. Had someone said something to him? Had he sensed something in talking to one of my colleagues?

That fall, he came east for Rachel's bas mitzvah, and the following spring, he called to say that he wanted me to come over to his place as soon as I arrived in Palm Springs.

"I have something to tell you," he said over lunch. "I have prostate cancer."

"What?" I said. "Since when?"

"It was diagnosed several weeks ago."

"How serious?" I asked.

"Well, they say that for men my age, prostate cancer often advances very gradually. But I seem to have a rather aggressive variety. My doctor says I'm a candidate for surgery, but I gather that has potential side effects which I'm not ready to accept."

I didn't press him on the subject, but it was the first sign that I had detected in years that there might be someone new in his life.

"So what are you going to do?" I asked.

"My doctor wants to get me into a trial that involves radiation and a hormonal drug called Lupron," he said.

"Is there anything I can do?"

"No, I'm in good hands. But you can promise me something: If it ever comes to it, I want to go like Jackie O."

"Huh?"

"Remember when Jackie Kennedy died? She was at home in Manhattan and they said that she went peacefully, surrounded by her family? If you ask me, she chose the time and terms of her death. I think when there was no hope left and the pain got to be too much, they upped the morphine and put her out."

"So what you're asking is . . ."

"I'm not asking you to do anything," he said. "I can take care of myself. I've looked into sources in Mexico. I just want you to know that if something like that ever happens, it was as I wished it."

"Okay, I guess . . ." I said, not knowing whether to conclude that my father was being crazy or profound, or both.

My mother retired, graciously, at the age of seventy-two.

Wheaton College had abolished mandatory retirement a few years earlier, so she could have stayed on even longer. But a young colleague in the French Department was coming up for tenure, and she wanted to clear the way for her appointment. Her right hand had also begun to shake, visibly enough that students noticed when she wrote on the blackboard. Her doctor told her it wasn't Parkinson's but a condition called "essential tremor" that only affected the movement in her hand, but it embarrassed her and she didn't want to cause anyone alarm.

Her last graduation was in 1999, six months after I was named editor of *Newsweek*, and Wheaton's president, Dale Rogers Marshall, invited me to give the commencement address. When I looked out at the seniors, I saw almost as many men as women, the result of the college's decision to go co-ed a decade earlier. At first my mother had opposed the idea because she thought it would negate all the hard work that she and her colleagues had done to create a "balanced curriculum." But when the boys started to arrive, she realized that they, perhaps even more than the girls, would benefit from the efforts to integrate the study of women into all of the college's courses.

From the speaker's podium, I asked my mother to stand up and be applauded, and I thanked the Wheaton community for helping to rescue a divorced single mother with two young boys. "Hillary Clinton says it takes a village to raise a family," I said. "In our case, it took a campus."

When she had first told me she was thinking of retiring, I had spent several restless nights worrying about where she would live. Would she return to France to be near her sisters? Would she want to move to New York to be closer to her grandchildren? But I needn't have worried, since she already had a plan. She told me she was going to move to Providence and get an apartment within walking distance of the Friends Meeting, so that the place where she lived could be as close as possible to her spiritual home.

She was due a modest pension, enough to live on frugally but less than she would have saved if she hadn't had to support my brother and me on her own or hadn't had so much personal stress that it took her three decades to finish her doctorate. During one of their arguments over child support in the 1960s, my father had said that he didn't have the money he owed her then but that sometime in the future he might be able to pay her back. So she asked me what I thought about the idea of trying to collect from him now.

"I don't know about that," I said, trying to be gentle. "I doubt that he will be very receptive. Do you really want to reopen those wounds?"

But she was determined to give it a try, and it had the result I feared. My father didn't even respond to her directly; he had his lawyer write a nasty letter saying he was under no financial obligation to her and was prepared to take legal action if she pursued the matter any further.

"I'm sorry, Mom," I said when she showed me the letter.

"Yes, it's very sad." She sighed. "I don't know why Syl has to be like that. But I needed to try, if only for my sense of pride."

She moved to Providence and lived a quiet life of solitary retirement until, a decade later, she made a trip to Pennsylvania to donate Grandpapa's papers to the Swarthmore College Peace Collection. On the way, she visited her old friend Trudy Enders, who was widowed and had recently moved into a Quaker retirement community near the Delaware River. She enjoyed the visit so much that she e-mailed me afterward to suggest that it might be time for her to move there too. And so, at age eighty-four, she started making plans to end her life in the company of her oldest friend in the world, the one she had first met in the "Incubator for monkey eggs" when they were both a year old.

18

Her Chinese name was "Hsiu-Li," which sounded phonetically like "Shirley," so that's what he called her. She was tiny, especially next to him, with delicate bones, a round face, and short black hair. I discovered that they first met in the early 1990s, when he was thinking about retiring to Palm Springs and wandered into her little restaurant in town. He loved the food and was struck by her energy and friendliness, so he did what came naturally: He started making conversation. In her broken English, she told him her life story, how she had come to America from Taiwan as a divorced single mother, bringing her two boys, James and Jason, and had opened a business on her own.

Then one day, she wasn't there. He went back, night after night, but no Shirley, and he worried that she had gone for good. But she was just visiting relatives in Taiwan, and when she returned he was overjoyed and relieved and realized that he was in love. He declared his affections, and she returned them. She moved into his condo, and he no longer had to cook for himself or watch sports alone. She served him Chinese meals with multiple courses from a rotating platter in the little dining area, sat with him while he rooted for his USC Trojans and Pittsburgh Steelers on the huge TV set, and stayed up playing poker with him when he couldn't sleep. Unlike other women he had been with, he never verbally baited or bullied or berated her, because there was no point; as an old friend familiar with those tendencies put it to me, "He couldn't reach her in that way."

Eventually she started spending summers with him in Maine, which is how she came to accompany him to the airport in Portland when I arrived for a visit with my family in August 2000. It was late on a Sunday morning, and he had organized a brunch to introduce us to their friends. It was at another of his finds, a soul food restaurant called the Freedom Cafe in Waterville, where he had been tickled to find the tastes and smells of his childhood and soon became close with the owners. Everyone was very nice, and the fried chicken and sweet potato pie were delicious, but there was something about the whole production that bothered me. I felt like he was showing us off to his friends, and to Shirley, as his Successful Son and his Attractive Daughter-in-Law and their Adorable Children, while he was the doting Patriarch of the Family, which of course is not at all the role that he had played in real life.

I grew more irritable when we reached his cabin in Canaan. He had the rest of the day all mapped out for us: We were going to watch sports, then go fishing. I asked if we could tune in to golf—it was the last day of the PGA Championship, and Tiger Woods was in the lead—but he sniffed that he hadn't ordered golf as part of his satellite TV package because it held no interest for him. I was left to monitor the tournament on his computer, and it went into a playoff just as he announced that it was time to go out on the water. I asked if we could wait, but he declared petulantly that we would miss sunset over the lake. He pouted and said that he would go alone with the kids. Minutes later, I looked out the window and saw them untying his motorboat from a little dock. As yet I knew nothing about how much "Junior" had suffered when Granddad left him at home while he went off with his cronies, memories that made my father yearn to take his own sons and grandchildren fishing.

My own memories were of the Red Barn, the roadside diner with the huge portions of fried clams and blueberry pie where he had taken me when I was in college. But when I asked if we could go there, he scoffed that it had gone downhill and insisted that we eat at another restaurant. He wanted to take us bargain-hunting at the local outlet stores, and I humored him by buying a pair of black walking shoes. But even the shopping got on my nerves, because it reminded me of how little he had provided for my brother and me over the years while he was busy indulging himself.

"Maybe we should just leave now!" I huffed to Alexis when we were alone.

She encouraged me to stick it out. "It's only a few days," she said.

In the end, I managed to keep my foul temper hidden and we had what passed for an officially pleasant visit. It wasn't until we were on the ninety-mile ride back to the airport that I finally realized what was bugging me. As I looked out the car window at the miles and miles of unpopulated woods, I thought: What is he doing here, anyway? Why Canaan? How did someone who had taught at leading universities on both coasts, lived in Africa, and traveled around the world, end up in a place like this? I knew he loved his little house and found the locals friendly, but what about us? What about his family? Weren't grandparents supposed to go out of their way to visit their grandchildren, not the other way around? Apart from the few times he had come to New York for family events, why was I the one who had to keep trekking to Palm Springs or to the middle of nowhere in Maine to see him?

"When do you think you'll come again?" he asked as he said good-bye, only stoking my sense of grievance.

"I don't know," I said, not about to make promises I wouldn't keep. "I'll see you in California in the spring."

Then Alexis and the kids and I picked up our bags and headed toward the security gate at Portland International Jetport, passing through a single X-ray machine by guards who were gossiping and

appeared not to be paying much attention. A year later, I would remember that scene when I learned that the Egyptian student Mo-
hammed Atta had chosen to start his voyage at that little airport in
Maine, before connecting in Boston with an American Airlines Boe-
ing 767 headed for New York.

When I saw the first footage of that plane hurtling into the upper
floors of the North Tower, my first thought was: "That's where I proposed to Alexis!" I had a sudden, awful vision of what it must have
been like for the diners at the Windows on the World that morning,
enjoying the sunny skytop views of New York over breakfast, as the ex-
plosion rocked the building and flames shot up past their windows. I
wanted desperately to talk to my wife, but she was at a conference in
Washington with Rick Smith and his top salesmen, and it was impossible to reach any of them because all phone connection outside of
Manhattan had been cut. I called Rachel's and Matthew's schools to
make sure that they were safe. Then, as I watched the second plane
plow into the South Tower on live television, I went to work planning
Newsweek's coverage of the worst terrorist attack in U.S. history.

"So what are you thinking?" Don Graham asked when he finally
got through to me.

"We can't wait until the weekend," I said. "We have to publish a
special issue now, in the next twenty-four hours."

For the rest of the day, the magazine's headquarters off Columbus
Circle in Manhattan looked like a cross between a newsroom and a
trauma ward. By noon, staffers who had been downtown to witness
the devastation began staggering into the building, having walked all
the way uptown because all the subways and buses were out of com-
mission. One of our senior editors, George Hackett, a usually unflap-
pable Yankee who lived in Greenwich Village, was trembling and in
tears from the shock of watching the towers collapse. Photographers
covered with ash and debris from Ground Zero arrived with their
haunting digital images: of the "leapers" who jumped from the towers rather than be burned alive; of the atomic bomb–like mushroom

cloud that rose as the skyscrapers imploded upon themselves; of the thousands of people running through the soot-dark streets, panic etched on their faces as if in a horror movie. What about our folks? I kept asking as the day went on. Was everyone okay? Fortunately, they all were.

When I finally took a day off three weeks later, for the Jewish New Year, I reflected that we at *Newsweek* were fortunate in another sense: We didn't have time to feel the depth of anxiety and depression that gripped so many Americans in the days after 9/11 because we were busy working. In twelve days, we had published sixteen million copies of four separate magazines, selling a previously unheard of eight million copies on newsstands around the world. We had also run two stories that were widely seen as being among the finest pieces of reporting and analysis done in the immediate aftermath of the attack: a seven-thousand-word investigation called "Trail of Terror" on the intelligence failures that kept us from capturing Osama bin Laden or detecting his murderous scheme; and a groundbreaking essay by my colleague Fareed Zakaria, "Why They Hate Us," on the roots of fundamentalist rage in the Islamic world.

For the magazine, it put to rest, at least for a while, the recurrent media sniping that newsmagazines had become irrelevant dinosaurs. And for me, it meant that I was no longer seen foremost as a novelty. In the three and a half years since I had been named editor, coverage of my stewardship had continued to focus on the "first African-American" angle. A reporter from *GQ* had spent a day at the magazine and written how unusual it was to see a mostly white staff taking direction from a black boss at our news meetings. *Savoy* magazine had published a profile called "The Anonymous Newsman," asking why I was not a household name in black America. Although I had commissioned numerous cover stories on what I saw as smart, provocative racial topics—affirmative action, multiracial identity, class disparities within the black community, and the rising power of black women—I still wanted to be known for being the best editor I could be, period. And at last, when *Newsweek* won the

Ellie for overall magazine excellence for our coverage of 9/11, the reporters who called to interview me didn't ask a single question about my skin color.

In those three and a half years, there had been moments of great joy and unexpected sorrow in my personal life. On a trip to Israel to see Alexis's father, Sidney, receive a lifetime achievement award for his service to Ben Gurion University, we had taken our children to Yad Vashem, the Holocaust memorial. In the rocky edifices of the Garden of the Righteous, we had searched the names of Gentiles honored for helping Jews survive the Holocaust and found the inscriptions for Grandpapa and Grandmaman: Edouard and Mildred Theis. I had seen Rachel stand before the congregation at our synagogue and become a bat mitzvah, giving a speech that offered a precocious theory as to why God had almost destroyed the human race in her Torah portion, the story of Noah and the Ark. "Maybe he still didn't have enough experience being God," she said.

I had also absorbed the grim news that my college roommate Joe Dalton had died of complications from a lifetime of diabetes, after cutting off contact with everyone he knew from Harvard and spending his last years as a shut-in in his hometown of Clendenin, West Virginia. And my friend Eric Breindel had passed away at the age of forty-two of disease that was certainly connected to his addiction to heroin in college and law school, a habit that he had kept hidden from most of us who knew him then. He had been arrested for buying five half-gram bags of smack for $150 from an undercover cop on the street in Washington and suffered the humiliation of pleading guilty in a D.C. courthouse in front of his parents, but he had never lost his powerful ambition and ability to connect with other people. Eventually he bounced back to run the editorial page of the *New York Post,* becoming a protégé of some of New York's most powerful businessmen and politicians and, in a small world coincidence, dating Lally Weymouth, Don Graham's sister.

Less than two months before 9/11, I had edited a memorial tribute to Don and Lally's mother, Katharine Graham. Over the July

Fourth weekend, Lally had invited Alexis and me to a gala birthday party that she threw every year for her mother at her home in the Hamptons. The next day, her friend Barbara Walters had hosted a brunch in Mrs. Graham's honor, and afterward Alexis and I had offered her a ride back to Lally's. When we pulled into the driveway, I got out of the car and offered to walk her to the house, but she proudly refused my help. The next week she flew to a gathering of media executives in Sun Valley, Idaho, and, still insisting that she could get around by herself, suffered a fatal fall when no one was around, ending one of the most remarkable lives in the history of U.S. publishing.

Over the next year, as George W. Bush began putting America on the path toward a second war in Iraq, I was determined to show that I had learned the lessons of the Monica Lewinsky episode. This time I trusted my gut instinct that the president was moving too fast, with faulty intelligence, and I pushed for a series of skeptical cover stories: on Bush's messianic sense of religion; Dick Cheney's role in selling the conflict; Ahmed Chalabi, the darling of hawkish neoconservatives whom I labeled "Our Con Man in Iraq"; and the faulty planning for the postwar reconstruction that was costing America hundreds of billions of dollars. They earned *Newsweek* another Ellie for overall excellence and a rare tip of the hat from my father.

"You really deserved this one," he said when I told him about the award.

"You mean we didn't deserve it the last time?" I replied.

"Yes, but doing great journalism after 9/11 was like shooting ducks in a barrel," he said. "This time you stuck your neck out, while everyone else was burying theirs in the sand."

Although I had purchased a subscription for him, he almost never commented on what was in the magazine, and I had always wondered why not. Did he have so many critical things to say that he was holding his tongue? Was he simply not reading it? But now, at last, I knew that he was, perhaps more closely than I had ever imagined.

• • •

Three weeks after the start of Operation Iraqi Freedom, I flew to Palm Springs to attend my father's wedding to Shirley Kao. This time around, he asked Paul and me to be his best men, and we gladly accepted. For some reason, he wanted us all to wear yellow ties, so on the way to the airport I stopped at a men's store to buy one.

The ceremony took place on the patio of his latest find, a restaurant called the Enchanted Garden in a small outdoor shopping plaza in Palm Springs. About thirty of his friends sat on folding chairs to watch the exchange of vows, and afterward he announced that he and Shirley were going to dance to "our song." He loaded a tape into a boom box, and the air filled with the sugary sound of Justin Timberlake and 'N Sync singing "This I Promise You." Afterward there was another dinner at his favorite Chinese restaurant, next to a Best Western on a highway north of town.

As it turned out, that year—2003—was a memorable one for both sides of my family. In August, Alexis and I took our kids to a reunion of the Theis clan organized by my cousin Manouche, who had become a schoolteacher and lived in a town called St. Die, in the Vosges, south of Alsace. My oldest cousin Olivier, the redhead who left me on top of the mountain when I was fourteen, had died of cancer, after fifty years lived with the same abandon with which we hurtled down the slopes of the Alps. But my mother's seven sisters were all there, along with most of their twenty-three children and dozens of their grandchildren. Remembering my own teenage struggles with the language, I had worried that Rachel and Matthew might have trouble communicating with their high-school French, but as it turned out most of their second cousins spoke passable English and they all shared the international idioms of their generation: the Internet, rap music, and movies.

In September, Matthew became a bar mitzvah. My mother drove down from Providence and my father flew in with Shirley, and we all watched with pride and emotion as Matthew read from the Torah and gave a speech linking the stories of his slave ancestors and Grandpapa's World War II valor to the closing chapters of the Old Testament, where a dying Moses instructs the Jews he had led out of bondage in Egypt to "choose life" as they were about to cross over into the Promised Land.

A month later, I was back in Palm Springs for the American Magazine Conference, an annual gathering of publishers and editors that I was chairing. My father had gone back to work, as a volunteer at the Boys and Girls Club of Palm Springs, offering college guidance to local high-school students, and he seemed happy to have something to look forward to every day besides playing tennis and watching sports on TV. Although he appeared to be putting on more pounds every time I saw him, he reported that the "salutary effect" of Shirley's cooking had done wonders in keeping down the level of worrisome protein cells in his prostate.

It wasn't until I returned to Palm Springs in the spring that I discovered that things weren't going quite as well as I thought. Rachel came with me, taking a break from applying to college, and when we invited my father and Shirley and an old Princeton colleague named Richard Falk out to dinner, I was alarmed by how much heavier he had gotten in just six months. There were several steps up into the poolside restaurant, and he had to stop to catch his breath after each one. *He must weigh almost four hundred pounds!* I thought to myself. It turned out to be an entertaining meal, with my father and Falk treating Rachel to a droll assessment of Princeton. But the next day, he came to the tennis tournament and pulled me aside to speak privately. He told me that he had quit the Boys and Girls Club, convinced that a younger rival was trying to undermine him, and that he and Shirley had decided to put their desert condo on the market and move full-time to Maine.

"We've had some setbacks in our investments," he said. "I'm afraid that the life of Riley on two coasts is no longer feasible."

"Does that make sense?" I asked. "Won't the winters in Maine be hard? Aren't your doctors here in California?"

"We've weighed those considerations," he said, "but Maine is the place where we feel at home. *She Ke Nan* nourishes our soul."

He was referring to the name that he had given to his cabin, which I hadn't bothered to learn was a blessing in Hausa, the language of northern Nigeria, meaning "go in peace."

I had seen my father go through so many highs and lows over the years that his latest development didn't exactly surprise me, but it did make me melancholy. I knew it meant that I wouldn't see him as often, after all the years of visiting Palm Springs. And it left me sad because, yet again, just when I thought he had finally pulled his life together, it seemed to be coming apart. I couldn't help suspect that his tribute to *She Ke Nan* was just a cover story: that he simply needed the cash, and that he was selling the place in Palm Springs because he could, while there was no real market for his little soul-nourishing refuge in the bowels of Maine.

Rachel ended up going to college at Harvard, but her first year there was tense and lonely. One of the few things she enjoyed as a fresh-man was joining in Kuumba, the university's interracial gospel choir, so when she asked us to come to its spring concert Alexis and I de-cided to skip a big journalist dinner in Washington and fly to Cam-bridge to offer her moral support. As I was rushing out of the office on Friday night, I quickly glanced over the stories that had just landed in my computer. Among them was a brief Periscope item reporting that an internal military review had confirmed allegations that a guard at Guantanamo Bay prison in Cuba had stuffed a Koran down a toilet in an effort to rattle a Muslim interrogation subject.

"Make sure Washington is sure about that Koran item," I asked, and the next day our reporters cleared it with government sources.

Then I put the matter out of my mind and focused on visiting my daughter, not realizing how much trouble that hundred-word story would cause. As it began circulating in our overseas editions in the following week, the suggestion that Americans were desecrating the Muslim holy book set off deadly riots in Pakistan and Afghanistan, and dozens of militant protesters were shot by police. Then, eleven days after the item appeared, the Pentagon's spokesman called me to deny the charge. I asked the reporter—Michael Isikoff, the same investigative correspondent who had uncovered the Monica Lewinsky affair—to double-check, and this time his source backtracked, insisting that he had heard about the Koran in the toilet somewhere but couldn't be sure it was in the military report. As our Saturday deadline approached, I wrote an editor's note apologizing for the error and saying that we would keep investigating what had happened. But that wasn't enough to satisfy the Pentagon, which blamed *Newsweek* for the bloodshed and demanded that we officially take back the entire story.

When I woke up on Monday morning, headlines about the demands for a *Newsweek* retraction were on the front page of the *New York Times* and the cover of the *New York Post*. By the time I arrived at work, thousands of irate messages had flooded my computer inbox. "You're the ones who should be dead, you commies!" they said, more or less, in suspiciously similar language. "You have blood on your hands!" I turned on the TV in my office to see that we were the talk of cable news. "Heads will roll over this!" a right-wing pundit predicted. "I bet the editor of *Newsweek* is fired!" There was a shot of the floor of Congress, showing a representative calling for a boycott of the magazine.

My secretary appeared in the doorway, looking shaken. "You just got a death threat!" she said. "A man left a message saying that he was going to hunt you down!"

"Did he leave a name?" I said, dryly.

"No, but the guy sounded nuts," she said.

I called Alexis and told her what was happening. When I shrugged off the irate caller, she got angry."A death threat is serious!" she said. "I'm worried about the kids. What if they start looking for our home number?" We had never gotten around to it before, but now she declared: "That's it, we're ordering caller ID."

The *NBC Nightly News* with Brian Williams had invited me to come on the show to talk about the crisis, and as I sat in the green room I decided to swallow my pride and utter the "R word." After all, it was true that we could no longer stand by our story about the contents of the military review, even if we still didn't know the underlying truth about the Koran charge. I called *Newsweek*'s publicist and dictated a carefully worded statement: "Based on what we know now, we are retracting our original story that an internal military investigation had uncovered Koran abuse at Guantanamo Bay." Then I went on the set with Williams to break the news. Afterward, I was touched when Steve Capus, the show's executive producer, came out of the control room to thank me and offer his sympathy.

When asked about the retraction at the White House press briefing the next day, spokesman Scott McLellan suggested that we go further and write about all the positive things that guards did for prisoners at Gitmo.

"Who made you the editor of *Newsweek*?" Terry Moran, the White House correspondent for ABC News, barked out.

Seeing that, I breathed a sigh of relief. I could see that the press was looking for a new angle on the story, and that McLellan had just given it to them: Is the White House overplaying its hand?

Over the following weeks, I would get supportive messages from friends and colleagues commending me for defusing the crisis so quickly, including a handwritten note from Jack Welch, the retired boss of General Electric, who knew a thing or two about media firestorms. But I could sense how close I had come to being consumed by the flames, and I was emotionally shaken and physically exhausted.

"Remember what you said about 'uneasy lies the crown'?" I told my father when he called me from Maine to see how I was doing.

"Indeed," he said. "And you may still not have heard the end of this."

"God, I hope I have," I said. "It was scary there for a minute."

I felt badly in need of some time off. But I saw that other members of my staff were frazzled too, so I let them go on vacation and waited until the end of August to take a couple of weeks in the Catskills. While I was there, Hurricane Katrina blew into Louisiana and Mississippi, broke open the fragile levees over New Orleans and left thousands of homeless sleeping on the floor of the Superdome. Any other year, I would have rushed back to the office. But I remembered how I had felt over the Labor Day weekend eight years earlier, when Princess Diana died while Maynard Parker was on vacation, and I decided to let my deputy Jon Meacham handle the story, figuring that he would be grateful that I trusted him enough to leave him in charge.

When I was asked to step down as the editor of *Newsweek* seven months later, I didn't have the heart to tell my father. I knew what his line of questioning would be, and I didn't want to face it. He would want to know what was going on behind the scenes and share his Shakespearean suspicions. I told myself that it was going to be hard enough to leave the only place I had ever worked, and I didn't need him inflaming my emotions.

"Do you have a few minutes to talk about some long-range planning?" Rick Smith had asked cryptically when he phoned me in the spring of 2006.

"Sure," I said.

"Why don't you take a stroll up to my office?" he said.

When I sat down on the couch in Rick's office, six floors above mine in the *Newsweek* building, he came directly to the point. He said the financial future of the magazine was looking increasingly cloudy. "Selling ads around here isn't getting any easier," he said. Meanwhile, the Web sites of *Newsweek* and the *Washington Post* were starting to make money, and the company was having surprising financial success with *Slate*, the clever online magazine that it had recently purchased from Microsoft.

"Don thinks that we should be focusing our efforts online," Rick said. "He wants you to take a new job developing more sites like *Slate*."

"Okay . . ." I said warily, eyeing a copy of the cover on Hurricane Katrina on Rick's coffee table. "And when would Don like me to do this?"

"Oh, the timing is flexible," he said. "In six months or so. But to give you an idea of how serious Don is about this, he's willing to give you a percentage of the profit of anything that you create that's—"

"Actually profitable?" I said, arching my eyebrows skeptically.

"Right," he said.

"Well, that's an interesting proposition," I said. "To tell you the truth, I had been starting to think about what I might do next."

That was indeed the truth. I had been in the demanding top job for seven and a half years, longer than either Maynard Parker or Rick before me, and longer than any editor at *Time* in the previous two decades. In fact, at that moment the chief of all the Time-Life publications, a canny Southerner named John Huey, was looking for a new editor for our competitor and had been taking dozens of potential candidates out for exploratory meals.

The next week, Don Graham gave me a three-hour pep talk in his office at the *Washington Post* headquarters, and by the end of it I had agreed to accept the new Web development assignment. I told Alexis what was going on and gave my mother advance warning. But it wasn't until five months later, on the day before it was announced that I would leave *Newsweek* and turn over the helm to Jon Meacham, that I phoned my father with the news.

"Hmmph," he said. "Is this really what you want?"

"I think it will be great!" I said cheerfully, determined not to give him an opening. "I'm ready for a change." Then I told him that Graham had offered me a piece of the action, because I knew how interested he was in money.

For the next six months, I worked hard to turn Don's dream of creating a small Web publishing empire into reality. He had a friend who had sold him on the idea of an online magazine about environmentally friendly shopping, and I hired a small staff and produced a site that got written up in the *New York Times*. I contacted Henry Louis Gates Jr. at Harvard about creating a site on black politics and culture. Don was supportive of my efforts, inviting me to Washington for progress reports and visiting me in the tiny office where I had moved in the *Newsweek* building. But the rest of the *Post's* digital operation seemed mystified about what I was up to and reluctant to devote resources to projects that weren't already generating traffic and revenue.

Then, less than six months into the job, I got an e-mail out of the blue from Steve Capus, who a year earlier had been promoted from *Nightly News* producer to the president of NBC News. "Hey there," it said. "How are you doing? Wondering if you'd have time to catch up."

We met for a drink, and he asked if I would be interested in becoming his deputy, the number two executive in the news division. I was flattered by the offer but also surprised. I had a great deal of respect for Capus, from years of joint projects between NBC and *Newsweek*, but we didn't know each other socially. And I had never worked in TV.

"Don't you worry about that?" I asked.

"I need someone with news judgment and ideas and people skills," he replied. "You'll figure out TV."

The more I thought about it over the coming weeks, the more I was intrigued by the prospect. For all of Don's good intentions, I was finding the bureaucracy of the Washington Post Company extremely resistant to entrepreneurship. And after a half-year away from *Newsweek*, I missed being a journalist. Although I had spent my career in print, I had grown up watching news on television and on NBC in particular. When my father had taken me out of school that Friday in first grade after President Kennedy was shot, he kept the channel tuned all weekend to Huntley and Brinkley. I had spent the entire sweltering summer of 1968 after fifth grade in front of the TV set in Norton with my mother watching the riots after Dr. King's murder, Bobby Kennedy's funeral train, and the four NBC correspondents with their headsets on the floor of the Democratic Convention in Chicago covering the mayhem inside the International Ampitheater while all hell broke loose in Grant Park outside.

Yet I still found it an excruciating decision to make. It was almost thirty years since I had first gone to work for *Newsweek*, stepping off the plane in San Francisco for my first adventure as a summer intern. I had met my wife at the magazine, worked with my college buddies Jon Alter and Joe Contreras as we were all raising our kids, made other lifelong friends among my colleagues. Emotionally, it had come to represent the stable home I had never had as a child, and as a boss I relished making everyone there feel the same way about it. So for the two months that I kept talking to Capus and working out the agreement that would make me a senior vice president at NBC, I couldn't quite believe I was leaving.

When there was no turning back, I e-mailed Don Graham and asked if we could have lunch. We met at his office in Washington and he took me out to an Indian restaurant down the street. As we were leaving the *Post* building, an older gentleman with a round belly and white hair walked into the lobby, and Don greeted him warmly.

"How's life?" he said. "How are the wife and kids?"

He introduced us. "This man was a pressman here for forty years!" he bellowed.

The Washington Post Company is a family-owned business, and thousands of the people who have worked there over the decades have thought of themselves as part of the family. Don is a particularly parental figure, with his memory for names and the sweaters he wears around the office, like the dad on an old TV sitcom. But as we walked into the hot May sunshine, and I steeled myself to deliver the news that he would accept with regret but gracious good wishes, I realized that the *Post* wasn't my home after all. Don wasn't my father, any more than Maynard Parker or Rick Smith or any of my other *Newsweek* bosses and mentors or college professors had been. My family was my only real family, and for better or worse, my father was my only real father.

I say I realized it that day. But in truth, it took another three years before I accepted it in my heart. That was when I learned that the Washington Post Company was selling *Newsweek,* in the midst of a steep financial decline that got dramatically worse after I left. It was May 5, 2010, the date of my twenty-fifth wedding anniversary. Alexis and I had gone to Paris to celebrate, and we were about to go out to a restaurant for dinner when I turned on my cell phone and discovered dozens of messages from friends and former colleagues who were shocked and upset by the news.

Before leaving our hotel, I sent one of them a response. "That's very sad," it said. "Alexis and I both worked at *Newsweek* for twenty-five years. Now we're going out to celebrate our twenty-fifth wedding anniversary. I'm glad that at least one of those institutions has survived."

The week before I started talking to NBC, my father came to New York for the first time in four years. The occasion was a dinner for the Jane Goodall Institute, on whose board he began serving after meeting the British primate expert in L.A. and becoming so distracted that he got lost in traffic. I invited him and Shirley to stay with us, and he sounded so cheerful in his e-mails that I wasn't prepared for the sight of him. He was no longer just huge; he was gargantuan. Even with the help of a cane, he couldn't walk more than a few hundred feet at a time. He was suffering terrible pain in his hip, he told me, but his doctors said he was too heavy to qualify for an operation. Meanwhile, the throbbing had forced him to give up the one form of exercise he could still do—water aerobics—so he kept getting fatter.

When we went out to dinner, I had to hail a cab for him even though the restaurant was only three blocks away. He limped to the table, and the meal got off to a tense start when he sent back the tomato soup he had ordered as an appetizer. "This isn't what I asked for!" he snapped at the waitress. He finally relaxed after getting a dish he was happy with and started quizzing Alexis about her work and Matthew about school. Then, as dessert was served, he cleared his throat and addressed us in a grave tone.

"I want to discuss something very important with you," he said. "I had a dear friend in Nigeria named Hussaini Adamu. Mark, you met him when you were a baby, although as I recall you don't remember. He became the emir of Kazaure, and before he died we made a pact.

I vowed that if anyone in his family ever needed my help, I would give it to them, and he made the same pledge to me. In African culture, an oath like that does not die with us. It gets passed down through the generations. I tell you this because one day, one of Hussaini's heirs may call on you for a favor. Whatever it is, I want you to do your best to grant it."

He turned to Matthew. "This applies to you too," he said, "once your father is no longer here. As far as I am concerned, it's a matter of honor for the Whitaker lineage."

"Okay," Matthew responded politely. Then he shot me a confused look as if to say: How am I going to help someone in Nigeria?

The next night, my father put on a specially tailored black suit and a bright red pocket square and Shirley dressed in a matching red pants suit for the Goodall gala. They didn't get back from the Yale Club until just before midnight, and they talked glowingly about what a wonderful time they had. The next morning, they packed their bags and took a cab twenty blocks up West End Avenue to visit Michael and Barbara DeLaszlo. My father had long since made up with his old college friends, and they had offered to host him and Shirley on their last night in New York.

The following morning, Alexis and I were eating breakfast when the phone rang. It was Barbara DeLaszlo. In an alarmed voice, she said that my father had missed his flight because he was running a high fever. Her doctor was out of town, and she wanted to know if we could suggest a physician to check on him. Then she lowered her voice. "Syl's very upset because he's run out of Vicodin," she whispered. "He says he needs it for his hip, but he seems to be taking an awful lot of painkillers!"

Alexis called a doctor we knew, who interviewed my father about his symptoms over the phone and prescribed antibiotics and several days of rest before he tried to get on a plane. Afterward, she expressed surprise that he only seemed to know medical specialists and didn't have a general practitioner who kept track of his medical records. So when I went to the DeLaszlos' to see him, I gave him an earful about it.

"I've never gotten around to it, with all the traveling back and forth between Maine and California," he said.

"Well, it's important," I said. "Someone should know your entire medical history and everything you're taking."

"Heard and noted," he said curtly.

"Look, Dad, I'm serious," I said.

"Okay, Mark, I get the message," he shot back in an exasperated tone.

At the time, I suspected that my father might not have a GP because he was pill shopping. But it was only in the course of my reporting that I discovered what pills he was shopping for: not just Vicodin, but OxyContin. That spring, he was finally cleared for a hip replacement, but it didn't go well. Afterward he was in even more pain, and he responded by going to more and more doctors for stronger and stronger medication. When my brother wanted to visit Maine that summer, he asked him not to come until he got another Oxy prescription filled. And while Paul was there, he was in a stoned stupor for much of the stay, snapping out of it only from time to time to play poker.

He might well have remained in that narcotic daze, but for two events. First, his tiny but deceptively tough wife, Shirley, put her foot down and demanded that he get off the Oxy, if not the Vicodin. And then, by summer's end, he developed a new addiction. He began obsessively following the election campaign of 2008 and the unlikely rise of the first black candidate ever to have a realistic chance of becoming president of the United States.

19

After selling the condo in Palm Springs, my father and Shirley still went west for the winter, renting a cheap little apartment near San Diego. So when Maine held its presidential primary caucuses in February 2008, they had to cast absentee ballots. On the night of the vote, a friend who was the local Democratic Party chairman called them with the results from their district: Barack Obama 59, Hillary Clinton 58.

"Your two votes put Obama over the top!" he reported.

The next day, my father e-mailed a group of friends to share the story, punctuating it with one of his puckish word plays. "Over the top?" he said. "I'm over the Moon!"

It was hardly a foregone conclusion that he would be an Obama supporter. In 2000, he had backed John McCain, the candidate who was on his way to becoming the Republican nominee this time around. He found McCain a refreshing straight shooter, and he once asked me to get his autograph when he heard that we would both be guests at a Henry Kissinger dinner party. Like millions of

African-Americans, he was skeptical when Obama first declared his candidacy and doubted that America was ready to elect a black president. But after the Illinois senator won the first primary caucus in the virtually all-white state of Iowa, my father became a believer, and from then on he followed the contest compulsively, cheering Obama on but also watching warily for developments that could knock him off his stride.

"Can you talk to him?" he asked, without saying hello, when he called me on a Saturday morning in mid-March.

"Dad, is that you?" I said.

"Can you talk to him?" he asked again.

I glanced at the clock. It was eight o'clock in the morning, or five o'clock in San Diego, the hour when, every morning since he had stopped drinking, he awoke and brewed his first pot of coffee.

"You mean Obama?" I asked, sensing what he was calling about.

"Yes, can you talk to him?"

"Of course I can't talk to him," I said. "I'm a journalist, remember? I don't take sides or give advice."

"Okay, okay," he said. "But this is very bad for him."

"No, it doesn't look good," I agreed.

The day before, the controversy over Obama's minister had exploded into a full-blown crisis for his campaign. I had read several profiles of the Reverend Jeremiah Wright a year earlier and thought to myself that he could be a ticking time bomb. Obama had written eloquently about the spiritual lessons he had learned from the charismatic pastor, but he had skated over the fact that Wright's sermons were full of left-wing rhetoric and racial indignation that was bound to play less well in the rest of America than it did among the progressive blacks and whites on the south side of Chicago.

When NBC's sister network MSNBC hosted a Democratic primary debate in Cleveland in late February, I had urged our moderators, Brian Williams and Tim Russert, to press Obama on the subject. But most of the press corps had only jumped on the story that week, after incendiary clips from Wright's angriest sermons began making the rounds of cable television. Now everywhere you turned, there was the robed pastor shouting "God damn America!" for its treatment of black people and thundering that the 9/11 attacks were "chickens . . . coming home to roost" for America's support of Israel.

"Shirley went to the mall yesterday," my father said. "You can just imagine what the white people here are saying. This is going to give every white voter who had the slightest reservation about Obama a free pass to say 'See, I told you so.'"

"Right, and his response so far has been pretty weak," I said.

"Very weak!" he said. "In fact, the ship may be going down. But this could still be an opportunity for Obama. He could give a speech . . . a speech about the realities of race in America. He's in a unique position to explain it from every perspective, black and white, young and old."

"I'm not sure a speech can save him," I said skeptically.

"Maybe not," he said, "but it could be a teaching moment. If you can't speak with him, I think I'll reach out to Sam Brown."

"Sam Brown?"

"He's an old friend. I think he's raised money for Obama."

"All right, good luck," I said.

"Bye!" he said, hanging up abruptly.

As soon he got off the phone with me, he wrote the following e-mail to Sam Brown, a former anti–Vietnam War activist who had become a successful businessman and run the Peace Corps for Bill Clinton:

Dear Sam:

Forgive my presumption, which is outweighed by the urgency I strongly feel, plus that I lack any other opportunity to reach Senator Obama.

Denying or minimizing awareness of or connection to Pastor Wright does not wash, even for one who, like me, remains a committed supporter. At the same time, the very essence of

something profound which Obama represents is at stake. He
must now find the voice inherent in his own experience and
enormous gifts and strength, to articulate not merely that he
does not agree with the bitter pronouncements and provocative
utterances of Pastor Wright, but rather that he, Obama,
understands the bridge which his own voice represents between
the historic feelings of Wright's and his own generation and
younger.

To do this, Obama need neither denounce nor embrace
Pastor Wright's perspective and energy, nor apologize for it.
What he must do is to convey the hopeful alternative to which
his own experience and career has led him. There is a profound
moment here, to educate deeply, as well as to redeem his
presidential hopes. . . . This crisis will not "blow-over"; it must
be surmounted with a superior message. Otherwise I believe his
candidacy is doomed. . . .

> *Please help him if you can. My best*
> *regards,*
> *Syl Whitaker*

Later that morning, Sam Brown e-mailed back to say that he
found the idea intriguing but that he wasn't close enough to Obama
to offer suggestions. Meanwhile, I e-mailed Tim Russert, NBC's
Washington bureau chief and moderator of *Meet the Press*. Without
citing the source, I said that I had been talking to a black Obama
supporter who worried that the Wright scandal could finish his
candidacy and that I hoped he would tackle the issue hard on his
broadcast.

"Topic A, brother," Tim responded.

What none of us knew that morning was that Obama was preparing to deliver exactly the kind of speech that my father envisioned.
The candidate had been toying with the idea for months but he
had only decided to link it to the Wright furor on Friday night. By

Saturday, only he and his closest aides knew what was coming, and the speech wasn't officially announced until Monday. On Tuesday morning, Obama stood before a row of American flags at the National Constitution Center in Philadelphia and talked movingly about how all sides saw race in America, just as my father had imagined. In the following days, it became clear that the speech had not only spoken powerful truths but rescued his candidacy at a moment when it could easily have slipped below the waves. And as I watched it all unfold, I could only marvel at how uncanny my father's intuition had been.

He had told me about his latest cancer checkup a month earlier. He sounded philosophical about it, but the news wasn't good. A CAT scan showed that malignant cells had spread from his prostate gland to his frontal lymph nodes. His doctor, an Australian named David Quinn who ran the Norris Cancer Center at USC, informed him that he had reached the end of the road for "hormonal refractive" treatment. For almost a decade, he had followed a regimen of radiation supplemented with a man-made hormone called Lupron, which I discovered had been at least partly responsible for his prodigious weight gain and also had the more pleasant side effect of taking some of the aggressive edge off his volatile personality. Now he would have to investigate other drugs and clinical trials. But Quinn still measured his chances of survival in "years, not months," he reported, and he felt reassured and in capable hands. "My spirits are good," he said. "We will know more in a few months."

Not knowing what else I could do for him, I asked if he would like to see some doctors at Sloan-Kettering. Alexis and I had some high-level contacts there: The deputy chief of medicine was the husband of one of her friends from journalism school, and we knew the oncologist who had treated Maynard Parker. At first he resisted, saying that he trusted his own doctors. But in April, he had a more encouraging checkup, showing that his PSA count had dropped again, and Dr. Quinn endorsed the idea of seeking a second opinion. Wanting to enjoy a restful summer in Maine, he started communicating with a prostate cancer specialist at Sloan-Kettering named Dr. Michael Morris about an appointment in the fall.

Two months later, on a quiet Friday the thirteenth in June, I was eating lunch at my desk at NBC headquarters in Rockefeller Plaza when the deputy Washington bureau chief, Wendy Wilkinson, called me in a panic. Tim Russert had gone downstairs in the bureau to record the lead-ins for *Meet the Press* and had collapsed in an audio booth. Medics had arrived and taken him away in an ambulance, but they had been unable to revive him. As soon as I got the briefing from Wendy, I called Steve Capus, who had gone home to prepare for a weekend trip. But by the time he got back to the office, it was too late: Russert had been pronounced dead at the hospital. Brian Williams was on assignment in Afghanistan, so it fell to Tim's old friend Tom Brokaw, the former network anchor, to break the sad news that America's most respected TV political analyst was gone.

The next day the skies opened up across the eastern seaboard, deepening the sense of gloom for everyone who worked at NBC. I had planned to fly to Washington to visit with grieving staffers in the bureau, but thunderstorms grounded my shuttle flight for six hours. By chance I ran into Bennett Freeman, my old friend from Oxford, going through airport security, and we spent the time on the tarmac catching up and talking about Tim, whom Bennett had met years earlier while dating a producer who worked for him. The next morning, the entire bureau and dozens of NBC alumni gathered to watch Brokaw preside over an emotional taping of *Meet the Press* devoted entirely to Russert's memory. Afterward everyone stayed around to talk, cry, and hug Tim's widow, Maureen Orth, and their son, Luke.

I reminded Maureen that I had first met her, via phone, when she was a *Newsweek* writer and I was an intern in San Francisco reporting an item about Led Zeppelin. I also told her that my father sent his condolences.

"Do I know him?" she asked.

"His name is Syl Whitaker," I said. "He says he knew you in the sixties, when you were at Berkeley. He was teaching at UCLA and dating a friend of yours named Sally."

"It was a long time ago . . ." she said, sounding too drained and upset to search her memory for long-forgotten names.

Alexis and I stayed in Washington to attend Tim's moving funeral and memorial service, then flew to Europe for the wedding of my youngest French cousin: Magali Grand, the third daughter of my aunt Denise, the eighth sister who was born after my mother and the five others came to America in 1940. Denise had married a Protestant farmer from the Camargue region in the south of France, and the festivities were taking place in the small village where they lived outside of Nîmes. As Alexis and I were heading out to the rehearsal dinner, I received an e-mail from Steve Capus. "Will you have anytime to talk in the next day or so?" it said. I e-mailed back that I would call him the next day, after the wedding.

The ceremony took place at the town's Protestant temple, a small chapel with an elevated wooden pulpit like the one from which Grandpapa preached the lessons of the Sermon on the Mount in Le Chambon-sur-Lignon. Magali's mother and sisters and girlfriends all sported stylish hats that reminded me of the hats that Grandmother Edith wore to church in Pittsburgh. Denise's brother-in-law hosted a wedding dinner at his ranch, and when I called Capus back on my cell phone from the reception he asked if I would be interested in becoming NBC's new Washington bureau chief.

As I reflected on all the reasons to accept the assignment—the honor of replacing Tim Russert, the challenge of running the biggest TV news operation in the nation's capital at such a historic time—I also thought about how pleased my father would be. I knew that he had never gotten over my exit from *Newsweek* and that he was an avid watcher of all the political shows on NBC and MSNBC. And sure enough, he was thrilled when I told him the news, and on the day the appointment was reported in newspapers and on websites across the country, he sent me congratulations that, for once, came with no qualifications or lectures or dark warnings. His e-mail said simply:

Dear Mark,

> *Now that the official announcement is out, I can tell you officially that I am deeply proud of you, and all that you have accomplished. Shirley joins me in sending our love and best wishes.*

Love, Dad

I went to work at my new job, shuttling back and forth between Washington and New York and the campaign conventions and debates, while my father prepared for his visit to Sloan-Kettering in October, a week before the presidential vote. He contacted Michael and Barbara DeLaszlo, and they made plans for a small reunion dinner with old friends from Swarthmore. He e-mailed me that he and Shirley would stay for the weekend, then fly back on Monday to be in Maine for Election Day.

Two days before they were scheduled to travel, I got an urgent call from Shirley.

"Your dad have stroke!" she said.

"A stroke?" I said. "When? What happened?"

"He can't move arm and leg! Ambulance take him to emergency!"

I called Maine General Hospital and was told that he was still in intensive care. It took several hours before I was given a room number, and when I got through a nurse told me that he was trying to sleep, so I waited until the next morning before calling again.

"Hello?" said Shirley's voice.

"It's Mark," I said. "Is Dad awake? Can he talk?"

Several minutes passed, and there was whispering and rustling in the background. Then I finally heard his voice.

"Hiii, Maaark," he said in a tired slur. "Sooorry about the trip to New York. Can you tell Doooctor Morris that I caaan't come?"

"Of course," I said. "Don't worry about that. Are you okay?"

"I'm nooot sure that would be the word I would use," he said. "I guess you could saaay I was set up for this. . . ."

All of a sudden I flashed back to my childhood memories of Granddad, crumpled in his wheelchair at the St. Barnabas home.

"There's aaaa nurse here," he said. "Haaave to say bye. Here's Shirley."

She got back on the phone.

"He sounds pretty good, under the circumstances," I said, trying to emphasize the positive.

"He sleep very bad," she said. Then she lowered her voice. "I think because no Vicodin!"

Over the next week, I called him every day at the stroke rehabilitation ward in Waterville. I spoke with his doctor, an osteopathic physician named Celia McLay, and offered to go to see him, but she suggested that he might be better prepared for a visit after some physical therapy. I told her that I had a lot to do before Election Day but that I would fly up to Maine as soon as it was over.

"Yes, your dad told me about your new job," Dr. McLay said. "He's very proud of you. He points at the TV when you come on."

"I'm just glad he can recognize me," I said.

"Oh, your dad is still all there mentally!" she said. "He's such a fascinating man! So cultured! And so witty!"

Leave it to Dad, I thought, to be lying half-paralyzed in a stroke ward in the middle of Maine and still be charming the birds out of the trees.

Dr. McLay asked to speak with my brother and me about where he would go after he left the hospital, which I took as an encouraging sign. The house by the lake was out of the question, as long as he couldn't walk by himself. Shirley had located a small apartment to rent in Waterville for the winter. But Paul and I were worried about whether our tiny stepmother could care for him alone, now that he was half-paralyzed as well as obese, and I was concerned about how he would maintain contact with Dr. Quinn.

"Do you think he'll ever be able to fly back to the West Coast?" I asked. To my surprise, Dr. McLay said she thought it might be possible after a few months of therapy. We agreed that Shirley would need assistance getting him on and off an airliner, and Paul consulted his appointment book to see when he could take time off from his psychology practice.

On Tuesday, November 4, 2008, Barack Obama was elected the forty-forth president of the United States. It was a remarkable achievement for a once lonely mixed-race child with his own experience of parental abandonment, and an especially thrilling day for African-Americans of my father's generation who never thought they would live to see one of their own in the Oval Office. As I watched the returns come in, I suddenly realized that he hadn't been able to vote. But when I called him at the hospital, he informed me, in the most cheerful voice I had heard in days, that he and Shirley had cast their ballots by mail a month before because they had decided after the Maine caucuses that early voting was good luck.

I stayed in Washington for the rest of the week to monitor NBC's coverage of the election aftermath, and then on Sunday, as political reporters across America finally stopped to catch their breath, I boarded a plane for Bangor, rented a car from Hertz, and headed west toward Maine General.

He was on the third floor of a building on the Thayer Campus, a drab hospital complex on a sparse stretch of land outside Waterville. I stepped out of the elevator and announced myself at the admitting desk, and a small, middle-aged nurse pointed me down the hallway. The door to his room was ajar. As I knocked, I saw him lying on his side on the bed, his all but naked body rising like a brown mountain under the hospital sheets. Above him was suspended a contraption that I realized, upon closer inspection, was an enormous harness attached to a steel pulley.

"Hi, Mark," he said in a voice that sounded weary but clearer than it had in the days after the stroke. "You're early."

Shirley emerged from a little bathroom, holding a bedpan. "You here already!" she said. "Nurses coming to help Syl sit up!"

Two tall blond nurses walked into the room, and my father shifted his head to introduce them.

"This is the son I told you about," he said. "And these are my guardian angels."

"Your faaatha is such a flirt!" one of the nurses said in a thick Maine accent.

I didn't want to see what was going to happen next or to compromise my father's dignity, so I excused myself and stepped into the hallway while the two nurses went to work with the harness and pulley. It took them about ten minutes to lift his inert body, which a doctor would later tell me weighed more than 450 pounds, off the bed and into a wheelchair.

For the next hour, I sat on the bed next to him and we talked. His speech was labored, but he was alert and lucid and droll as ever. He said that he had lost all movement in his left leg and most of his left arm, making it impossible to walk or to get of bed unassisted. But he could still wiggle a few fingers, which gave the doctors hope. He groused about the two hours of physical therapy he was subjected to every day. He described how attentive Shirley had been, staying by his side all day and sleeping in the hospital room at night, and he confessed how much he worried about being a burden to her. We talked about the electricity of the election, and he shook his head in disbelief that America had actually chosen a black president. He quizzed me about my job at NBC and what the famous anchors and reporters he saw on television were like away from the cameras.

I had forgotten that it was Sunday until a lanky young man with sandy blond hair appeared in the doorway of the hospital room.

"Would you like to pray?" he said with an evangelical air.

"I'm a Quaker," my father said.

"So am I!" the young man answered.

My father shot me a skeptical look.

"Which Meeting?" he asked.

The young man smiled righteously. "I go to different ones," he said.

"I see," my father said, in a tone suggesting that he had been to all the Meeting houses in the area and had never seen the fellow. "Portland or North Fairfield?"

"Ahhh, Portland," the man said. "Maybe I can drive you there sometime."

"That's all right," my father said. "I'm a North Fairfield man."

"Well, if you ever want to pray, the nurses know where to find me," the man said, beating a hasty retreat.

My father waited until he was gone and then shook his head. "A Friend indeed!" he said. "Well, I'm not in need!"

Shirley asked if I wanted to see the rehabilitation center, and I walked alongside the wheelchair as she pushed it down the hallway to a room lined with what looked like training bars in a ballet studio. The floor was littered with odd-looking benches and chairs and rubber straps and other pushing and pulling devises. A trim man with black hair came over and introduced himself as the physiotherapist.

"Welcome to my chamber of horrors," my father said. "This is my torturer in chief."

When we got back to his room, the small nurse I had met at the receiving desk popped her head in the doorway and reminded him that it was almost time for his three o'clock cleaning. I took that as a polite warning that the visiting hours were over.

"Is this your son the TV star?" the nurse asked.

I nodded. "Nice to meet you," I said, "but I work behind the scenes in TV. I only go on the air once in a while when they need me."

"Well, your dad thinks you're a star!" she said. "I'll give you a few minutes to say goodbye."

"Don't you like being on TV?" my father asked as soon as she left.

"It's fine," I said, "but my job is to support the real stars in my bureau. Besides, I can see that it becomes an addiction, and I'd just as soon not get hooked."

He gazed at me for several seconds, and I noticed his upper lip starting to quiver. Then tears filled his eyes and suddenly he was sobbing. He looked over helplessly at Shirley, who pulled a wad of tissues out of a Kleenex box by his bedside and came over to wipe his face.

"I've been thinking a lot about that, Mark," he said. "I want you to know that I don't care if you become a star. I just want you to take care of yourself. That's all that matters."

"I agree," I said coolly, instinctively pulling back from his show of emotion.

We hugged goodbye and I kissed Shirley on both cheeks, in the French manner, and I promised to come back as soon as I could. I located my little rental car in the parking lot and pulled away from the hospital, wondering yet again how my father had ended up so far from anywhere. During the hour-long drive back to the Bangor airport, I kept thinking about his parting words.

"Take care of yourself . . ."

"Take care of yourself . . ."

"Take care of yourself . . ."

That was it. That was all I had ever wanted to hear. Why had it taken fifty years for him to say it? Why had it taken me fifty years to hear it? Then unexpectedly, as Route 95 stretched before me, I began to sob too.

I left Maine feeling more optimistic about my father's prospects, but as soon as I got back to Washington things started getting strange. Every time I called the rehab ward, I was told that he was away at another branch of the hospital. Then one day I phoned and was informed that he was no longer in the room that I had visited. I couldn't get through to Dr. McLay, so I called the hospital switchboard. An operator told me that C.S. Whitaker Jr. was now in the cancer wing.

When Dr. McLay finally returned my phone message, she explained that he had been undergoing a lot of tests. It was so difficult to move him, given his weight and the effects of the stroke, that the hospital had decided to relocate him permanently to the oncology ward.

"So has his cancer spread?" I asked.

"They can't tell, which is why they keep ordering more tests."

"Won't this set back his stroke rehab?"

"Unfortunately, yes," she said. "But it's out of my hands."

When I finally tracked down his new room number and got through to him, he sounded melancholy and anxious. The next day, as I got off a plane from Washington to New York, I listened to a message on my cell phone from a man with a New England accent named Bert Corrigan. He identified himself as a friend of my father's and asked me to call him urgently.

"Your dad's desperate," Corrigan said in a worried voice when I reached him. "His new nurses are abusing him."

Abusing him? I thought. I had just been at the hospital, and the nurses in rehab were eating out of his hand.

I called his new room and my father answered. "What's wrong?" I asked. "Bert Corrigan called me."

"They hate me here," he said. "My nurses are trying to kill me!"

"I doubt they're trying to kill you, Dad," I said.

"Shirley's here. She'll tell you."

He handed the phone to Shirley.

"Nurses only help Syl every hour!" she said. "But he need to move every fifteen minutes or in bad pain! Syl complain and they get mad and don't come back for hour and a half!"

I tried to picture what was going on. The cancer ward must have been much more crowded than the stroke center. The nurses were probably stretched too thin to visit my father four times an hour to readjust his mammoth frame, and they were less susceptible to his charm than his rehab "angels." He was frightened about what the tests would show and was high on medication, or maybe not high enough, if he wasn't getting painkillers and he was suffering from withdrawal.

"Mark, you have to talk to someone!" he said pleadingly when Shirley put him back on the line.

"Okay, I'll look into it," I promised.

I called Jim Schmidt, a retired white businessman from New Jersey who had become one of my father's best friends in Maine. His daughter was an administrator at the hospital, and she had helped arrange for my father to get VIP treatment after his stroke. Jim said she was out of town but gave me her number, and I left a message explaining the predicament.

The next day, I woke up to two voice-mails on my cell phone. The first was from Jim's daughter, and the second was from Barbara DeLaszlo.

"I have some answers for you about your dad's nursing situation," said the first message.

"Mark, I'm so sorry," said the message from Barbara. "So very sorry."

I called Jim Schmidt's daughter first.

"I've talked to the head nurse in the oncology ward," she began, "and she's going to make a new schedule for your father—"

I interrupted her. "I just got a message from an old friend of my father's saying how sorry she was. Do you know what she meant?"

There was silence on the phone for several seconds.

"I wasn't sure how much you knew. . . ."

"About what?"

"The tests came back. Your father's cancer has spread to his lungs and liver. I'm afraid it's untreatable."

I sucked in a mouthful of air and blew it slowly through my cheeks. "I had an idea this was coming," I said, "but it's still a shock to hear those words."

"They say he still has time," she said. "All that weight may help him hang on a few months longer."

When I reached him that evening, he was in a morphine daze and just barely coherent.

"Dad, I'm so sorry," I said.

"It's okay," he said softly. "I guess it's my time to go home. . . ."

I suddenly remembered Grandmother Edith: "He led such a *good* life, and now he's going home. . . ."

"I . . . I just want one more . . . one more winter. . . ." he said.

"It sounds like you might . . ." I began.

"One more winter for Shirley's sake."

He sounded ready to drift off to sleep, so I told him that I'd check back the next day. But things got crazy at work, and it wasn't until Wednesday, the day before Thanksgiving, that I called again.

"How's Dad?" I asked when Shirley picked up the phone.

"He in coma," she said calmly.

"A coma?" I said. "But I thought the doctors said he had more time."

"He no eat anymore," she said. "Put him in coma."

Until then I had been stoic about what was happening to my father, but the idea that Rachel and Matthew and Alexis might not be able to talk with him again made me more upset for them than I had been for myself. I had envisioned taking them to Maine and sitting by his bedside and having another visit like the one we had had after Election Day.

At least they could see him one last time, I thought. I reached the "end of life specialist" who had been assigned to his case, and she told me that his store of fat might give him another week or two, even though he was no longer taking sustenance. So I started looking into flights to Maine for the Sunday after Thanksgiving.

My mother was visiting us for the holiday, and she responded pensively when I told her the news. But I didn't feel comfortable discussing my feelings about my father with her, and I didn't want to upset the kids by discussing the clinical details. I decided to wait until she left on Saturday morning to finalize our travel plans.

I awoke early, as usual, and had breakfast and several cups of coffee and read the Saturday papers before I noticed my cell phone in the kitchen pantry. I turned it on to check my voice-mail.

"You have one unheard message!" came the greeting, then the time code—"2:30 a.m. . . ."—and then Shirley's voice.

"Syl gone now," she said. "He die in peace. I tell him, 'Okay, Syl, okay, you can go now. I love you. James and Jason love you. Mark and Paul love you. You can go now.'"

20

Tout comprendre, c'est tout pardonner.

It must have been during my teenage year in France that I first heard that expression, although perhaps not. Perhaps it was when I finally took my cousin Anna's advice and read *War and Peace*. But never mind. To understand all is to forgive all: That's the adage that we all know. Yet if I learned anything from my journey, it's that sometimes it has to happen the other way around.

I said that I began to report my family story a year after my father died, over the next Thanksgiving holiday. But the truth is that I first had the idea five years earlier, while he was still alive. I approached both my parents to see if they would talk to me, and they were both wary.

"Oh dear." My mother sighed. "I'm afraid the story would make me look very weak."

"I'll talk to you under one condition," my father said. "I don't want to be the villain of the piece."

Confronted with those reluctant responses, I threw up my hands in exasperation and told myself that it wasn't worth it. I didn't want to face my mother's fruitless regrets or my father's surly defensiveness. They were bound only to infuriate me and to dredge up old resentments. Better to stay focused on my busy job and the life I had made for myself and not to kid myself that any of us were ready to confront the past.

So it's no accident that it was only after he was gone, and then another year had passed, that I was moved to try again. And when I did, I found out how much I had gotten wrong, beginning with how I had interpreted those two remarks.

When my mother said she had been weak, it turned out that she wasn't just living in the cobwebs of remorse. She was describing an objective conclusion that she had reached after decades of hard-won enlightenment. And when I interviewed her and read the scores of letters she wrote over the years, I discovered someone very different from the naive, unworldly prisoner of the ivory tower that I had always seen her as. I found a woman who was unafraid to tell painful truths and to face difficult facts and, when presented with them, never tried to censor but to insist only on accuracy. In my mind, I always thought that I had become a journalist in defiance of my mother and her well-meaning but sheltered worldview. I came away realizing that my reportorial instincts may have been more of an inheritance than I knew.

In my determined search for a stable career and family life, I also thought that I was providing for myself what my parents had failed to give me. I didn't see how much I was relying on the example of the shy, fourteen-year-old girl who arrived in America on a storm-tossed ocean liner and—with the glaring exception of her wager of the heart with my father—spent the rest of her life looking to find a safe harbor and, having reached it, to avoid putting it at risk. In embracing my wife's faith, I had dwelled on the shortcomings of Quakerism rather than recognizing the values that my mother had passed on by resolutely driving my brother and me to Friends Meeting in Providence every Sunday, even in the depths of her depression. And I had spent so many years being mystified at her inability to find another man that

I had forgotten the sense of family that she still managed to bequeath us, by taking us to France and exposing us to Grandpapa and Grandmaman and the rest of the Theis clan.

And the villain of the piece? (Ironic that he should put it that way, isn't it, given that it had all started with a college play?) Certainly, that's how I had seen my father for much of my life, as Alexis reminded me when I told her that I wanted to tell his story.

"But you were so angry at your father!" she said. "Don't you remember?"

I did remember, of course, but by then I had had enough of that anger. I had had enough of it for a lifetime. As a chubby kid, I had consumed entire boxes of doughnuts in depressed anger at his absence. As a coatless teenager, I had used rebellious anger toward him to keep me warm. I had written a summa cum laude college thesis and climbed to the top of *Newsweek* with sublimated anger. Unlike his volatile, self-destructive variety, mine was quiet and purposeful, but deep down a rage was burning nonetheless. There were even times when I thought that it wasn't just love for my wife and children that made me so driven to be a good husband and father. It was also as an elaborate form of revenge. I was getting back at him by proving that I could succeed in all the ways he had failed, and that I could do it without his help. "You weren't a man!" I had taunted him as a teenager, and I was going to show him what it meant to be a real man.

But now he was gone, and I realized that anger wasn't going to help me anymore. I was sick and tired of feeling sick and tired too. *God grant me the serenity to accept the things that I cannot change and the courage to change the things I can. . . .* Well, I couldn't change what had happened, but I could change how I chose to remember him.

And by letting go of my anger toward him, I was led to the discoveries of what I owed my father as well. I found the letters that showed how much I worshiped him as a child and how he had taught me the knack for connecting with other people that I would mislay as a lonely teenager but find again as a sociable adult.

I documented the sense of ambition and imagination that I had emulated, in ways conscious and unconscious, in my own journey around the world and my adventures as a journalist. I reconstructed the wry lessons in human behavior and institutional politics that helped guide me through the ranks of *Newsweek* and NBC, and I recognized the times that he was watching my back when I thought he was just being paranoid. In a perverse way, I realized, he had done me a favor by offering so many cautionary tales about how *not* to behave. But I saw that he had also given me a priceless gift: the model of a black man who was proud of his racial identity but determined never to be confined by it.

In the process, I came to see him differently too, as not just the villain of the play or the tragic victim of fatal flaws. "I guess I was set up for this," he had said when I phoned him after his stroke, and at the time I had chosen to see the bitter irony in that statement. He had mocked fate by trying so hard not to be like his father, and yet there he was, a sad cripple just like Granddad. With his drinking and his rages and his crashes from meteoric heights, he had repeated the self-destructive drama of his parents' lives, and even done them one worse. But after a year of reporting, I had a different view. Now I saw the ways in which he managed to have the last laugh, after all, at least in the ways that counted most.

With Shirley, he was finally able to rewrite his tortured relationship with his mother. He had found someone who would love him uncritically, and whom he could love in kind, in a way that his pride and Grandmother Edith's vanity and both of their sharp tongues made it impossible for the two of them to achieve. As he lay immobile in that hospital bed in Waterville, looking up at the harness and steel pulley, he could also take comfort that Shirley would never leave his side. He ran no risk of ending up like Cleophaus Sylvester Whitaker Sr., in an old-age home dictating his memories to a nurse.

And at the end, putting aside anger had allowed me to be there for him. When Grandmother had cried out for him from her hospital bed in her last years of life, he had been too distraught and fragile in his sobriety to go to her side. When Granddad had died, he had been too furious and unforgiving to come back from Africa for his funeral. But I had made the trip to Maine. I had sat by his wheelchair and we had the kind of talk that we both would have wanted to have if we had known that it would be our last. I had honored my parent and comforted the sick, and now I understood why both are considered such important laws in the Jewish tradition. That last visit had helped him to die, peaceful in the knowledge, as Shirley whispered to him in his final moments, that his sons loved him despite everything that had occurred between us. And for me, it had made it easier to carry on the business of living.

So yes, Tolstoy was right: *Tout comprendre, c'est tout pardonner.* But sometimes you have to forgive first, before you can begin to understand.

The Smart and Edwards Funeral home was a plain clapboard building along a stretch of rural highway outside of Skowhegan, Maine, so many worlds away from the stately Whitaker Funeral Home on Bennett Street in the Homewood Brushton district of Pittsburgh or the shabbily genteel Edith M. Whitaker Funeral Home on Climax Street in Belzhoover. His body had been cremated there in December, but Shirley had decided to delay the services until May, so his ashes could be buried in the spring weather that he loved. In the days after his passing, the funeral director had asked me to write an obituary to be published in the local newspaper, and I had bought a death notice in the *New York Times*, thinking wistfully that if his life had taken a different turn I wouldn't have had to pay for the recognition. And from a lawyer for a bank in Maine, I had discovered the last sad facts about his finances: He had died without filing a will and left behind a reverse mortgage on his cabin, *She Ke Nan.* Shirley couldn't afford to pay it off, meaning that another one of his quirky dream houses would have to be surrendered to the bank.

Finally, on the weekend before the national holiday, Alexis, Rachel, and Matthew and I flew to Portland and drove north for my father's memorial day. Smart and Edwards hadn't opened its doors yet, so everyone who had arrived for the service was still standing in the parking lot. First I glimpsed my brother, who with his sunglasses and tall, muscular physique looked like a bodyguard standing next to our stooped, eighty-two-year-old mother. I got out of the car and kissed them hello, then reached down to embrace Shirley. My aunt Cleo and my uncle Gene were there, both thinner and grayer than I remembered but still warm and cheerful. So was Bobby Smedley, the namesake of my uncle who died so tragically trucking steel to Buffalo on a cold December night. Then, out of the corner of my eye, I saw Barbara Callaway, who because her hair had gone so white in the years I knew her now looked remarkably unchanged.

"Hi, Barbara," I said as I went over to greet her. "It's been a long time."

"It certainly has," she said. "And my God, Mark, you've grown to look so much like Syl when he was younger!"

How did he end up in a place like Canaan? I had so often asked myself. If you look at a map of Nigeria, the emirate of Kazaure is a tiny speck near the border with Niger, almost as far north as his little town in Maine was on a map of the United States. When his friend Hussaini Adamu had died in the late 1990s, his son Suleiman had given him a three-legged seat carved out of African wood that had belonged to his father. My father called it "the emir's stool," and as he kept gaining weight in his final years and could no longer fit in many ordinary chairs, he carried it with him wherever he went. It was as if he had become the emir of his own private kingdom, and now we had all come there to bow down and chant "Rankadada!"

And sure enough, as we milled in the parking lot, a tall, striking black woman in African dress walked over and introduced herself. "I have been sent by the Adamu family to pay honor to your father," she explained in a Nigerian accent that resonated with royal reverence.

When the doors of the funeral home opened, we went inside and sat down in the parlor. Because he had been cremated, there was no casket, just an easel holding the handsome photo that had been taken of him when he earned his groundbreaking doctorate from Princeton. On each chair was a program with a more recent photo of him inside, looking like a huge white-haired black Buddha, along with the lyrics to "Amazing Grace." Otherwise there was no guide to the service, signaling that it would be a Friends ceremony and that anyone who felt so moved would be free to speak.

A tall, white-haired Quaker elder rose first, testifying to my father's religious faith and good works as clerk of the North Fairfield Meeting. Paul delivered a touching and funny eulogy that summed up his personality. "Dad was a world-class schmoozer" was a line that got a big laugh. Not wanting to compete with my brother, I remembered him by telling the stories of our last encounters. I choked up as I talked about his prescient vision of Obama's race speech, then I pulled myself together and conjured up our last conversation in the rehab ward. After describing how he had grilled the young evangelical who claimed to be a Quaker, I said: "That was Dad in a nutshell, combining spirituality and sly humor with a political scientist's demand for empirical evidence."

Barbara Callaway got up and spoke of the contributions that he made to African studies, only hinting at the personal feelings she still had for him when she said, "Syl was a great man in every respect." Jim Schmidt and a handful of other Maine friends whom I had barely met spoke about him as though they had known him for their entire lives. Then, after everyone had their say, we held hands and sang the familiar and in his case apt refrain: "*Amazing Grace, how sweet the sound, to save a wretch like me . . .*"

A small black hearse carrying the urn with his ashes led the way through the winding back roads to North Fairfield. Outside the Meeting house, folding chairs were set up around the small cemetery plot that he had picked out because of the way the sunlight hit it in the morning. Someone, I forget who, led us in another prayer, and then roses were handed out to place in the grave. Later the plot would be filled and covered with a handsome marble stone engraved with that Princeton graduation photo and the name "C.S. Whitaker." For the rest of eternity, passersby who wondered what the "C" and the "S" stood for would simply have to guess.

I glanced over at my mother as she was handed a flower.

"Do you want help?" I asked.

"Please," she said.

I took her trembling hand and we walked down the steep hill to the gravesite. She reached over and dropped the rose on the ashes of the man who had brought her so much pain—so much pain, she would tell me, but also the possibility of her greatest joys, the satisfaction of raising two sons and the happiness of doting on two grandchildren.

When the ceremony was over, we went inside for sandwiches and coffee in the Meeting house. The sight and smell of the little kitchen reminded me of the potluck lunches in the basement after services in Providence, in the years where our Sunday trips to Meeting were an escape from all the sadness of our life in Norton. Everyone ate and chatted and agreed how nice the ceremony had been and made promises to stay in touch.

On a small card table in the corner of the kitchen was a montage of photographs that Shirley had put together, and I went over to look at them. In one image, my father was sitting outside at a picnic table with her and her two sons. In another, he was aboard his beloved motorboat on the lake in Canaan, a fishing rod in his hand, a crushed white cap perched on his big round head, and a yellow life vest floating atop his enormous frame. There was a picture of him and me taken outside his condo in Palm Springs on the hazy day when he threw a party in my honor. And there, nestled in the middle of the collection, was another photo of the two of us that I had forgotten.

I carefully pulled the faded snapshot out of the collage and examined it to fix the time and place. It had been taken at George School, when I was fifteen or sixteen, in the years after I returned from the trip to France. It was a period filled with so many dark memories: of my father's drinking, of our nasty fights and our failed reconciliations. But in this photo he looked fit and handsome, with a short Afro, stylish aviator glasses, a fitted suede jacket, and an orange tie. Still skinny from dieting, I had on blue jeans and a bright orange sweater, and my hair was a curly mop. I couldn't tell whether I had amused him, or he had amused me, but his head was thrown back, and my shoulders were hunched forward, and we were both smiling.

Shirley saw me holding the snapshot and walked over.

"Syl like that picture," she said. "You keep it now, okay?"

"Thanks," I said, slipping the photo into my pocket. "I think I will."

Acknowledgments

In reconstructing the events in this book, I relied on interviews with the people who experienced them and on letters, autobiographical accounts, and e-mails written at the time. Among the sources, living and dead, to whom I am indebted are the following: Jeanne Whitaker, Syl Whitaker, Paul Whitaker, Barbara Callaway, Edith Whitaker, C.S. Whitaker Sr., Cleo McCray, Eugene McCray, Della Whitaker, Edouard Theis, Louise Theis, Trudy Huntington, Michael DeLaszlo, Barbara DeLaszlo, Paul Berry, Annie Guerin, Edgar Cahn, H.H. Wilson, Neil Tyfield, Mary Tyfield, Richard Sklar, Julian Franklin, Wendy Gray, Gretchen Ellis, Badi Foster, Charles Harris, Joseph Contreras, Eric Breindel, Jonathan Alter, Laura Levine, Alexis Gelber, Sidney Gelber, Anita Gelber, Emily Korzenik, Congressman John Lewis, Maynard Parker, Rick Smith, Steve Capus, Sam Brown, Dr. Celia McLay, Jim Schmidt, Bert Corrigan, James Kao, Jason Kao, and Shirley Kao.

I also drew on the following works and authors for additional details and context relating to key episodes in this book: *Lest Innocent Blood Be Shed*, by Philip Hallie, on the wartime heroics of Le

Chambon-sur-Lignon; *Some Form of Peace,* by Marvin Weisbord, on my father's adventures at the Pine Mountain work camp and other tales of Quaker courage; *African-Americans in Pittsburgh,* by John M. Brewer Jr., on black life in my father's home town in the decades before and after he was born; *A Taste of Power: A Black Woman's Story,* by Elaine Brown, on the Black Panther movement and the 1969 shootout at UCLA; *Hope!: The Story of Geraldine Owen Delaney, Alina Lodge and Recovery,* by Dick B., on the AA program that helped my father stop drinking; *Investigating Clinton,* by Michael Isikoff, on *Newsweek's* reporting of the Monica Lewinsky scandal; and the finding in *Whitaker v. Board of Higher Ed. of City of New York,* my father's lawsuit against Brooklyn College, written by Judge Jacob Mishler.

I could not have undertaken this project without the aid of my assistant at NBC in Washington, Phally Lambert, the bureau librarian, Marcie Rickun, or my CNN assistant Kate Swan. Steve Capus, the president of NBC News, kindly gave me permission to write the book and Jim Walton, the president of CNN, allowed me to finish it. And I will always be grateful to Katharine Graham, Don Graham, Rick Smith, and Lally Weymouth for the support and opportunities they gave me during my years at *Newsweek.*

Lynn Nesbit, my agent and friend, was the first person to encourage me to write about my parents, and I'm thankful that she was still interested when I finally got around to it. Alice Mayhew, my editor, immediately appreciated the kind of memoir I was trying to write and gave me invaluable advice as to how to make it better. At Simon & Schuster, I am grateful to Jonathan Karp for his wise counsel, as well as to Roger Labrie, Lisa Healy, Elisa Rivlin, Rachel Bergmann, Michael Accordino, Nancy Singer, Tracey Guest, Rachelle Andujar, and their teams for the expert job they did in editing, designing, and getting the word out about the book. Along the way, Lee Aitken, Bob Barnett, Erroll McDonald, and Sarah Crichton all gave me valuable feedback and encouragement.

I wrote this story for my parents but also for my children, Rachel and Matthew, so they would have a better idea of where they came from and why they are so precious to me. And I could not have done it without the love and support of my wife, Alexis, who made me want to have a family of my own, after all, and who gave me a place to call home.

Index

About the Author

Mark Whitaker is Executive Vice President and Managing Editor of CNN Worldwide, where he directs editorial coverage for all of the network's television channels and digital sites in the United States and around the globe. Previously he was a Senior Vice President and Washington Bureau Chief for NBC News, where he also appeared frequently as a commentator on NBC and MSNBC programs. He began his career in journalism at *Newsweek* magazine and was an award-winning reporter, writer, and editor before becoming the first African-American ever to lead a national newsweekly as editor of *Newsweek* from 1998 to 2006. He and his wife and two children live in New York City.

Reading Group Guide

My Long Trip Home
Mark Whitaker

INTRODUCTION

In *My Long Trip Home*, Mark Whitaker, a renowned journalist and editor with more than thirty years of experience reporting on the world around him, turns his eagle eye inward. *My Long Trip Home* traces the fascinating paths of Mark's parents and grandparents, from the French countryside during World War II to segregated, wartime Pittsburgh, before settling in with his own personal story. Mark's father, Syl, struggled mightily with alcoholism and anger issues; Mark's mother, Jeanne, wrestled with depression and financial hardship raising two young sons on her own; and Mark spent much of his childhood angry at his parents for separating and confused by their bitter divorce. But after years of emotional turmoil, Mark began to make peace with his family's past, doing so in time to have one last meaningful visit with his father before his death. In this family memoir, Mark explores and retreads the many paths that converged to create his own life, and discovers the healing power of forgiveness and compassion along the way.

Topics & Questions for Discussion

1. Mark Whitaker is a journalist by profession. In what ways did his journalistic instincts come through in *My Long Trip Home*?

2. How was the narrative in *My Long Trip Home* enhanced by first exploring the family history of both of Mark's parents? How would the story have been different if Whitaker had written only about his own life?

3. Why do you think Whitaker wrote this memoir?

4. How did the photos affect your experience of reading *My Long Trip Home*? Did you feel differently toward people described in the book after seeing their photos?

5. *My Long Trip Home* is, in many ways, a story of American history as well as familial history. How did important movements and events in American history alter the trajectory of the Whitaker and Theis families?

6. Syl was a great charmer and a wonderful conversationalist. What were the hidden downsides of these outwardly positive traits?

7. When Mark's parents learned that he wanted to write a book about their family, his mother expressed concerns that "the story would make me look very weak," and his father said, "I don't want to be the villain of the piece." (p. 335) Do you think Mark successfully honored each of their wishes? Why or why not? Do you think his parents would feel that they were accurately depicted?

8. Whitaker doesn't express much self-pity, but by all accounts he had a difficult childhood and adolescence. What coping mechanisms did he use to get through the hard parts of his life?

9. How did Whitaker's understanding of race and of his racial identity, shift as he grew up? What role did his father play in shaping his racial identity? His mother? Reflect on your own adolescence. How did your racial identity shape you as a person?

10. How did racism—both subtle and overt—shape and influence C.S., Edith, Syl, and Mark's careers? Have you ever been confronted with racism in your personal or professional life?

11. How did Whitaker express his anger throughout the years? How did his feelings toward his father evolve as he grew older?

12. Syl once told his son: "Human nature is to abuse power . . . most people who abuse power don't think they are doing it. They've justified it based on their own view of the world." (p. 285) Do you think Syl abused power? In what ways? What was Syl's own view of the world that enabled him to justify the abuses?

13. Geraldine Owen Delaney, the head of Alina Lodge, said that "of all the ways alcoholics fooled themselves, the greatest delusion was control." (p. 219) How did this delusion of control manifest itself in Syl's life? Why do you think Syl finally stopped drinking?

14. How did feminism and the women's movement impact Whitaker's mother? If you were alive during the feminist movement in the 1970s, were you reminded of anything from your own personal experiences? How do you define feminism?

15. Both the Whitaker and Theis families have legacies of heroism and strength in the face of adversity. In what ways did Jeanne, Syl, and Mark carry on those legacies?

16. What factors—emotional, familial, genetic, situational—do you think contributed to Whitaker's success in life? What forces and people helped him as a person?

17. In describing his motivation for leaving Swarthmore, Whitaker writes: "Just as I had been at George School, I was driven by a desire to find something—I didn't know exactly what—that I thought I was missing." (p. 182) What do you think he was missing? Did he ever find it?

18. Is there a hero or heroine in *My Long Trip Home*? Why or why not? If yes, who do you think it is?

19. How differently would the Whitaker family story play out if Whitaker's parents met as young adults today? Consider the effects of the civil rights and women's rights movements on our current culture and society.

20. Whitaker writes of his time spent in France as a teenager: "I was also learning something even more important that year: that not all families are destined to be unhappy." (p. 276) Do you think families are destined to be happy or unhappy? How can you choose happiness as a family?

21. According to Whitaker, during Syl's tenure at Princeton, he would focus discussions and dissuade distractions in meetings by asking, "But what is the noble purpose?" (p. 169) What do you think is the "noble purpose" of *My Long Trip Home*?

ENHANCE YOUR BOOK CLUB

1. *My Long Trip Home* is, among many things, an exercise in meticulous genealogical research. Take a moment to reflect on a family story or memory that makes you smile, and do a bit of digging. Who are the characters in this memory? Do you tell this story often? If you have access, look through old photographs, letters, postcards, or journals for supporting evidence, and bring your finds to your book club. If you're able to speak with older relatives, ask them about their favorite family stories as well. Did you uncover anything surprising about your past? What qualities or traits in your family history do you most admire? For reference, consult the author's own suggestions for genealogical research (www.cnn.com/2011/10/17/opinion/whitaker-family -story/index) and the National Archives' genealogical research tools and tips (www.archives.gov/research/genealogy/index).

2. Mark Whitaker has had a long and distinguished career as a journalist and editor. Get a behind-the-scenes look at the journalism industry by scheduling a newsroom tour with your local TV news affiliate. How did the tour change your perception of journalism and TV news? What types of people do you think thrive in that environment? Do you feel differently about Whitaker after learning more about his profession?

3. Mark's family has strong French and African ties. Explore both cultures in the most delicious way possible: food! Host an international potluck for your book club by preparing dishes from France and Nigeria, as well as any other countries you have a personal connection to. Consult www.epicurious.com/recipes menus/global/recipes for more recipe ideas.

4. Both Syl and Mark benefited from scholarships during their college years. Get into the spirit of supporting education and

volunteer to read to children at a local school or through a charity near you. Visit www.reachoutandread.org for more information.

5. *My Long Trip Home* retraces history and shares family stories from earlier generations. Look forward and imagine your descendants want to write about your life. What personal story would you want to pass down to them? Share your story with your book club. Do any common themes emerge?

A Conversation with Mark Whitaker

You explained in an interview that, though you were initially ashamed by the unpleasant aspects of your family history, "Once I'd embarked on the book, I found that coming to it as a reporter gave me a kind of detachment that I needed." Did you ever try to write this memoir with more of a visceral, emotional connection? What made you decide to approach your family's story with a reporter's detachment?

I started writing the story from memory, because that's what I thought you did as a memoirist. But I quickly realized that there were many things about my family's story that I didn't know, or thought I knew but wasn't sure if I had right. That's when I began approaching the story as a reporter—interviewing sources, collecting documents, verifying details. Because that's what I've been trained to do, it made the project much easier and more enjoyable for me. But I think it also made it easier for people to talk to me, particularly in revisiting the painful episodes, because they could see that I wasn't trying to judge anyone but to search for the truth.

You did an enormous amount of research for this memoir. What discoveries most surprised and thrilled you? What information did you find most disappointing or frustrating?

My most pleasant discoveries were about my grandparents and my grandfathers in particular. I learned that my father's father, who I knew as a stroke victim late in his life, was an incredibly dynamic man who had been born on a tenant farm in Texas, the eleventh child of a former slave, and risen by force of will and personality to became one of Pittsburgh's first black undertakers. I also learned more about the heroism of my mother's father, a French Protestant pastor who helped hide Jews from the Nazis during World War II. My saddest discoveries were about my father—not just the extent of his alcoholism, in the years when I didn't see him much, but how needlessly unforgiving he was to so many people in his life.

In any memoir that requires detailed recounting of the past, the author's memory (and that of his subjects) is truly put to the test. How much, if any, of your story came from assumptions, rather than concrete evidence? Do you feel your journalistic instinct for a fact-based narrative altered your writing style in any way?

In many ways, the narrative voice of the book comes from that disparity between what I remembered or assumed and what I discovered in the course of my reporting. It's there in the first paragraph of the first chapter—"Growing up, I always took it for granted that it was my mother who was first attracted to my father. . . . But when I went back and investigated, it turned out that it was the other way around. . . ." And that interweaving of memory and reporting continues throughout the book.

You mentioned in an interview on *The Colbert Report* that you wrote this book without an advance or any publisher's commitment. Was your final goal always to publish this memoir, or did you initially write the manuscript for your own satisfaction?

I started writing a year to the day after my father died, after waking up in the middle of the night with an epiphany that I wanted to tell his story. At first I just wanted to see what came out, and I wasn't sure if it would add up to a book that anyone else would find interesting. Once I had written two hundred pages, I sent it to a literary agent friend, and she suggested that I finish a first draft before submitting it to publishers. So I didn't know for sure that it would be published until that first draft was finished, at which point I rewrote the whole thing twice to make sure that it would also be a satisfying experience for readers who didn't know me.

What was it like to share *My Long Trip Home* with your family for the first time? What do you think your father would say about this book?

I interviewed all the surviving members of my family at length for the book: my mother and my brother and my father's older sister, among others. So none of them was surprised about what I said about them, although they all learned other family details they had never known before. They were all very supportive, although my mother in particular was a stickler for accuracy. What would my father have thought? I hope he would have understood that ultimately the book is meant as a tribute to him and to my mother, and that he would have been proud to have a record of all of us for posterity. But he could be very thin-skinned and argumentative, so I'm sure there are many details with which he would have quibbled.

Why do you think you suddenly felt ready to write this book when you did, a year to the day after your father died? What kept you from writing it earlier?

For many years, I told myself that I was too busy with my career to write a book. But the truth is that I was also ashamed. I thought that the only part worthy of a book was the romantic part—the interracial romance, the talks of black Pittsburgh and the French Resistance. Yet I also thought it would be dishonest to leave out the painful part after my parents divorced. Of course, now that it's done I see that it's the pain and recovery and reconciliation that most people relate to, and that makes the story universal.

What traits or qualities are you most proud of in your mother and father? What important lessons did they give to you that you hope to pass on to your children?

Ultimately, the book is about what I got from both of my parents, not just what I didn't get. From both of them, I inherited a reverence for learning, and love of language and writing. From my father,

I learned a wry skepticism about human nature and institutions and some of the positive as well as negative virtues of social charisma and charm. From my mother, I inherited a basic survival instinct and a faith in myself that started with her faith in me. Of all those gifts, that last one is the one I have most wanted to pass on to my own children.

If you could go back in time and visit your younger self, what would you say to your ten-year-old self?

I would have told my ten-year-old self: It's not always going to be this bad! You won't always be fat. You'll get to see your father again, and he will eventually have a place in your life. Your horizons won't be limited to this little town where you're living now. Your mother will get happier. You won't always fight with your brother. In fact, you have a lot to look forward to! You are going to have a very rich and full life and a happy family of your own some day. And that all turned out to be true, although I'm not sure I would have believed it at the time.

You said in an interview with _Reuters_, "I wanted to prove myself on my own, both vis-à-vis my parents and my race." Do you think your children feel the same way?

Absolutely, and my wife and I encourage that. We thought it was important for our two children to learn about their black and Jewish heritage, because they are both by birthright. But we also made it clear that as adults, they would be free to forge their own identities and to associate with the friends and mates and communities they choose for themselves. And so far I think they've made very sound choices in that regard. But I also think that children of interracial and interreligious backgrounds are a lot more common and accepted than they were in the past, and that's a good thing.

What advice do you have for people struggling to overcome a turbulent childhood or a difficult family situation? Was writing and researching a form of therapy for you?